Vol. XCV

No. 3

SO-BAV-676

Bible Expositor and Illuminator

SUMMER QUARTER

June, July, August 2023

Christ Proclaims the Kingdom

UNIT I: Understanding God's Kingdom

UNIT II: Responding to God's Kingdom

UNIT III: Entering God's Kingdom

Editor in Chief: Kenneth Sponsler

Edited and published quarterly by
**THE INCORPORATED TRUSTEES OF THE
GOSPEL WORKER SOCIETY
UNION GOSPEL PRESS DIVISION**

Rev. W. B. Musselman, Founder

Price: $7.69 per quarter*
*shipping and handling extra

ISBN 978-1-64495-312-9

LOOKING AHEAD

This quarter's lessons will focus on God's kingdom. All of our lessons are taken from Matthew, Mark, and Luke's Gospels. The first four lessons form a unit that focuses on understanding God's kingdom.

Our first lesson is from Matthew's account of Jesus' Beatitudes. In the Beatitudes, the principles of the secular world are reversed; so they seem quite alien from a worldly perspective. Our second lesson is also from Jesus' Sermon on the Mount. Jesus came to establish a kingdom of righteousness that perfectly fulfills God's law. The third lesson, from Mark chapters 3 and 6, is about God's kingdom and its victory over the kingdoms of this world. Our fourth lesson examines three parables about how God's kingdom grows.

Lessons 5 through 10 form our second unit, which is about how we are to respond to God's kingdom. Lesson 5 is taken from Luke's account of Jesus' model prayer. The Lord's Prayer sets an example for us about the priorities of God's kingdom. Lesson 6 deals with Jesus' teachings on humility. Lesson 7 deals with Jesus' story of the rich man and Lazarus. The Scriptures are sufficient to produce saving faith; those who reject their witness would not be persuaded by even the greatest miracle. Lesson 8 is about Jesus' parable of the sheep and the goats. Those who minister to needy believers minister to the Lord Jesus Himself. Lesson 9 deals Jesus' use of parables and what it takes to understand their meaning 10 examines the role of forgiveness in a Christian's life; if our sins forgiven by God, we will in turn be forgiving toward those who wr

Our final unit of study for this quarter focuses on entering Go God restores the lost, deals with us justly, and honors the hu proud.

Lesson 11 is about Jesus' parable of the prodigal son. welcome repentant sinners into His kingdom, no matter strayed from Him. Lesson 12 is about Jesus' parable of ers. God is faithful in dealing with all His servants gener cusses Jesus' story of the Pharisee and the tax collec their own righteousness will be condemned, but tho sinfulness and call upon the Lord for mercy and f

May God bless you abundantly through this Word, the Bible.

The Invincible Kingdom of God

TODD WILLIAMS

In 1986, King Mswati III became the sovereign monarch over the African kingdom of Swaziland (now called the Kingdom of Eswatini). While we generally understand what a kingdom is, the word "kingdom" is rarely used in contemporary settings. It typically brings to mind castles, walled cities, and knights riding out in shining armor. Of the handful of modern nations who have a king, very few allow him any real authority. It is crucial to recognize, however, that it is as a kingdom with an absolutely sovereign King that we must understand God's rule and reign. He is not an elected official, and He does not need popular support to accomplish His will. This reality is behind much of this quarter's teaching.

It is helpful to recognize that when Adam disobeyed God's command in Eden, he turned the whole human race into rebels against God (Rom. 5:12, 19). No one is born with a heart that is loyal to the divine King (3:9-18). The only way anyone becomes a subject in this righteous kingdom, therefore, is for the person to humbly seek a pardon from God. No individual becomes a loyal subject without first experiencing a profound change of heart like the prodigal son (Luke 15:17-20; cf. Acts 3:19). Nevertheless, most of the lessons in this study expose a sad reality: many people make a mere show of being citizens in God's kingdom without having a real change of heart (see lessons 4, 6-13).

The true and loyal subjects of God's kingdom are those whose hearts have been energized by God's Spirit. Their desires and values have been completely turned upside down (Matt. 5). Since the people of this world are ruled by Satan (I John 5:19), there is a striking difference seen in those who serve God (Matt. 5:16; II Cor. 6:14-15; Eph. 5:11-13). Followers of God love their enemies and pray for those who persecute them (Matt. 5:44). They are meek and merciful (vss. 5, 7). When they mourn, they find comfort (vs. 4). When they hunger and thirst for righteousness, their passion is satisfied (vs. 6). They truly have ears to hear the truth (Matt. 13:16). None of these things are true of worldly people.

This stark difference is represented prominently in Jesus' parables. God's followers are those who accept the invitation to the banquet (Luke 14:21-23), who provide the drink of water to Christ's followers (Matt. 25:37-40), and who seek God in humility (Luke 15:18-19; 18:13). Rebels against God are, on the other hand, represented in Jesus' parables by the tares (Matt. 13:25), by those who refuse to attend the banquet (Luke 14:18-20), and by the unforgiving servant (Matt. 18:32-33).

So what is it that Christ was proclaiming when He said, "The kingdom of heaven is at hand" (Matt. 4:17)? At the very least, He was announcing that the unassailable power of God's kingdom was poised to strike a death blow to the powers of darkness. Christ's exorcisms proved that the advance of God's kingdom against Satan could not be halted. Through Christ's teaching and miracles of healing, He countered the ruin and woes brought on humanity through Satan's work. Christ brought a message of light, life, and goodness to a world fraught with hatred, hostility, and bitterness.

As you study this quarter's lessons about God's kingdom, you will see a focus on the practical outworking of God's kingdom power in the lives of His

(Editorials continued on page 186)

SCRIPTURE LESSON TEXT

MATT. 5:1 And seeing the multitudes, he went up into a mountain: and when he was set, his disciples came unto him:

2 And he opened his mouth, and taught them, saying,

3 Blessed *are* the poor in spirit: for theirs is the kingdom of heaven.

4 Blessed *are* **they that mourn: for they shall be comforted.**

5 Blessed *are* the meek: for they shall inherit the earth.

6 Blessed *are* **they which do hunger and thirst after righteousness: for they shall be filled.**

7 Blessed *are* the merciful: for they shall obtain mercy.

8 Blessed *are* **the pure in heart: for they shall see God.**

9 Blessed *are* the peacemakers: for they shall be called the children of God.

10 Blessed *are* **they which are persecuted for righteousness' sake: for theirs is the kingdom of heaven.**

11 Blessed are ye, when *men* shall revile you, and persecute *you,* and shall say all manner of evil against you falsely, for my sake.

12 Rejoice, and be exceeding glad: for great *is* **your reward in heaven: for so persecuted they the prophets which were before you.**

13 Ye are the salt of the earth: but if the salt have lost his savour, wherewith shall it be salted? it is thenceforth good for nothing, but to be cast out, and to be trodden under foot of men.

14 Ye are the light of the world. A city that is set on an hill cannot be hid.

15 Neither do men light a candle, and put it under a bushel, but on a candlestick; and it giveth light unto all that are in the house.

16 Let your light so shine before men, that they may see your good works, and glorify your Father which is in heaven.

NOTES

Upside-Down Kingdom

Lesson Text: Matthew 5:1-16

Related Scriptures: Psalm 24:1-6; Isaiah 66:1-2;
Luke 6:20-26; Hebrews 11:36-38

TIME: A.D. 28   PLACE: mountain near Capernaum

GOLDEN TEXT—"Blessed are they which do hunger and thirst after righteousness: for they shall be filled" (Matthew 5:6).

Introduction

Matthew, who was also known as Levi (Matt. 9:9; Luke 5:27), was a tax collector who had left his business to follow Christ. He was one of the twelve apostles and in characteristic fashion humbly referred to himself as a tax collector, or publican (Matt. 10:3). Many have noted that Mark is a book of action that does not stress the lengthy discourses that Jesus sometimes used in His teaching. Matthew, however, included several lengthy discourses in his book. He also repeatedly used the phrase "kingdom of heaven" as he presented Jesus as the Messiah-King.

The first of the discourses in Matthew is what we know as the Sermon on the Mount (chaps. 5—7).

The Sermon on the Mount describes the kind of righteousness Jesus expects of His followers. It must exceed the righteousness of the Pharisees (Matt. 5:20) and will be realized fully in Christ's kingdom. It is also a standard we should strive for.

LESSON OUTLINE

I. THE INDIVIDUAL HEART—
   Matt. 5:1-6

II. RELATIONSHIPS WITH
    OTHERS—Matt. 5:7-12

III. RELATIONSHIPS WITH THE
     WORLD—Matt. 5:13-16

Exposition: Verse by Verse

THE INDIVIDUAL HEART

MATT. 5:1 And seeing the multitudes, he went up into a mountain: and when he was set, his disciples came unto him:

2 And he opened his mouth, and taught them, saying,

3 Blessed are the poor in spirit: for theirs is the kingdom of heaven.

4 Blessed are they that mourn: for they shall be comforted.

5 Blessed are the meek: for they shall inherit the earth.

6 Blessed are they which do hunger and thirst after righteousness: for they shall be filled.

Spiritual instruction (Matt. 5:1-2). {The implication in these verses is that Jesus drew away from the multitudes in order to instruct His disciples privately. When we read Matthew 7:28, though, we conclude that many had gathered and listened in while He taught, so that by the end of His teaching session there was another multitude present.}Q1

{There seem to have been three levels of followers throughout Jesus' ministry. There were the twelve men He chose to prepare for taking the gospel throughout the world; there was a larger group of believers also sometimes referred to as disciples; and, finally, there were the crowds that followed Him out of curiosity or with some other motive.}Q2 From among the Twelve, there were three we sometimes refer to as His inner circle of disciples. These were Peter, James, and John. They shared some experiences that none of the others did.

"Modern sociological experts say that a person is limited to twelve truly significant relationships at a time, and only a maximum of three of these at most can go to the deepest levels of intimacy" (Weber, *Matthew,* Broadman and Holman). It seems that Jesus had a specific plan in mind when He chose twelve men to accompany Him throughout His years of ministry on earth. Others often listened to what He was saying to His disciples, and at times He spoke to the crowds, but much of the time He was instructing the Twelve.

On this occasion Jesus seated Himself, the disciples gathered around, and He opened His mouth to give them instruction in righteousness. The mountain was probably a high hill northwest of the Sea of Galilee.

Spiritual need (Matt. 5:3-4). The Beatitudes form the introduction to Jesus' message, and there is a parallel development of their thoughts in the body of the message. They are also progressive in thought, with each one logically following the one preceding it. They are not meant to be cute clichés but rather truths to be lived. {The word "blessed" literally means "happy," but it is more than a surface emotion. It is a deep sense of being blessed by God in a way that leads to genuine contentment and peace in the heart.}Q3

{The first characteristic of righteousness mentioned is being poor in spirit. This does not refer to those who are physically poor. It speaks of the person who recognizes that in himself there is no merit or righteousness, that is, nothing to make him worthy of heaven.}Q4 It is the recognition that one is unable to become righteous without help from God. The recognition of this condition of spiritual poverty is the attitude that leads one to salvation, and the person who is saved enters the kingdom of heaven.

Those who mourn (vs. 4) are those who see their spiritual poverty and become deeply sorrowful over it. This is a godly sorrow that leads to genuine repentance. It is mourning over sin and the spiritual bankruptcy it has caused. Repentance and confession bring the comfort of forgiveness. David wrote, "Blessed is he whose transgression is forgiven, whose sin is covered. Blessed is the man unto whom the Lord imputeth not iniquity, and in whose spirit there is no guile" (Ps. 32:1-2).

Spiritual maturity (Matt. 5:5-6). It is wrong to equate meekness with weakness. Meekness is sometimes defined as strength under control. {A meek person can in reality be a very powerful person, but he is one who is spiritually mature and gracious enough to use his strength positively and constructively instead of negatively and destructively.}Q5 Meekness is not looking down on oneself and feeling worthless, either. A meek person realizes that God has given him certain authority as His child and that he is free to use it.

Such a person does, however, submit completely to the will of God and uses his freedom and authority only as God wants. It is this unquestioning submission that most characterizes the meek person. Both Moses and Paul were meek (cf. Num. 12:3; II Cor. 10:1), and in both of them we see strong leadership abilities used under the guiding hand of God. Neither sought personal gain. Both wanted people to know the joy of obeying God. The reward for such submission will be realized in the coming kingdom, when Christ rules on earth.

{It is characteristic of the meek that they have an appetite for the things that make them more pleasing to God and more conformed to His righteousness. We know what it is to be very hungry or thirsty. When we experience either, our body craves what it has been missing and desperately needs. Food or drink becomes the center of our thoughts and the focus of our determination. We reach a point at which nothing else matters as much as satisfying the hunger or thirst driving us to distraction.}[Q6]

This kind of insatiable longing for righteousness will be answered. We will find ourselves being completely satisfied as we read God's Word, pray, worship, sing, and study what others have written in explanation of His Word.

RELATIONSHIPS WITH OTHERS

7 Blessed are the merciful: for they shall obtain mercy.

8 Blessed are the pure in heart: for they shall see God.

9 Blessed are the peacemakers: for they shall be called the children of God.

10 Blessed are they which are persecuted for righteousness' sake: for theirs is the kingdom of heaven.

11 Blessed are ye, when men shall revile you, and persecute you, and shall say all manner of evil against you falsely, for my sake.

12 Rejoice, and be exceeding glad: for great is your reward in heaven: for so persecuted they the prophets which were before you.

Spiritual outreach (Matt. 5:7-8). In Luke 6:36 Jesus is recorded as saying, "Be ye therefore merciful, as your Father also is merciful." Psalm 62:12 says, "Also unto thee, O Lord, belongeth mercy: for thou renderest to every man according to his work." God is merciful, and we should be most grateful that He is! On our own we deserve nothing, and apart from His grace and mercy we would never have the hope of heaven. The person who exhibits mercy will be rewarded with mercy.

An often heard statement is that God's mercy is His withholding from us what we deserve. We deserve hell because of our sin, but God removes that punishment from us when we receive His Son as Saviour. {Our natural tendency is to be selfish and unforgiving toward those who have wronged us. We want them to get what they deserve because of what they have done. The righteous attitude is a forgiving attitude, and as we exercise it, we will have a greater sense of God's forgiveness.}[Q7]

Those of us who have experienced God's mercy have been cleansed from our sins. We need to live in purity of heart, which reflects the status we have with God. Perhaps the climactic truth in the Beatitudes is that the pure in heart will see God someday. It is also true that the person who lives with a pure heart can see God now in ways others do not. They recognize His presence in daily situations and realize His provision, protection, and guidance in every circumstance.

Spiritual privileges (Matt. 5:9-10). We live in a troubled world in which people long for peace. We know there will not be real peace among nations until the Lord Jesus reigns on earth. But we also know that {individuals who have trusted Jesus Christ as their personal Saviour are at peace with God regarding their eternal destiny and that it is possible for them to live at peace with others. Furthermore, it is the person who loves the Lord dearly and is endeavoring to live according to His Word who can help others find peace.}[Q8]

Being at peace with God, living in peace with others, and helping other people find peace are evidence that a person is a child of God. The best way to help others find peace in their hearts is to lead them to saving faith in Jesus Christ, who said He is the one who gives peace that the world cannot give (John 16:33).

Jesus then spoke about suffering from oppression because of our beliefs. The key thought here is that the persecution comes specifically because of our taking a stand for righteousness. Some students experience this at school; many adults experience it in the workplace. There is a real animosity in many unsaved people for those who profess belief in Christ. It is a Satan-promoted animosity coming from his hatred of God. In his determination to oppose everything God is and stands for, he promotes persecution of God's children.

The ability to endure persecution gracefully is evidence of a genuine faith that will result in a believer's eternal existence in heaven. Those who have identified themselves with Christ, who suffered the greatest persecution of all, can be confident of a glorious deliverance someday.

Spiritual endurance (Matt. 5:11-12). The proper perspective on persecution is amplified in these verses. It is a blessing to know our testimony is so effective that it is noticed and opposed by those who do not believe. The followers to whom Jesus originally spoke these words were going to experience tremendous opposition from the Roman government. By the time of the apostle Paul's ministry, Nero was the emperor, and he displayed a deep-seated hatred of Christians. While we know Nero as a notorious emperor, others would be just as bad.

Jesus promised great blessing to those who were reviled, persecuted, and slandered. In fact, He told them they should rejoice and be exceedingly glad, for a great reward awaited them in heaven. "If God is as real as He claims, if the Bible is true, if heaven is to be gained, then there is no temporary earthly trouble or persecution that can thwart the child of God from the eternal glory that lies ahead" (Falwell, ed., *KJV Parallel Bible Commentary,* Nelson).

As Jesus' followers experienced persecution, they would be following in the footsteps of the highly regarded Old Testament prophets. This was an encouragement to them, for the prophets were viewed as godly men who lived by the highest standards.

RELATIONSHIPS WITH THE WORLD

13 Ye are the salt of the earth: but if the salt have lost his savour, wherewith shall it be salted? it is thenceforth good for nothing, but to be cast out, and to be trodden under foot of men.

14 Ye are the light of the world. A city that is set on an hill cannot be hid.

15 Neither do men light a candle, and put it under a bushel, but on a candlestick; and it giveth light unto all that are in the house.

16 Let your light so shine before men, that they may see your good works, and glorify your Father which is in heaven.

Spiritual influence (Matt. 5:13-14). {Three figures are used to illustrate the believer's influence on the world: salt, light, and a city on a hill.}[Q9] Salt does several things. It adds flavor, it causes thirst, it acts as a preservative, it melts ice, and it helps in the healing of wounds if used properly. As believers, we have a tremendous opportunity to make a significant difference in the lives of the people we know.

We should improve life by providing a spiritual flavor unknown by the unsaved. We should cause others to thirst for the joy of life we possess. We should be a means of preserving and maintaining godliness in the midst of a dark, godless society. We should provide the warmth that melts hard, resistant hearts, giving them encouragement to come to God. We should be an avenue of healing to those around us who are broken and bruised by the harshness of life. There are multitudes of broken hearts all around us who need help.

Pure salt will maintain its flavor. In Israel, however, most of the salt was mixed with other minerals. In certain circumstances this mixture could lose its flavor, making it worthless for seasoning. When that happened, it was used to cover roads to keep the grass from growing there. It is possible for us to become useless to others if our hearts are cold and uncaring. Instead of being useless, we should be like lights shining for the Lord in this dark, evil world. We should be so obviously different from the world that we are like a city on top of a hill that cannot be hidden.

Spiritual light (Matt. 5:15-16). Jesus chose to expand on the illustration of light by explaining how light is most effectively used. {You should notice that Jesus did not say this is what believers should be but what they already are. Because we are in Christ, we are very different from the world. Every true believer is a light in this dark world simply because he knows the truth.}Q10 Light reveals reality and truth because it enables us to see what is around us as we walk.

Since believers are lights in this world, any believer who does not function as a light in revealing spiritual reality and truth is actually acting contrary to his new nature. Such a person is like the light that has been lit and then hidden under a basket, offering no help to anyone in the home. Such a light is useless to everyone present, and a Christian with no testimony is useless to his Saviour and those near him who are separated from God. We are challenged, therefore, to let our testimonies shine for God.

Our faith is most easily seen through our good works. When unsaved people can clearly see that we live with a higher and more noble standard than do those of the world, they will be drawn to what we have. As this occurs, God is truly glorified.

—Keith E. Eggert.

QUESTIONS

1. Who was listening to Jesus at the beginning of the Sermon on the Mount, and how did that change?

2. What three basic types of followers do we see in Jesus' ministry?

3. What is the true meaning of "blessed" in these verses?

4. What does "poor in spirit" (Matt. 5:3) refer to?

5. What is the meek person like?

6. What does it mean to "hunger and thirst after righteousness" (vs. 6)?

7. What is it about us that keeps us from being naturally merciful, and why should showing mercy be important to us?

8. What are the characteristics of a peacemaker?

9. What three pictures illustrate the effect we should have on the world?

10. Why did Jesus not say we *should* be lights in this world?

—Keith E. Eggert.

Preparing to Teach the Lesson

People are always looking for something to make them happy, but lasting pleasure-based happiness is elusive and always just out of reach. This week we explore the concept of true happiness according to Jesus.

TODAY'S AIM

Facts: to explain Jesus' view on experiencing true happiness.

Principle: to explain that when we do what God wants, we will experience true happiness.

Application: to urge students to seek God's will rather than their own happiness.

INTRODUCING THE LESSON

In our world today there is an increased emphasis on the search for immediate pleasure and gratification. This, however, never leads to true happiness. The Bible tells us that true happiness comes when we are linked with God in our search to be happy, for He already has laid out guidelines for us.

DEVELOPING THE LESSON

1. The setting for the sermon on happiness (Matt. 5:1). It is interesting that Jesus used every opportunity to teach about the values of the kingdom of God.

On this particular day, Jesus and His disciples saw the crowds gathering out of curiosity, as they always seemed to do when He was present. As He taught His disciples on this occasion, the multitudes listened in. What He taught fascinated them, for what He said was very different from what they were hearing in their synagogues.

We are told that this sermon was preached on a mountain. I have had the privilege of visiting the traditional location of the Sermon on the Mount. The hillside slopes down gradually so that a great number of people could sit on the grass and easily hear one who was teaching them. In the deep valley below, the sowers sowed their seed. Jesus used such natural locations to fortify His teaching, for they often provided earthly illustrations He could use.

2. Those whom God blesses (Matt. 5:2-10). Jesus began His sermon by speaking of blessedness, or true happiness. Happiness is a universal desire. There is no one who does not want to be happy. Jesus related the concept of being happy to knowing God's blessing daily.

In this sermon Jesus made a series of poetic statements that made it easy for His hearers to remember what He taught. In the first of these, He stated that the poor in spirit would be given the kingdom of heaven. These people recognized that they needed God deep within. It is easy to live our lives without realizing that we need God; we thus lose God's blessing. Do we know that we need God?

God also blesses those who mourn. This indicates deep sorrow, particularly sorrow for one's sins. It demonstrates a state of repentance. God's response to a heart that sorrows about sin is the gift of His comfort.

God blesses those who are meek. Meek people are gentle and lowly. God hates pride. He promises the earth to the meek. They will fully enjoy the earth as heirs of Christ's future kingdom. Meekness does not mean powerlessness; rather, it means submitting one's strength to God. Ask the students whether they know any meek people and why they think they are meek.

God will bless those who want to live by God's standards of justice and righteousness. He will satisfy them. Those who show mercy to others will be blessed by God as well, for they themselves will find mercy.

Those who are clean and pure in their hearts will see God. This is the promise for the believer in Jesus. The Jewish people were afraid to see God lest they die. Jesus offered them what their religion could not—the ability to be in God's presence.

Peacemakers will be called God's children, for they express God's nature of making peace. Those who share the gospel of peace with others have a special relationship with God.

Those who live for God will certainly be persecuted. This is foretold for all those who live for God (cf. Phil.1:29; II Tim. 3:12). Ask your students whether they are willing to be persecuted, for that is their portion when they really live for God. But the great compensation for living for God is His kingdom.

3. A reward waits for you (Matt. 5:11-12). The Christian is called to endure persecution. It comes with the calling. Its reward is God's blessing. This is the crux of this sermon. With God, we can be truly blessed, or happy, no matter what we go through. Being mocked, persecuted, and defamed is part of the Christian disciple's struggle.

Jesus reminds us that when that happens, we are in good company, for it happened to the prophets too. The reward for faithfulness awaits us in heaven. We must be willing to wait through our trials for God's ultimate blessing.

4. Salt and light (Matt. 5:13-16). In this section Jesus used two very common images to describe His followers. They are like salt, which provides flavoring for food. Citizens of the kingdom of God provide a flavor that infiltrates the world for God. Salt that has lost its saltiness is without any value and fit only to be trash.

Light is another image Jesus used to talk about the followers of God. They are the light for others so that they can see the life of God and follow Him too. Those who live by kingdom values are to be like a light set upon a high place so that all can benefit from that light. They are to be like a city on a high mountain that all can see.

In Jesus' day there was no electricity, so oil lamps had to be lit and put at a high level so that all could see by that light. Christians today are to be that kind of light for the world. Their good works are to testify to the work of their wonderful heavenly Father.

ILLUSTRATING THE LESSON

The world offers happiness but never delivers. God offers us a humble and difficult path, but He assures us of true happiness.

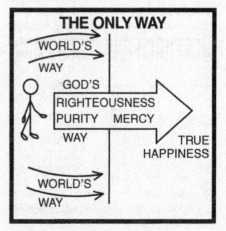

CONCLUDING THE LESSON

Our lesson has shown us that true happiness comes only with seeking God and His ways rather than happiness itself.

ANTICIPATING THE NEXT LESSON

Next week we consider how we are to live in light of God's perfect kingdom.

—*A. Koshy Muthalaly.*

PRACTICAL POINTS

1. We must always see ourselves as weak and totally dependent on the Lord (Matt. 5:1-4).
2. To be like Christ means we must be gentle in all our relationships (vs. 5).
3. A desire to live righteously will be seen in our merciful treatment of others (vss. 6-7).
4. We who know the peace of God must seek to share it with others (vss. 8-9).
5. We should see persecution for our faith as an opportunity to honor the Lord (vss. 10-12).
6. Good works are not a means of elevating ourselves, but a way of glorifying God (vss. 13-16).

—Jarl K. Waggoner.

RESEARCH AND DISCUSSION

1. Is "blessedness," or true happiness, something we should pursue, or is it the result of pursuing other things (Matt. 5:1-11)?
2. Why is meekness not often considered a virtue today? In what ways can we actively practice it?
3. How can we pursue righteousness without becoming legalistic or self-righteous?
4. In what practical ways can we be "peacemakers" in our world?
5. Should we expect to be persecuted for our faith (Matt. 5:12; cf. John 5:18; I Pet. 4:12-13)? Should we be concerned if we experience no persecution?
6. Can you cite outstanding examples of people who let their light "shine before men" (Matt. 5:16)?

—Jarl K. Waggoner.

ILLUSTRATED HIGH POINTS

Blessed (Matt. 5:3-11)

The word "happiness" presents a picture of pleasure, delight, gladness, contentment, or exhilaration.

A child receives a toy, a wife sees her husband return from a business trip, a long-lost friend is able to visit your home—all are joyful experiences. Success in academic pursuits and advancement in one's profession are also examples of what people call happiness and satisfaction.

"Blessed" is the familiar New Testament term for happiness. The Beatitudes are the direct teaching of the Saviour, and they demonstrate that happiness is not always related to a material entity or a happy occasion. In reality, Jesus' words illustrate that real happiness depends on how a person has responded to God's provisions for a happy life and how close he is to the Lord.

There is no true and lasting happiness without having trusted in Christ as one's Saviour and Lord. That type of happiness has eternal qualities, not just temporal ones.

Rejoice (vs. 12)

A familiar phrase that Christians have been hearing for a number of years at Christmastime is "Wise men still seek Him." Many of our contemporaries, however, miss the whole point of Christmas. There is even "Christmas in July," and it is valued because many non-Christians look forward to Christmas all year as a time of joy.

People repeat the phrase "Merry Christmas" without seriously thinking of what it could mean for them.

Knowing Christ makes it possible to have joy throughout the year. Indeed, we can rejoice at any time and in any circumstance.

—P. Fredrick Fogle.

Golden Text Illuminated

"Blessed are they which do hunger and thirst after righteousness: for they shall be filled" (Matthew 5:6).

It is not only the church that recognizes magnificence in the teachings of Jesus; many outside the faith give Him credit for His instruction also. They may not want to grant Him His due as the Son of God, but they marvel at the words He spoke.

One Scripture passage known far beyond the church is the Sermon on the Mount. It is in this sermon that we find this week's golden text. The immediate context is a section known as the Beatitudes because it is a series of blessings uttered by our Lord on some very special people in the eyes of God.

The term "blessed" refers to happiness, and Jesus singled out certain people who would be given that wonderful blessing because of something in their lives. The ones specifically referred to in our golden text are those who recognize sin for what it is and for what it does to the human soul. They are those whose lives were once filled with sin.

Like most people in the world then and now, these are people who likely pursued first one sin and then another, thinking that by doing so they would find the good life. Satan is clever in disguising sin that way. As a fly or worm with embedded hook looks very tempting to a hungry fish, so temptation is presented to us, promising happiness and satisfaction.

Not every person who sins recognizes it for what it is. Look at society today, and you will agree. In Jesus' day the religious leaders, such as the Pharisees, were sinners but could not see it in themselves. On the other hand, many of the publicans (tax collectors) and other sinners did know that they were sinners and often responded positively to Jesus (cf. Matt. 21:31; Luke 7:36-50).

Those who see sin for what it is and hate what it does to the human condition are those who long for something better. They know there is something better, but they also recognize their inability to change. They long to be righteous but find that righteousness eludes them.

These are the people who, when presented with the good news of Jesus, embrace Him as the One they longed for all the time they were trapped in Satan's web. They find in Christ a liberty they could only dream about before and a power to walk a different path that only disciples of Jesus can tread. The gnawing void and craving within them is filled with the presence of God and with a joy and blessedness that sin promised but could not provide.

Jesus can pronounce a blessing on someone who thirsts and hungers after righteousness because such a person is drawn to Christ. Anyone who comes to Him is welcomed with open arms (John 6:37). He finds in Christ freedom from the eternal penalty of sin, acceptance and worth as a person, a guiding light in a world dark with sin, a power to live so that God can bless, a way to escape the temptations that continue to dog the path of a believer, and a Friend who knows what it is like to be human.

To such a person comes an inner sense of joy and happiness that may be dampened on occasion but, like an eternal flame, is never extinguished. It is called eternal life.

—*Darrell W. McKay.*

Heart of the Lesson

What does it mean to be happy? Some people think it means having no worries or cares. Real life can never be completely absent of problems, though. If a person depends on circumstances for his happiness, he will be living a roller-coaster type of life. From one moment to the next, he will be up and down in a dizzying pattern.

Our text talks about true happiness and how to have it.

1. Kingdom norms lead to happiness (Matt. 5:1-12). Jesus taught that a person is blessed, that is, happy, when he lives the qualities of God's own people.

Jesus' formula for happiness is unlike anything the world might suggest. He said a happy person is one who knows he has no good within himself and thus relies on God. The happy person is humble and pure and merciful. He longs to be more like Christ, helping make peace wherever possible. He is ridiculed and persecuted because of his stand.

This type of life does not fit our common picture of happiness. Where is the wealth, the ease, the success, and the fame?

Jesus talked about eternal rewards for this kind of Christian character. He said those who are living this way are already part of the kingdom of heaven. They will be comforted and filled. They will receive God's mercy and be called the children of God. They will see God. What could be better than that?

2. Kingdom witness leads to fulfillment (Matt. 5:13-16). Jesus called on His followers to be salt and light to the world around them. Salt preserves, gives flavor, and helps heal. Christians should be representatives of righteousness to those around them. The salt of a Christian's witness can lead to a thirst in an unsaved person for the things of God.

Of what use is salt if it has no flavor? It can be used to melt ice, but it certainly cannot season our food anymore. It is no different from its surroundings, so it is worthless. It is the same for Christians. If we live the same way as those who do not know Christ, how are we pointing the way to Him?

Jesus also called us to be the light of the world. Light shows the dirt. Light illuminates our world so that we can see. Light also exposes error. Jesus called on us to shine our light so that it can be seen by all.

What good is light if it is hidden? Jesus called us to be His shining lights, reflecting Him before others. When we do good works, it should not be for our own praise. Rather, any good we do should honor and glorify God.

These verses, known as the Beatitudes, stand in direct contrast to the earthly wisdom and ideas of our world.

Instead of stepping over others to get higher on that ladder of success, we should live as Christ did. He knew who He was and never puffed Himself up. He lived with everlasting values foremost in His mind.

The Christian character qualities in this text present a beautiful mosaic of what a true follower of Jesus looks like. He is a humble, hardworking, wise person who longs to be more like Christ each day.

When we become more like Jesus, we will experience true happiness. Will it be smooth sailing? Far from it! Jesus' life certainly was not an easy one. Why should we expect ours to be? Instead of unsatisfying emptiness, though, we can have a life of fulfillment here on earth and even more so in heaven.

—*Judy Carlsen.*

World Missions

The story of the planting and growth of the church among the Wallamo tribe in Ethiopia is one of the most remarkable stories of the spread of the gospel in modern times. One Sudan Interior Mission (now SIM) worker called it "a grand second to that recorded in the book of the Acts of the Apostles" (Cotterell, *Born at Midnight*, Moody).

It did not seem that way at first; there was no glory or victory as the missionaries entered Ethiopia on Christmas Day 1927. Dr. Thomas Lambie led a team of veteran workers from Kenya and other nations in the region. Dr. Lambie was a remarkable missionary pioneer, physician, and hospital builder.

Restricted by the Ethiopian government to working in the north, the missionaries prayed about reaching the primitive Wallamo tribe in the south.

Life in Ethiopia was fairly pleasant. It was a poor country ruled by a royal household. The missionaries were particularly welcomed for their medical skills. They brought aid for the blind and for the lepers, but very few converts were counted.

The motto of SIM is By Prayer. Prevailing prayer obtained the consent of the king to enter the Wallamo country. Fifty-five workers moved rapidly to establish stations, but converts came no easier in the south than they had in the north.

On October 3, 1935, Italian forces invaded Ethiopia. Though it was far from a rich prize, Mussolini was seeking to establish Italy as a formidable power in a world that echoed with the dangerous ambitions of Germany, Russia, and Japan. Ethiopia, defended by tribesmen with spears and swords, was no match for the Italian juggernaut. Even though Ethiopia had inferior weapons, though, it held out for seven months.

Dr. Lambie was appointed director of the Red Cross for all of Ethiopia. He led a heroic, lifesaving work until the occupation was complete. The Italian army closed all the mission stations and ordered the workers to the capital, Addis Ababa. It was the end of the Ethiopian outreach. There was barely one convert for each of the ninety-two missionaries in ten years of labor (Cotterell).

There was no news out of Ethiopia during the next six years. In May 1941 a young SIM worker reentered the country with the British army. The Wallamos learned of his return, and the news spread like wildfire. The missionary was startled to learn there were seventy groups of believers worshipping in structured churches!

What made this most amazing was that the burgeoning Wallamo church had only the Gospel of John in their own dialect. They had been forced to use the Amharic Scripture of the Coptic church, an unfamiliar tongue. Serious translation work was undertaken at once.

Author F. Peter Cotterell closed his engrossing book with an analysis of the large, growing Wallamo church. He wrote, "Why did it all happen? The immediate answer is simple. A sovereign God willed it to be so."

Some years later, SIM was forced to leave the infant church in East Sudan under similar circumstances. The believers suffered horribly under an oppressive regime. When the missionaries returned, they found phenomenal growth in numbers and in vitality.

—*Lyle P. Murphy.*

The Jewish Aspect

Early in His ministry, Jesus began to announce that the kingdom of heaven was near, or in His words, "at hand" (Matt. 4:17). John the Baptist also had spoken of the nearness of the kingdom (3:2), and Jesus continued to refer to the kingdom.

Jesus' and John's audiences were Jewish. In both cases, when they spoke of the kingdom, they were speaking of realities very precious to their audience, although they were realities greatly misunderstood.

Both the context and the setting of the Sermon on the Mount point to the interpretation that this kingdom refers to the eventual reign of Christ on earth. This coincides with the promise that the meek will inherit the earth (Matt. 5:5). The word for "earth" is the Greek word $g\bar{e}$, which also can be translated "land." The "meek" of Israel will inherit the land and reign with Christ.

This future kingdom is described in various Old Testament passages. One central feature is that it will have Jerusalem as its capital. The nations will flow to Jerusalem to worship the King as He reigns from the throne of David (Ps. 2:6-9; Isa. 2:1-4; Dan. 7:13-14; Zech. 8:3-8; 14:16-21). This messianic King will rule with all of God's people (Jer. 30:9; Ezek. 34:23-24; Hos. 3:4-5).

Ezekiel foretold that there will be physical changes in the earth in the messianic kingdom (Ezek. 47:1-9). He also wrote that a new temple will be built in Jerusalem (40:1—46:24).

During the future kingdom, there will be prosperity (Jer. 31:12-14), health, and long life (Isa. 65:18-23). Peace will cover the earth and even extend to the animal kingdom (11:6-9; 65:25).

The future kingdom will be characterized by a deeper spirituality for Israel. God's law will be written on the hearts and minds of the people, and they will be truly devoted to the Lord (Jer. 31:33-34; Ezek. 36:24-27). The knowledge of the Lord will be worldwide (Isa. 11:9).

Jesus' message in the Beatitudes describes the inward nature of the people who will inhabit the kingdom. Stanley Toussaint has pointed out that "the basis of each blessing in every case is a reference to some phase of the Jewish kingdom prophesied in the Old Testament" (*Behold the King,* Multnomah).

The promise of the kingdom as an inheritance ties verses 3, 5, and 10 of Matthew 5 with the promises found in Ezekiel 39:25-29 and Daniel 2:44 and 7:27. Part of the Old Testament promises of the kingdom involved God's covenant with Israel concerning her eternal possession of the land (Jer. 31:3-5, 8-10, 35-37; Ezek. 39:25-29; Amos 9:15).

Jesus' teachings about the kingdom were largely rejected by the Jewish people of Jesus' day. They did not understand what He was saying. But a blessed future awaits for all who come to Christ in faith. When Christ comes again, the promises of the kingdom will come to full fruition. What a glorious day that will be. He will rule on the earth, and Israel will take her proper role among the nations.

As we read the Beatitudes, we should bear in mind that its lessons are fully applicable to believers today. As fellow citizens of the kingdom, we need to take these principles to heart and live them out.

—*Carter Corbrey*

Guiding the Superintendent

We constantly struggle with the concept of relevance. We are continually challenged to adhere to God's infallible revelation, which we are rightly told is absolutely relevant in today's culture. Yet the world's system tempts us to believe otherwise. It constantly and loudly proclaims its belief that the Bible is outdated and irrelevant in today's culture.

One practical example of this competition for people's devotion revolves around the concept of happiness. The world of advertising asserts that happiness is the result of pursuing materialistic hedonism. God's Word reveals that true happiness is achieved by developing character qualities modeled by the Lord Jesus Christ.

This week's lesson text details these character qualities and firmly proclaims that they result in true happiness.

DEVOTIONAL OUTLINE

1. Favored by God (Matt. 5:1-12). When Jesus saw how many people were following Him, He seized the opportunity to teach them about kingdom happiness.

Jesus taught that people who are favored by God have the following characteristics: they embrace their unworthiness before God, they weep over their personal sinfulness, they exhibit gentle self-control, they long for justice to be done everywhere, they have compassion on others, they are zealous for moral purity, they pursue achieving peace whenever possible, and they gladly endure harsh opposition.

None of these characteristics are ones that we normally pursue. The world tells us to value ourselves above all else, to go easy on ourselves regarding our flaws, to assert ourselves, to look out for number one, to seek pleasure at any cost, to fight for our rights, and to not take any guff from anyone. All that sounds natural, but it is a recipe for chronic unhappiness, which is exactly what we see all around us in the world today. Jesus points us to a radically better way.

2. Spiritual impact (Matt. 5:13-16). Jesus taught His followers that their lives were to have spiritual impact. They were to be salt and light in the world. Salt is a preservative, and light both exposes things hidden in darkness and illumines the path to safety.

Jesus warned His followers that it was possible to forfeit their calling to spiritually impact their world, and He challenged them to fulfill their calling by demonstrating lives marked by obedience to the Father's will. The result of their obedience to His challenge would be that others would "glorify your Father which is in heaven" (vs. 16).

AGE-GROUP EMPHASES

Children: Children need to know not only that God loves them but also that He wants to teach them how to do things that bring Him glory.

Youths: Young people often find meaning in life by forming cliques or joining tight-knit groups. Membership in such a group or clique often requires visible evidence, such as tattoos or clothing in a certain color. Have your teachers remind their young students that membership in God's kingdom demands a lifestyle that brings glory to God.

Adults: The body of Christ is in desperate need of mature Christian adults who are not ashamed to demonstrate the character qualities of kingdom living. Encourage your adults to be spiritual role models.

—*Thomas R. Chmura.*

SCRIPTURE LESSON TEXT

MATT. 5:17 Think not that I am come to destroy the law, or the prophets: I am not come to destroy, but to fulfil.

18 For verily I say unto you, Till heaven and earth pass, one jot or one tittle shall in no wise pass from the law, till all be fulfilled.

21 Ye have heard that it was said by them of old time, Thou shalt not kill; and whosoever shall kill shall be in danger of the judgment:

22 But I say unto you, That whosoever is angry with his brother without a cause shall be in danger of the judgment: and whosoever shall say to his brother, Raca, shall be in danger of the council: but whosoever shall say, Thou fool, shall be in danger of hell fire.

27 Ye have heard that it was said by them of old time, Thou shalt not commit adultery:

28 But I say unto you, That whosoever looketh on a woman to lust after her hath committed adultery with her already in his heart.

38 Ye have heard that it hath been said, An eye for an eye, and a tooth for a tooth:

39 But I say unto you, That ye resist not evil: but whosoever shall smite thee on thy right cheek, turn to him the other also.

43 Ye have heard that it hath been said, Thou shalt love thy neighbour, and hate thine enemy.

44 But I say unto you, Love your enemies, bless them that curse you, do good to them that hate you, and pray for them which despitefully use you, and persecute you.

NOTES

A Perfect Kingdom

Lesson Text: Matthew 5:17-18, 21-22, 27-28, 38-39, 43-44

Related Scriptures: Acts 14:8-18; Romans 9:30—10:4;
I Corinthians 3:11-15; James 2:10-13

TIME: A.D. 28   PLACE: mountain near Capernaum

GOLDEN TEXT—"Think not that I am come to destroy the law, or the prophets: I am not come to destroy, but to fulfil" (Matthew 5:17).

Introduction

Since each evangelist (Matthew, Mark, Luke, and John) presented the life and work of Jesus Christ from a unique perspective, each writer emphasized certain aspects of the Lord's teaching and ministry. The Gospel of Matthew was directed toward a Jewish audience.

Some have suggested that Matthew presents Jesus as the new Moses. Just as there are five books of Moses (the Law), so there are five major discourses in Matthew. Just as Moses received God's law on a mountain, so Christ delivered His new law from a mountain. Picking up from last week, we look at another portion of Jesus' Sermon on the Mount.

Whereas Moses conveyed God's law to the new nation of Israel, Jesus raised the sights for His followers. Israel was God's chosen people, but they were still an earthly kingdom and prone to earthly shortcomings. Jesus was looking toward God's perfect kingdom. It has not yet come in full, visible power, but all followers of Christ represent the King. We need to reflect His light to the world around us.

LESSON OUTLINE

I. THE LAW FULFILLED—
  Matt. 5:17-18

II. THE LAW INTERPRETED—
  Matt. 5:21-22, 27-28

III. THE LAW OF LOVE—
  Matt. 5:38-39, 43-44

Exposition: Verse by Verse

THE LAW FULFILLED

MATT. 5:17 Think not that I am come to destroy the law, or the prophets: I am not come to destroy, but to fulfil.

18 For verily I say unto you, Till heaven and earth pass, one jot or one tittle shall in no wise pass from the law, till all be fulfilled.

Not to destroy (Matt. 5:17). Since Jesus did not follow the traditions of the Pharisees, we can easily see how He might be accused of being a lawbreaker. The scribes and Pharisees were the guardians of the law. Anyone refusing to accept their traditional interpretations was subject to being castigated as a sinner (Matt. 12:2; John 9:16).

In the verses that follow this part of the Sermon on the Mount, Christ made several contrasts between His teaching and the interpretation of the scribes and Pharisees. He addressed such topics as murder (Matt. 5:21-22), adultery (vss. 27-30), divorce (vss. 31-32), and the taking of oaths (vss. 33-37).

Among Jews, what Christians call the Old Testament is divided into three sections: Law, Prophets, and Writings (cf. Luke 24:44). Sometimes the Scriptures were simply referred to as the Law and the Prophets, as they are in Matthew 5:17.

While some may have thought that Christ came to destroy the Law and the Prophets, this was not the case at all; rather, He came to fulfill them. {"By fulfillment is meant not just the carrying out of predictions but the accomplishment of the intention of the Law and the Prophets. In contrast to the Pharisees, Jesus brought out the true and deeper meaning of the Law, and he actually lived up to its intention" (Allen, ed., *Broadman Bible Commentary,* Broadman).}Q1

Since Matthew was concerned to show that Jesus of Nazareth is the long-awaited Messiah prophesied in the Old Testament Scriptures, he often reminded his readers that certain events occurred because they were prophesied (cf. Matt. 1:22; 2:5-6, 15, 17-18; 4:14-16; 8:17).

All will be fulfilled (Matt. 5:18). To further impress upon His hearers that He did not come to destroy the law, Christ declared that the minutest

details of the law would be fulfilled in Him.

{A "jot", or *yod,* was the smallest letter in the Hebrew alphabet. The smallest Greek letter, *iota,* is still used today to express something very small. The "tittle" was the least stroke of a pen that could change one letter to another.}Q2 It was as if Christ were saying that every *i* in the law would be dotted and every *t* crossed by Him.

The thrust of Christ's statement was that every part of the Law and the Prophets would be fulfilled in Him before the end of time. Unlike every human before or since, Jesus of Nazareth perfectly obeyed God's law (Heb. 4:15); therefore, He alone could be accepted by the Father as a sacrifice for sinners.

THE LAW INTERPRETED

21 Ye have heard that it was said by them of old time, Thou shalt not kill; and whosoever shall kill shall be in danger of the judgment:

22 But I say unto you, That whosoever is angry with his brother without a cause shall be in danger of the judgment: and whosoever shall say to his brother, Raca, shall be in danger of the council: but whosoever shall say, Thou fool, shall be in danger of hell fire.

27 Ye have heard that it was said by them of old time, Thou shalt not commit adultery:

28 But I say unto you, That whosoever looketh on a woman to lust after her hath committed adultery with her already in his heart.

Do not kill (Matt. 5:21). From the beginning of time, man has understood that there was a prohibition against the taking of human life (Gen. 4:10; 9:6). This was reinforced by the teaching of the Ten Commandments (Ex. 20:13) and the body of the Mosaic Law, which required capital punishment for this and certain other crimes (21:12-17; 22:18-20). The taking of any life is a serious matter and should never be viewed lightly. Sadly, human life is often undervalued today.

The warning about being in "danger of the judgment" (Matt. 5:21) had to do with the system of courts and judges found in ancient Israel (Deut. 16:18; 19:11-20). As in modern times, those who took the lives of others were subject to the criminal justice system under which they lived.

Of course, there will be a final judgment before which individuals will have to answer for their actions. Even if they escape the justice of men, they will one day stand before God (II Cor. 5:10; Rev. 21:8; 22:15).

As bad as murder is, it is not unforgivable. Moses (Ex. 2:12), David (II Sam. 12:9), and Paul (Acts 26:10) were guilty of murder. Thankfully, "the blood of Jesus Christ his Son cleanseth us from all sin" (I John 1:7).

Do not be angry (Matt. 5:22). As the Son of God, Christ spoke with divine authority: "But I say unto you." This, in fact, was what impressed the crowds who listened to Him on this occasion, for "it came to pass, when Jesus had ended these sayings, the people were astonished at his doctrine: for he taught them as one having authority, and not as the scribes" (7:28-29).

Though the human propensity to get angry is not wrong in itself, many do so "without a cause" (5:22). Of course, we can usually justify why we get angry, but most of the time it is rooted in our own pride and selfishness. Even the Lord became angry—but not without real justification (Mark 3:5; 11:15).

Again, the word "judgment" (Matt. 5:22) likely refers to the local judges,

not necessarily the final judgment. The point of our Lord, however, was to show that both overt acts (such as murder) and the inner motivation that leads to such acts (unrighteous anger) are serious matters.

{The meaning of the Aramaic word "Raca" is somewhat uncertain, but it could be translated "empty-head" or "good-for-nothing." It was a term of contempt reserved for those considered utterly worthless.}[Q3]

The Greek word for "council" is the word used for the Great Sanhedrin, which met in Jerusalem and was the highest court in the land (Deut. 17:8-13). Each village and town also had a sanhedrin, or council, to adjudicate local matters (16:18).

Again, Christ's point was that treating others with contempt puts one in grave danger. {And to declare another a fool was to place one's soul in danger of eternal punishment (Matt. 5:22).}[Q4] Since "the fool hath said in his heart, There is no God" (Ps. 14:1), to label another person a fool was to relegate him to the level of an atheist. Certainly, nothing worse could be said of an individual.

{"The word, *Gehenna,* rendered *hell* . . . is the Greek representative of the Hebrew *Ge-Hinnom,* or Valley of Hinnom, a deep, narrow glen to the south of Jerusalem, where, after the introduction of the worship of the fire-gods by Ahaz, the idolatrous Jews sacrificed their children to Molech. Josiah formally desecrated it [and] it became the common refuse place of the city, into which the bodies of criminals, carcasses of animals, and all sorts of filth were cast. From its depth and narrowness, and its fire and ascending smoke, it became the symbol of the place of the future punishment of the wicked" (Vincent, *Word Studies,* Eerdmans).}[Q5]

Lust forbidden (Matt. 5:27-28). That the Ten Commandments clearly sanctify the marriage bond is seen in the declaration "Thou shalt not commit adultery" (Ex. 20:14). In its broadest sense, this referred to all sexual activity outside the marriage relationship. It is obvious that many give little regard to obeying this commandment in today's world (cf. Heb. 13:4).

What is at the root of this prohibition? Is it not keeping one's mind and heart pure? {While a man may keep himself from actually physically committing adultery, it is much more difficult to keep one's thought life pure. Make no mistake about it, though—those who have committed adultery have been guilty of lustful thoughts prior to any physical act of immorality.

Christ went to the very heart of the matter, the lustful mind.}^Q6 Because of their emotional makeup, most men will find this to be more of a temptation than will most women. Even so, women can be tempted with lustful thoughts too.

"Jesus is not saying that lustful desires are identical to lustful deeds, and therefore a person might just as well go ahead and commit adultery. The desire and the deed are not identical, but, spiritually speaking, they are equivalent. {The 'look' that Jesus mentioned was not a casual glance, but a constant stare *with the purpose of lusting.* It is possible for a man to glance at a beautiful woman and know that she is beautiful, but not lust after her. The man Jesus described looked at the woman *for the purpose of feeding his inner sensual appetites* as a substitute for the act. It was not accidental; it was planned" (Wiersbe, *Bible Exposition Commentary,* Victor).}^Q7

THE LAW OF LOVE

38 Ye have heard that it hath been said, An eye for an eye, and a tooth for a tooth:

39 But I say unto you, That ye resist not evil: but whosoever shall smite thee on thy right cheek, turn to him the other also.

43 Ye have heard that it hath been said, Thou shalt love thy neighbour, and hate thine enemy.

44 But I say unto you, Love your enemies, bless them that curse you, do good to them that hate you, and pray for them which despitefully use you, and persecute you.

Eye for eye (Matt. 5:38). The concept of an eye for an eye comes from the Mosaic Law (Ex. 21:23-25; Lev. 24:20) and is sometimes called the law of retaliation. {Under the old covenant there were numerous and detailed instructions concerning what punishments should be meted out for various offenses, but the punishment always fit the crime. This law did not justify personal vengeance or vindictiveness, however. In fact, the purpose of this law was not just to secure justice in the case of an offense; it also was designed to restrict personal and unlimited retaliation against an offender (Deut. 19:4-7).}^Q8

While personal vengeance against an enemy may seem normal and natural to many, it is not our Lord's way (Lev. 19:18). He calls us to a higher law, the "royal law" (Jas. 2:8) of love.

Turn the other cheek (Matt. 5:39). In contrast to the retaliatory spirit that is so prevalent among humans, Christ asks us to respond humbly as He did.

The Lord's statement "Resist not evil" might give us the impression that we are to allow evil to go unchecked in our world. This command applies to individuals, however, not government. In short, it means the Christian must not respond to evil with evil. When tempted to retaliate, we must rise above a vengeful spirit. The only way evil can be conquered is to overcome it with good (Rom. 12:16-21).

{When treated badly, most find it difficult to turn the other cheek. Doing so takes great strength and courage. When hurt, we think that it will make us feel better to get back at the one who caused us pain, but it does not. It only lowers us to the level of the one who has mistreated us (Prov. 20:22).}[Q9]

Love your neighbor (Matt. 5:43-44). While the law did say, "Thou shalt love thy neighbour" (Lev. 19:18), it did not state that one's enemies were to be hated. Even so, this was a common teaching among the Jewish rabbis, who drew a sharp distinction between one's neighbor and one's enemy. In the parable of the good Samaritan, Jesus clearly responded to this misreading of God's law (Luke 10:25-37).

"It is astonishing, that the scribes fell into so great an absurdity, as to limit the word *neighbour* to benevolent persons: for nothing is more obvious or certain than that God, in speaking of our neighbours, includes the whole human race" (Calvin, *The Gospels,* AP&A).

{Jesus taught us to live by standards higher than those of the scribes (Matt. 5:20). Christ said that instead of hating our enemies, we should love them. He said that instead of cursing those who curse us, we should bless them. Instead of hating those who hate us, we should do good to them. Instead of persecuting those who persecute us, we should pray for them (vs. 44).}[Q10]

Of course, these concepts are as radical today as they were when Jesus delivered the Sermon on the Mount. Putting them into practice is difficult, to say the least. Our Lord never said that following Him would be easy, though.

Keep in mind that Christ was speaking to individuals and was not attempting to regulate human governments. Even if a nation adopted in principle that it would love its enemies, there would always be those who would refuse to do so. If, however, enough individuals within a nation practiced Christ's teachings, it would revolutionize the character of that nation and how it related to other countries. For the time being, though, we can only anticipate such universal peace, which will be realized only when Christ returns (Isa. 2:1-5; Hos. 2:18; Zech. 9:10; Rev. 11:15).

—John A. Owston.

QUESTIONS

1. In what ways did Christ fulfill the law?
2. What was a "jot" and a "tittle" (Matt. 5:18)?
3. What is the meaning of the word "Raca" (vs. 22)?
4. What kind of danger is one in when calling someone a fool?
5. What is the background behind the Greek word translated "hell"?
6. How did Christ strengthen the prohibition against adultery?
7. What was Jesus targeting when He warned against lustful looks?
8. What was the idea behind the "eye for an eye" concept from the Old Testament?
9. Why is it so difficult to turn the other cheek?
10. Why is it not acceptable to hate one's enemies?

—John A. Owston.

Preparing to Teach the Lesson

Wherever human societies have developed, codes for individual and group conduct have followed. These come from human experience and reasoning. But God also has spoken. Jews were governed by the Mosaic Law given by God at Mount Sinai. Jesus Himself lived under that code, but He also breathed new life into it by pointing His followers to the code of grace that would underlie the perfect kingdom He was bringing to earth. This lesson deals with some aspects of the new approach for living that Jesus introduced.

TODAY'S AIM

Facts: to know what Jesus proposed for changing people's thoughts and actions as He sought to move them from legality to love.

Principle: to show that the inner law of love superseded the outer law of legal ordinances.

Application: to help believers be governed by the law of love in their relationships with others.

INTRODUCING THE LESSON

An old adage states that "the road to hell is paved with good intentions." While people tend to procrastinate in doing the right things until it is too late, often even their intentions fall short of what is called for. According to the dictionary, an intention is "a determination to act in a certain way" (merriam-webster.com). An intention therefore becomes a motivating mental and emotional force.

When Jesus talked about intentions, He wanted to go beyond the mental and emotional aspects to the spiritual aspect. Perhaps He was thinking of Proverbs 23:7, which states of man, "As he thinketh in his heart, so is he."

Maybe He thought of Proverbs 4:23: "Keep thy heart with all diligence; for out of it are the issues of life." This lesson deals with some of those issues.

DEVELOPING THE LESSON

1. Intention I (Matt. 5:17-18). If we look at our five texts for this lesson as intentions, the first one has to do with Jesus Himself. He lived under the Mosaic Law and was the only person ever able to adhere to it perfectly. He declared that He had no intention of destroying it; instead, He came to fulfill it.

He did this not only by living a perfect life but also by paying the penalty for sin that the law demanded. This was done in the culmination of His ministry on earth when He died on the cross. His intention was clearly expressed in Mark 10:45: "The Son of man came not to be ministered unto, but to minister, and to give his life a ransom for many."

2. Intention II (Matt. 5:21-22). Jesus obviously was thinking of the sixth commandment—"Thou shalt not kill" (Ex. 20:13; Deut. 5:17)—when He said that a murderer was in danger of judgment. However, He went beyond the act itself to the anger that leads to murder. He equated that with the act itself and said that a person ruled by such anger would be judged too.

Have various sources for your students to consult when considering the terms "Raca" and "fool" in the latter part of Matthew 5:22. Share any meanings you have discovered, such as idiot, simpleton, good-for-nothing, or contemptuous person. Just as the use of "Raca" would make one liable to appear before the Sanhedrin for punishment, so also the use of "fool" could put a person in danger of hellfire. Discuss the hatred in the heart that would prompt using these terms.

3. Intention III (Matt. 5:27-28). Jesus later took up the matter of adultery, probably referring to the seventh commandment (Ex. 20:14; Deut. 5:18). Here again He directed people to the evil in the heart that produces the lustful look at a woman. He equated the desire to commit adultery with participating in the act itself. Once again He showed that intention is a crucial factor.

4. Intention IV (Matt. 5:38-39). Jesus later moved on to the issue of violent wounding, referring to "an eye for an eye, and a tooth for a tooth." He was referring to Exodus 21:24-25. Have your students turn to this passage and take note of the full series, which adds "hand for hand, foot for foot, burning for burning, wound for wound, stripe for stripe." Discuss what it means to turn the other cheek in a situation like Jesus described.

5. Intention V (Matt. 5:43-44). When Jesus spoke of loving one's neighbor, He was reminding His hearers of Leviticus 19:18, which says, "Thou shalt love thy neighbour as thyself." The Pharisees taught that one should hate his enemies. They misused such passages as Deuteronomy 23:3-6, which speaks about the Ammonites and Moabites and their mistreatment of Israel and ends with "Thou shalt not seek their peace nor their prosperity all thy days for ever."

Jesus sought to raise people to a higher level when He said people should love their enemies, bless those who cursed them, do good to those who hated them, and pray for those who despitefully used them and persecuted them. Have your students turn to Romans 12:17-21 to see Paul's instruction on this subject. Only a heart intent on love can do all this.

ILLUSTRATING THE LESSON

Our texts make it clear that there are two kinds of hearts. An evil heart produces destruction, taking of life, adultery, wounding, and cursing. A loving heart produces fulfillment, saving of life, morality, healing, and blessing.

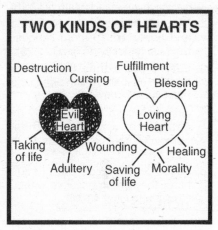

TWO KINDS OF HEARTS

CONCLUDING THE LESSON

Direct the attention of your class to Matthew 5:48 as the conclusion to this part of Jesus' Sermon on the Mount: "Be ye therefore perfect, even as your Father which is in heaven is perfect." Explain that no human being except Christ could ever be sinlessly perfect. What the term "perfect" means is spiritual maturity, and that develops throughout a believer's life.

Performance does not always measure up to a person's position in Christ, but the intention and effort for striving toward maturity should be present. Challenge your students to walk in the light and experience continual cleansing from sin by the blood of Christ (I John 1:7).

ANTICIPATING THE NEXT LESSON

Our next lesson looks at the calling of the Twelve and at the glimpse of Christ's victorious kingdom that their initial ministry assignment afforded. Death will be swallowed up in victory!

—Gordon Talbot.

PRACTICAL POINTS

1. God's Word is more solid and long-lasting than the very ground on which we stand (Matt. 5:17-18).
2. We need to take the sins of anger and hatred much more seriously than we typically do (vss. 21-22).
3. Lust is not a trifle that we can dismiss casually; it can bring us to ruin (vss. 27-28).
4. Jesus calls us to do exactly the opposite of what the world and our own impulses urge us to do (vss. 38-39).
5. Jesus' commands are not just hard; they are impossible without God's help (vss. 43-44).

—*Kenneth A. Sponsler.*

RESEARCH AND DISCUSSION

1. If Jesus did not abolish the law but upheld it to the smallest detail (Matt. 5:17-18), how is it that we are not "under the law" (Rom. 6:14)?
2. If a believer calls someone a fool, does he lose his salvation and become consigned to hell (Matt. 5:22)? What point was Jesus making?
3. Do you think there is anyone alive (other than Jesus) who has not committed adultery in his heart (vs. 28)? How do we overcome this sin?
4. What are some practical ways that we can turn the other cheek in today's world (vs. 39)?
5. How successful do you think Christians have been at loving their enemies (vs. 44)? How can we improve in this?

—*Kenneth A. Sponsler.*

ILLUSTRATED HIGH POINTS

But to fulfil (Matt. 5:17)

Faith Church was started by a small group of people with a burden for a gospel witness in their community. At first they were able to rent the music room in the local high school for a nominal fee. As the congregation grew, they were able to purchase a converted mobile home on a great location next to a major highway. The quarters were cramped, but the people made do.

In a few years Faith Church was able to construct a new building better suited to meet the needs of the congregation. The old building had served its purpose. It continues to provide supplemental Christian education space, but it no longer is used for public worship services.

Turn to him the other also (vs. 39)

Being a pastor's wife is not always easy. Judy often found herself on the wrong side of the president of the church women's group. The senior woman made snide remarks right to her face, and it seemed fairly obvious that there was negative talk behind the scenes as well. Many evenings Judy would come home from the women's meetings hurt and frustrated. She felt that she needed to keep attending because of her position in the church.

Rather than fight fire with fire and return evil for evil, Judy took a different approach. She baked a beautiful blueberry pie and delivered it to the home of the woman who had been treating her so badly. The woman did not know what to say. The kind gesture did not seem to make much of a difference in the older woman's behavior, but Judy had the satisfaction of taking the high ground and living in the spirit of Jesus' commandment to turn the other cheek.

—*Bruce A. Tanner.*

Golden Text Illuminated

"Think not that I am come to destroy the law, or the prophets: I am not come to destroy, but to fulfil" (Matthew 5:17).

Christ affirmed that the Jewish scribes and Pharisees sat in "Moses' seat" (Matt. 23:2), and yet in the same discourse He called them hypocrites and a brood of vipers (vss. 13, 33). Their ancestors had murdered the prophets; using strong language, Jesus urged the Jewish religious leaders to finish, or "fill up," what their predecessors had started. (The Greek for "fill up" in verse 32 is the same as that translated "fulfil" in our golden text.) Jesus' strident tone against the men in "Moses' seat" is very likely the reason why people might have thought He was opposed to the Law and the Prophets.

Jesus set the record straight: He was opposed only to evil people who pretended to honor the Law and Prophets; in truth, He had come to *fulfill* the Law and Prophets, a common way of designating the entirety of the Old Testament Scriptures.

Let us think about the fulfillment Jesus spoke of. In what ways did He fulfill the Law and the Prophets? First, we should recognize that God's Law was a reflection of His holiness. As God's Son, Jesus was truly the embodiment of divine perfection. Everything He thought, said, and did was perfectly aligned with God's holiness and truth. When John the Baptist hesitated to baptize Jesus, the Lord responded that He must fulfill all righteousness (Matt. 3:15). This was something He continually did throughout His life and ministry (Luke 24:44).

The fact that Jesus did fully obey the Law has extreme implications for our salvation. His perfect obedience provides us with a righteousness that is not our own (I Cor. 1:30; Phil. 3:9). He did all that was necessary to remove the Law's condemnation for everyone with faith in Him (Rom. 10:4; Col. 2:14).

A second way that Christ came to fulfill the Law and Prophets relates to the types and shadows contained in the Old Covenant. The sacrifices and elaborate rituals required by the Mosaic Law truly did not have spiritual meaning in and of themselves (Heb. 10:1). These offered only a rudimentary understanding of spiritual truth, but they are explained fully in the Person of Christ (Col. 2:16-17). The myriad Old Testament animal sacrifices point to Jesus' efficacious sacrifice on the cross (Heb. 10:8-10).

Finally (at least for this short treatment of the subject), Jesus fulfilled the messianic prophecies contained in the Law and the Prophets (and the Psalms—Luke 24:44). Jesus is the Prophet whom Moses said would come (Deut. 18:15-18). Jesus is the seed of Abraham through whom all the nations of the world are blessed (Gal. 3:16). He is the Lamb of God, who takes away our sins (Isa. 53:6-12; John 1:29). Literally hundreds of Old Testament prophecies apply directly to Christ (cf. Matt. 1:22; 2:17,23; 4:14; 8:17; 12:17; 13:35; 21:4; 26:54, 56; 27:9). These messianic foreshadowings are proofs showing that Jesus was exactly who He claimed to be: the King whom God intended to rule over His kingdom (Acts 2:32-37; 4:25-27).

The reality of Christ fulfilling the Law and the Prophets makes our faith sure and certain. It reveals that Christ's kingdom is the culmination of God's work throughout history. It is an affirmation of God's power to control this world and thwart Satan's schemes. But more than that, in a world that seems overrun by evil, it is the outworking of God's goodness.

—*Todd Williams*.

Heart of the Lesson

Following a man-made list of dos and don'ts makes many Christians feel secure. If they obey the dos and avoid the don'ts, they see themselves as being spiritual. In fact, they assume they are more spiritual than the person who does not follow any set list.

This rigid system is really legalism. It assumes that outward actions infallibly indicate inner motives. This is not true. A person can do all the right things but for the wrong reasons. This type of living makes a person proud. He thinks, *See how holy I am? I follow all the rules.* Inwardly, however, the person might be deceitful, unloving, and spiteful.

For example, a little girl was told to sit down. She did not want to sit down, but she knew she had better obey her mother. She sat down, but she also said, "I am sitting down on the outside, but inside I am standing up." Did the little girl have an attitude of obedience? Of course not. She outwardly obeyed, but inwardly she was rebelling.

No one can completely follow God's law except Jesus Christ. Only He has lived a perfect life here on earth; yet the religious leaders of His day still found much to criticize about Him—such as His disregard for their view of the Sabbath restrictions. Jesus did not allow Himself to be swayed by their view of what holiness entailed.

1. Jesus' role in the law (Matt. 5:17-18). Because of Jesus' different approach to the law, the scribes and Pharisees thought He was out to destroy the law.

Jesus told them that He had not come to do away with the law. Rather, He came to fulfill it. He would reveal its fuller meaning. The law had been a good start to show God's people what was right. It helped them see what God required of them, what His standards were; yet God knew there was no possible way for people to completely obey the law. That is why He sent His Son to earth—to bridge that gap between a holy God and sinful man.

2. The heart and the law (Matt. 5:21-22, 27-28, 38-39, 43-44). Jesus came to embody the law. How did this work?

Jesus explained what the law really required. This made a holy life seem even harder to live than before. Jesus was more interested in the attitudes and motives of the person than just the externals that others could see.

Naturally, the Pharisees did not like hearing Jesus' words about the need for proper inner motives. Strictly speaking, they should have been the most open to Jesus and His words, for they were the religious leaders of God's people. They should have been the most godly men around, but they were not. They were only out for man's praise, not God's approval of their hearts and lives. Jesus reserved His harshest judgments for these men, for they led the people further away from God rather than closer to Him.

Let us face the fact that for most it is relatively easy not to kill or steal or lie or commit adultery. Jesus took matters a huge step further, though, when He told the people that mere thoughts of hatred or lust were just as bad in God's sight as any sinful outward actions. God certainly is the only one who can judge a person's real motives and thoughts.

While it is true that the Bible says Jesus' followers are not under the law but under grace, it is even harder to live right with proper motives than to follow a list of dos and don'ts. It is only through Christ's power that we can please God.

Jesus Christ countered the Jews' religious philosophy by saying that the inner person is more important than outward obedience alone.

—*Judy Carlsen.*

World Missions

The Christian faith is not to be spread by armies, although that has been tried. It is not to be spread by financial enterprise, which also has been used more than is often realized. It should not be just the professionals who do the job, either. Rather, it should be ordinary believers who let their light shine by doing righteousness, living a life based on a true heart change.

We are tempted to think that missionaries are the paid emissaries who do the work and let the rest of us go about our lives undisturbed. This is not the biblical concept at all. Jesus spoke to ordinary people, exhorting each to be a missionary as God worked through him or her to give a practical exhibition of true righteousness.

This is in contrast with the ritual righteousness of the Pharisees. They would wear special clothing, eat a prescribed diet, and avoid people and objects that the religious authorities deemed defiling. Their carefully crafted regulations left them free to be deceitful and oppressive while technically not breaking their law.

Jesus urged men and women to have principles on which to act, not just technical restrictions that could be easily skirted. It is sincere heart religion that is the secret of Christianity's spread. Other religions have ritual but not inner transformation.

Missionaries are ordinary Christians who take the gospel to the lost wherever the Lord has led them. Supporters often enable them to live there without having to earn a living themselves. Of course, we all should be missionaries wherever we are and whether or not we are supported by anyone else.

With sincere concern for the lost, Christians have ministered to the sick and injured the world around. They have gone into the hottest and the coldest lands on earth with true servant's hearts. They have gone to disease-ridden and poverty-stricken areas with compassion and brought relief. Hospitals, clinics, and dispensaries have been started by them even before they built churches.

Christians go into lands not to rape and pillage but with moral standards that respect people and recognize their dignity and worth. Mission stations have been havens of light in dark areas. Some have seen their refusal to use violence as weakness and their refraining from oppression as naïveté, but that is not so. Rather, it reflects their love and kindness.

One of the most outstanding areas of Christian practice is promoting the worth of women. Where they were treated as slaves and beasts of burden, Christianity has brought them respect, encouragement, and protection. In places where no one thinks they can learn anything, Christians have begun schools for girls where they can demonstrate their intelligence.

Relief from mutilation, humiliation, and even death marks the path of the gospel. The truth has been resisted by those men who profited from evil, but light will conquer darkness. What Jesus taught strikes a responsive chord inside each of us as we recognize our own desire to be treated well and to be free from the vices and evils of a sinful society.

Missionary work starts in each of us and then spreads through our church to the local community where we live and from there to the larger field and worldwide. Our individual commitment to be involved in witnessing is something we should pray about earnestly.

I urge you to let the Lord work through you to help dispel the world's darkness.

—Philip J. Lesko.

The Jewish Aspect

Religions of the world are characterized by certain types of buildings. Protestant churches often have steeples. Roman Catholics have monasteries. Muslims have their mosques. Hindus have their temples.

In Judaism no set style of architecture prevails. Milton Steinberg observed that synagogues "are of almost every conceivable style and ornamentation" (*Basic Judaism,* Harcourt Brace Jovanovich).

One common element does exist, however, in Jewish synagogues. That element was there in Christ's day and is still present today. Steinberg states, "Every synagogue possesses, enshrines, and makes accessible at least one copy, in scroll form, of the book known as the Torah."

It was to the Torah, and its misinterpretation by the rabbis and the Pharisees, that Jesus referred in His Sermon on the Mount. He contrasted the traditions of the rabbinical interpretations with His approach, which focused on the spiritual intention of the Law rather than on mere externalities. Jesus called His audience back to the actual words of God rather than the interpretations of men.

The Jewish philosopher Philo, a contemporary of Jesus, honored the Torah, saying of Moses' words that "there may well be a hope that they will remain to all future time, as being immortal, as long as the sun and the moon, and the whole heaven and the whole world shall endure" (*On the Life of Moses* i i. 14). Agreeing with Philo's sentiment, Josephus (A.D. 37-100) wrote that "though we be deprived of our wealth, of our cities, or of the other advantages we have, our law continues immortal" (*In Answer to Apion* 39).

Jesus said that He did not come to destroy the Law or the Prophets (Matt. 5:17). He also confirmed that not even the smallest element of the law would pass away (vs. 18). God's law would instead be fulfilled in the life and teachings of Christ as He presented its true significance.

Jesus stated six times in Matthew 5 that "it was said" or "it hath been said" (vss. 21, 27, 31, 33, 38, 43). The phrase "it was said" was the common way that the Pharisees introduced their quotations from Scripture to support their teachings. In contrast to this rabbinical teaching, Jesus asserted, "But I say unto you" (vss. 22, 28, 32, 34, 39, 44).

Jesus took the rabbinic teachings on the vital subjects of murder and anger, adultery and lust, divorce and remarriage, oaths and communication, retaliation and graciousness, and love and maturity to a higher level of spiritual life.

Jesus spoke to the "multitudes" (Matt. 5:1) in this sermon, and He knew the importance of confronting the improper Pharisaical interpretations of Scripture. Josephus recognized that "the Pharisees have delivered to the people a great many observances by succession from their fathers, which are not written in the laws of Moses . . . [and] the Pharisees have the multitude on their side" (*Antiquities of the Jews* 13.10.6).

As sometimes occurs with religious teachers, the Pharisees emphasized their own interpretive traditions to such an extent that they were regarded as equal with the Old Testament Scriptures. Jesus focused on that rabbinic tradition, recognized it for what it was, and called His listeners back to the true intention of the Scriptures.

—R. Larry Overstreet.

Guiding the Superintendent

One of the temptations in the Christian life is to believe that godliness comes from abiding by certain rules and regulations. Many Christians believe that God is pleased when they dutifully fulfill their man-made checklists of daily spiritual tasks.

Spiritual disciplines are important, but it is possible to be dutifully immersed in them while neglecting significant internal issues such as the spiritual condition of the heart.

Jesus wanted His disciples to understand that fulfilling the law involved much more than external, dutiful obedience. He wanted them to pursue a demanding new approach to discipleship, an approach based on internal, heartfelt obedience.

DEVOTIONAL OUTLINE

1. The fulfillment of the law (Matt. 5:17-18, 21-22). Jesus told His disciples that He did not come into the world to destroy the law; rather, He came into the world to fulfill it. He also assured them that He would perfectly complete this task.

To illustrate what He was saying, Jesus stated that there is much more to obeying the command not to kill than simply refraining from homicide. The fulfillment of this commandment also involves refraining from illegitimate anger and verbal abuse.

2. Maintaining sexual purity (Matt. 5:27-28). When it came to the matter of adultery, Jesus wanted His followers to understand that it is not enough to abstain from adulterous acts. An obedient response to the seventh commandment requires a disciple to pursue a pure heart void of lust.

3. Turning the other cheek (Matt. 5:38-39). The Old Testament law dealt with just punishment (cf. Ex. 21:24; Lev. 24:19-20). Jesus stated that His followers are not to seek retaliation for wrongs endured but are to go so far as to return good for evil.

4. Loving our enemy (Matt. 5:43-44). Leviticus 19:18 commanded neighborly love. Jesus extended this to include even one's enemies. Followers of Christ are to display God's nature by ungrudgingly seeking the good of those who curse, hate, and persecute them.

AGE-GROUP EMPHASES

Children: Encourage your teachers to concentrate on the principle of love. They should teach the children that even though there are people in the world who do bad things, children who love the Lord can also love those people by praying for them.

Youths: Young people, especially young men, often believe that refraining from revenge or backing away from a fight is a sign of weakness. Many young men also believe that sexual purity is merely the practice of refraining from sexual acts. Challenge your young men to think differently about these issues. Help them understand that in many instances, enduring a painful situation without retaliation is a sign of godly strength. Help them also see that sexual purity includes restraint and discretion in what they look at and what they think about.

Adults: Some adults believe that the older they get, the easier life should be. Many translate this belief into the spiritual realm and begin to let down their guard. Challenge your adults to believe that fulfilling God's law involves a demanding, disciplined, heartfelt pursuit of holiness. That is what God truly desires from them.

—*Thomas R. Chmura.*

Scripture Lesson Text

MARK 3:13 And he goeth up into a mountain, and calleth *unto him* whom he would: and they came unto him.

14 And he ordained twelve, that they should be with him, and that he might send them forth to preach,

15 And to have power to heal sicknesses, and to cast out devils:

16 And Simon he surnamed Peter;

17 And James the *son* of Zebedee, and John the brother of James; and he surnamed them Boanerges, which is, The sons of thunder:

18 And Andrew, and Philip, and Bartholomew, and Matthew, and Thomas, and James the *son* of Alphaeus, and Thaddaeus, and Simon the Canaanite,

19 And Judas Iscariot, which also betrayed him: and they went into an house.

6:6b And he went round about the villages, teaching.

7 And he called *unto him* the twelve, and began to send them forth by two and two; and gave them power over unclean spirits;

8 And commanded them that they should take nothing for *their* journey, save a staff only; no scrip, no bread, no money in *their* purse:

9 But *be* shod with sandals; and not put on two coats.

10 And he said unto them, In what place soever ye enter into an house, there abide till ye depart from that place.

11 And whosoever shall not receive you, nor hear you, when ye depart thence, shake off the dust under your feet for a testimony against them. Verily I say unto you, It shall be more tolerable for Sodom and Gomorrha in the day of judgment, than for that city.

12 And they went out, and preached that men should repent.

13 And they cast out many devils, and anointed with oil many that were sick, and healed *them*.

NOTES

A Victorious Kingdom

Lesson Text: Mark 3:13-19; 6:6*b*-13

Related Scriptures: Matthew 10:1-15; 12:22-32;
Luke 11:14-23; I John 5:14-17

TIME: A.D. 28   PLACES: mountain in Galilee; Galilee

GOLDEN TEXT—"He ordained twelve, that they should be with him, and that he might send them forth to preach" (Mark 3:14).

Introduction

In Scotland, a young woman began teaching a Sunday school class of poverty-stricken boys. The most unpromising youngster was a boy named Bob. After the first two or three Sundays, he did not return; so the teacher went to look for him. Although the Sunday school superintendent had given Bob some new clothes, they were already worn and dirty when the teacher found him. He was given another new suit, and he came back to Sunday school. But soon he quit again, and the teacher went out once more to find him.

When she did, she discovered that the second set of clothes had gone the way of the first. "I am completely discouraged about Bob," she told the superintendent. They gave Bob a third suit of clothes, and this time he began to attend faithfully. It was not long until he became a Christian.

Who was that obstinate, ragged boy? He was none other than Robert Morrison, who later became the first Protestant missionary to China. He translated the Bible into Chinese and brought the Word of God to millions. When Jesus chose His disciples, they did not appear to be the most promising group; yet He knew they would grow and become powerful ministers, reaching thousands.

LESSON OUTLINE

I. **HIS SELECTIONS—Mark 3:13-19**

II. **HIS COMMISSION—Mark 6:6*b*-13**

Exposition: Verse by Verse

HIS SELECTIONS

MARK 3:13 And he goeth up into a mountain, and calleth unto him whom he would: and they came unto him.

14 And he ordained twelve, that they should be with him, and that he might send them forth to preach,

15 And to have power to heal sicknesses, and to cast out devils:

16 And Simon he surnamed Peter;

17 And James the son of Zebedee, and John the brother of James;

and he surnamed them Boanerges, which is, The sons of thunder:

18 And Andrew, and Philip, and Bartholomew, and Matthew, and Thomas, and James the son of Alphaeus, and Thaddaeus, and Simon the Canaanite,

19 And Judas Iscariot, which also betrayed him: and they went into an house.

The meeting on the mountain (Mark 3:13). {Jesus had reached a moment of tremendous importance: the time when He would choose those He wanted as His constant companions and learners who would carry on the ministry He was beginning.}^Q1 These men were going to be learning what kind of people they should be, what they should believe, how they should live, and what and how they were to teach others. They would eventually be the commissioned ones for beginning a worldwide outreach with the gospel. This was the initial organization for a campaign.

{Luke 6:12 says that before Jesus made His choices, "He went out into a mountain to pray, and continued all night in prayer to God." These appointments were not to be made without careful consideration, for the entire future of the ministry would be resting upon them.}^Q2 When we pray, we exhibit an attitude of dependence upon God. At this time Jesus was depending on His Father for the right decisions. Luke 6:13 says Jesus had many disciples but was going to choose from among them those He wanted as His apostles.

The Greek word translated "disciples" is *mathētēs,* and it signifies a learner. The word for "apostle" is *apostolos,* and it speaks of a delegate or ambassador. A literal rendering of this might be "one who is sent on behalf of and with the authority of another." Jesus' plan was to take a group of learners and prepare them to be His official representatives to the world.

It was these men who would become the leaders of the church in its establishment, organization, and beginning outreach in their communities.

The purposes for His choices (Mark 3:14-15). {There are two clearly stated purposes for Jesus' choice of these men. The first is "that they should be with him."}^Q3 It was going to take a while for this rough, untrained group to become what Jesus wanted. Luke 9:51-56 offers a good example of what He was dealing with. Upon traveling through Samaria, Jesus faced rejection. James and John, offended by this, asked, "Lord, wilt thou that we command fire to come down from heaven, and consume them, even as Elias did?" (vs. 54).

Jesus' response indicated that their attitudes were all wrong, even at this late stage of His ministry: "But he turned, and rebuked them, and said, Ye know not what manner of spirit ye are of. For the Son of man is not come to destroy men's lives, but to save them" (vss. 55-56). Their people skills still needed further honing if they were to be successful in future ministry. {The time the apostles spent with Jesus was a time of specific preparation that enabled them to carry His message to the world in the way He wanted it communicated.}^Q4

Anyone involved in any type of ministry must spend time alone with the Lord before engaging in that ministry. Whether it is preaching, teaching, singing, witnessing, or one-on-one evangelism, the heart must be ready first.

{The second purpose for Jesus' selection of the Twelve was to send them forth to preach, heal, and cast out demons.}^Q3 {The Greek word translated "power" in Mark 3:15 means "authority." It would be one thing to open their mouths and preach but quite another to have the ability to heal diseases and cast out demons. Since it is not natural for people to have such miraculous power, it was an authority conferred upon them by the Lord.}^Q5

The first of His disciples (Mark 3:16-17). {The first man named in the list of apostles is Simon, whom Jesus "surnamed Peter."}Q6 This does not mean that He changed his name but rather that He added another name to the one he already had. We often refer to him as Simon Peter. "Peter" is the Greek equivalent of the Aramaic name "Cephas" (John 1:42), a word meaning "stone" or "rock." Peter has been described by preachers as "the disciple with the foot-shaped mouth" because of the times when he spoke without thinking things through!

{Although Peter denied the Lord during His last days, he eventually became a leader of the early church and wrote two epistles that are included in our New Testament.}Q6 After His resurrection, Jesus made a special personal appearance to Peter, perhaps to encourage and strengthen him after his deep remorse for denying his Lord (Luke 24:34; I Cor. 15:5).

There was an initial interaction with Peter (along with his brother Andrew) and the brothers James and John in Mark 1:16-20. In our present text we learn that Jesus surnamed the latter two "Boanerges" (3:17). This surname apparently was an Aramaic idiom whose literal meaning is "sons of thunder." It is commonly assumed that this nickname gives an insightful indication of their personalities. Remember, they were the ones who wanted to call fire down upon the Samaritans who rejected Jesus.

The rest of His chosen ones (Mark 3:18-19). There are four lists of the apostles in the New Testament (Matt. 10:2-4; Mark 3:16-19; Luke 6:14-16; Acts 1:13). The Acts list consists of just eleven names, for by then Judas Iscariot was dead and had not yet been replaced. In all four lists, the first four names are the same, though with some change of order. Peter, however, is first in every case.

In each list the next group of four names is also the same but with a couple of changes in their order. Matthew listed himself after Thomas instead of before, as the other two Synoptic Gospel writers did. The Acts list is different from all three.

The third group of four begins with James the son of Alphaeus and ends with Judas Iscariot (with the exception of the Acts list). Matthew and Mark refer to Thaddaeus, while Luke and Acts refer to Judas the son of James. These are apparently two different names for the same person. This Judas, of course, should not be confused with Judas Iscariot.

About some of these men very little is known. In fact, most of them are not even mentioned again in the book of Mark. It is commonly assumed that Nathanael in John 1:45-51 was Bartholomew. Matthew 10:3 indicates that Thaddaeus's name was actually Lebbaeus, with Thaddaeus being his surname. What is perhaps the most significant bit of information, however, is the fact that all three of the Synoptic Gospel authors mention the fact that Judas Iscariot is most known for being Jesus' betrayer.

HIS COMMISSION

6:6b And he went round about the villages, teaching.

7 And he called unto him the twelve, and began to send them forth by two and two; and gave them power over unclean spirits;

8 And commanded them that they should take nothing for their journey, save a staff only; no scrip, no bread, no money in their purse:

9 But be shod with sandals; and not put on two coats.

10 And he said unto them, In what place soever ye enter into an house, there abide till ye depart from that place.

11 And whosoever shall not receive you, nor hear you, when ye depart thence, shake off the dust under your feet for a testimony against them. Verily I say unto you, It shall be more tolerable for Sodom and Gomorrha in the day of judgment, than for that city.

12 And they went out, and preached that men should repent.

13 And they cast out many devils, and anointed with oil many that were sick, and healed them.

Sending them out (Mark 6:6b-7). A chronological study of the life of Christ reveals that He made several itinerant tours around Galilee. The first is mentioned in Mark 1:35-39, the second in Luke 8:1-3, and the third is the one mentioned here. After choosing His disciples, Jesus took them on ministry tours to give them an opportunity to observe how He shared the gospel with others. The time had now arrived for them to go on their own. Jesus' ministry was multiplied through these sent-out representatives.

{The passage sounds very much like an official commissioning service. As He sent them forth, Jesus divided the disciples into pairs and apparently commissioned each pair individually as His representatives.}[Q7] It was a common practice for this type of activity to be done by two men rather than one, both for practical reasons and for legal ones (cf. Deut. 17:6; John 8:17). As special representatives of Christ, these men were to be viewed just as if He Himself were present giving the message they were speaking.

The first of Jesus' two purposes in choosing the Twelve had now been accomplished: they had been with Him and had learned much. Now the second purpose was being fulfilled: they were being sent out to preach and to have authority to exorcise demons from possessed people. From Mark 3:15, we know they were also given the power to heal diseases. A new phase of Jesus' ministry was about to begin. An expansion was taking place, making it possible for more people to be reached.

Describing their preparation (Mark 6:8-9). In Matthew 10:5-6 we learn that Jesus told the disciples they were to minister specifically to Jewish people on this tour, not to Gentiles or Samaritans. We learn other details from Matthew not included in the Mark account, including exactly what they were to preach and what other ministries they were to perform (vss. 7-8). The next instructions are the same as those in Mark and were given to inform the disciples that they were to totally depend on God for their supplies.

{They were to take only one staff, or walking stick,}[Q8] which was a common possession of most people. They were to rely on the one they had without preparing an additional one in case something happened to it (this seems to be the emphasis in the parallels in Matthew 10:10 and Luke 9:3). As far as other provisions were concerned, they were to trust that God would provide for them through the people they ministered to. They were not to take a bag of possessions for their physical needs, nor were they to take food or money.

{As for their clothing, they were to wear sandals (which was just ordinary footwear at that time) and to take only the tunic they were wearing.}[Q8] "Coats" (tunics) were knee-length, loosely fitting inner garments. An extra coat was often used at night as a blanket. All of these instructions give the impression that Jesus felt it was urgent for them to get on their way, for their message was so desperately needed throughout Israel.

Explaining their approach (Mark 6:10-11). Matthew 10:11 says, "And into whatsoever city or town ye shall enter, enquire who in it is worthy; and there abide till ye go thence." The disciples were to choose carefully where they would reside in each city, and they were to stay in the same place until they moved on. They needed to focus on their ministry instead of moving around looking for other places to stay. This might also indicate that they were to be content where they were without accepting more attractive offers that might arise later.

{Jesus let them know in advance that they could expect rejection in some places. The instruction He gave about shaking the dust off their feet stemmed from the Jewish practice of doing this when they left Gentile territory. This indicated that they felt such territory was defiled and unclean; thus, as they left it, they completely dissociated themselves from it.}[Q9] People who rejected the disciples and the message they presented were to be shown this symbolic act as a testimony against them.

This act in essence would show that by rejecting Jesus' disciples, the people were rejecting God and His message to them. This should have provoked serious thought on the part of those watching. It was the hope of Jesus and His disciples that this might cause some to reconsider and accept Him as their Messiah. If they would not, they would face great judgment.

Ministering as commanded (Mark 6:12-13). {"They were heralds of the gospel and had repeated success in expelling evil spirits from people. This demonstrated Christ's power over the supernatural world and confirmed His claim to being God" (MacArthur, *The MacArthur Study Bible,* Word). As the official representatives of Jesus Christ, everything the disciples did reflected back on Him and showed the people of Israel the validity of His claims. Their message was exactly what Christ was preaching and wanted spread.}[Q10]

The message of repentance had been given repeatedly since the days of John the Baptist (Mark 1:4, 14-15). Repentance is a turning from sin to God and is necessary for salvation. It is not a required "work" prior to salvation but rather an evidence of the work of God in one's heart. The Greek word means "to think differently." It is what follows a person's understanding of God's will. He will have a resulting change of direction.

The fact that these disciples had power to cast out demons and heal those who were sick shows that such miracles could happen apart from the personal presence of the Lord. It also shows that God cares about the total person, including physical, emotional, and spiritual needs. The God who cared then is the same God we serve now. When Jesus sent out the Twelve to minister to the needs of Israel, He showed His concern for all people.

—Keith E. Eggert.

QUESTIONS

1. What important decision did Jesus have to make at this time?
2. Why was it so important, and how did He prepare for making it?
3. For what two purposes did Jesus choose the twelve men He did?
4. Why was it so important that the Twelve spend time with Jesus before going out on their own?
5. What special authority did Jesus confer upon these men?
6. Who is named as the first disciple in each list, and what roles did he eventually fill?
7. What took place at the commissioning service Jesus held, and what was the result?
8. What instructions were the disciples given regarding what to take on their mission?
9. How were they to handle rejection when it occurred?
10. What did the men preach, and how did they validate their Master?

—Keith E. Eggert.

Preparing to Teach the Lesson

In our lesson this week we see how Jesus equipped the disciples and sent them out into the world. When Jesus sends us out in His service, He also first equips us for the work.

TODAY'S AIM

Facts: to show how Jesus equipped the disciples before He sent them out into the world to preach.

Principle: to emphasize that Jesus never sends us to do His work in the world without equipping us.

Application: to challenge students to strive to do God's work in God's power.

INTRODUCING THE LESSON

Before an important space mission is conducted, a lot of training and preparation takes place. The astronauts are selected carefully and then given training in simulated situations. When the big day arrives, they are well equipped for the mission before them. So it was with the mission Jesus gave the disciples. He had chosen the Twelve carefully and then prepared them for service in the world.

DEVELOPING THE LESSON

1. Jesus called the Twelve (Mark 3:13-19). As was His custom on many occasions, Jesus went up into a mountain to pray (cf. Luke 6:12). He then called to Him those He had handpicked for the ministry to work alongside Him. Twelve disciples were chosen for this task. Twelve seems to be a significant number in the Bible. Ask the students to list other sets of twelve in the Bible that they can remember. Twelve also seems to be a manageable number for training in a small group.

Notice also the kinds of people Jesus had chosen to send out. They came from all walks of life and social strata. Some were uneducated fishermen, one was a tax collector, and all of them had different personalities. God had a definite plan and purpose when He put them all together. This tells us that God can use any of us, no matter what our upbringing or background. As long as we are obedient, we can fit into God's plans for His kingdom.

Encourage the class to talk about what it means to answer the call of Jesus, and discuss the implications of following Him. Following Jesus at the expense of everything else does have an element of risk, but the rewards are unimaginably great.

Jesus called the Twelve so that He could send them forth for some very definite tasks. They would be called upon to preach. They also would be given power to heal sicknesses and to cast out demons.

Here the students can discuss the nature of God's call today. How does Jesus' call to His disciples compare with the call He has on our lives today? Bible teachers need to be aware of various denominational emphases in this very sensitive area.

2. Jesus equipped the Twelve (Mark 6:6b-11). Those whom Jesus calls, He equips for ministry and service. Note that He sent out the Twelve two by two. This reminds us that we need each other in ministry and that we can support one another.

Jesus also gave the disciples authority over demonic spirits and the forces of evil. Paul talked about our battles being "not against flesh and blood, but against principalities, against powers, against the rulers of the darkness of this world, against spiritual wickedness in high places"

(Eph. 6:12). When we follow Jesus, we are engaging in a battle with Satan and all his evil forces.

Jesus also wanted the disciples to learn to depend on God to provide for all their needs. When God sends us forth for ministry, He also provides for all our needs. The disciples were told to take nothing for the journey except a staff—no traveler's bag and no money. They were permitted to wear sandals and a tunic, which was common in their day, but were not allowed to take an extra coat with them.

Discuss with the students whether they would be willing to minister under such restrictions. What does God expect of us today?

The disciples were told to accept hospitality in a city and to stay with one family at a time where they were welcomed. If a city did not receive them well, however, they were to shake the dust off their feet as a sign that the people were rejecting the gospel and bringing condemnation upon themselves.

There is another implication here. We are warned that when we serve the Lord, we can expect persecution and hardship. Discuss with the students whether they know someone in ministry who is experiencing hardship because of stepping out for Jesus. Has the face of ministry today changed to the point that we have become so comfortable that there seem to be no hardships in following Jesus? If there is no hardship in ministry at all, are we then doing what Jesus wants of us?

3. Jesus sent the Twelve (Mark 6:12-13). Mark's report here is succinct and simple. Jesus sent the Twelve out, and they spread the Word of God faithfully. They cast out demons, healed the sick, and called on people to repent of their sins. They faithfully preached the gospel of salvation.

Jesus is the only way into the kingdom of God. We are to proclaim that message today. Only when Jesus comes into their lives are individuals eternally transformed.

When a person responds to the preaching of the gospel, wholeness of being results. That person becomes a new creature in Christ and enjoys what Jesus called the "abundant life" (cf. John 10:10).

ILLUSTRATING THE LESSON

When Jesus calls us for ministry, He equips us for service. He wants us to share the gospel of salvation with the world.

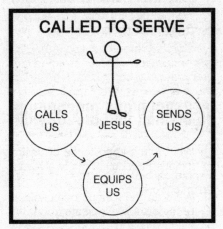

CONCLUDING THE LESSON

Every disciple is called to share in the task of evangelizing others. When Jesus calls us, He sends us out to make known the gospel of salvation so that others may come into His kingdom.

ANTICIPATING THE NEXT LESSON

Our lesson next week reminds us that there are both true and false followers among those who call themselves Christians.

—A. Koshy Muthalaly.

PRACTICAL POINTS

1. Spending time with Jesus is a prerequisite for any effective work for Him (Mark 3:13-14).
2. No work we seek to do can be successful without the authority and power of Jesus (Mark 3:15; cf. John 15:5).
3. Trust Christ; He knows you better than anyone else does (Mark 3:16-17; cf. Ps. 139:1-6).
4. Beware! No matter how auspicious the group, betrayers may be present (Mark 3:18-19).
5. Jesus supplies all that is needed for those whom He sends out (6:6b-7).
6. We may be sent to preach, but only Christ can change people's lives (vss. 8-13).

—Don Kakavecos.

RESEARCH AND DISCUSSION

1. What is the importance of Jesus' initiating the call of the twelve disciples?
2. What do the various personalities of the disciples indicate about the kinds of people God uses? How does this encourage you?
3. Why is spending time with Jesus so crucial to serving Him? In what practical ways can we spend time with Jesus?
4. Should we be surprised when those who seem to be followers of Christ defect? Why or why not (cf. I John 2:19)?
5. Why do you think that Jesus gave the Twelve the directions recorded in Mark 6:8-11? Are they still incumbent upon His followers today? Explain.

—Don Kakavecos.

ILLUSTRATED HIGH POINTS

Round about the villages (Mark 6:6)

Some of us who like gospel music decided to begin promoting concerts in our area. For these occasions we invited well-known quartets.

On one such night, the attendance was far below expectations. I made it a point to apologize to the visiting quartet, knowing they were accustomed to singing before much larger audiences. The leader patted me on the shoulder and told me not to be concerned, saying, "We sing the same no matter how many are out there." Then he added, "The Lord can bless even if there is just one."

We did invite the group back, and this time we had a fine crowd. Most of all, we felt God's presence. No community is too small for God.

There abide till ye depart (vs. 10)

A friend, a widow of many years now, lives in a nearby town. She spends much time in her garden, a major food source for her.

Lizzy has been active in her church seemingly all her life. She sings in the choir, teaches Sunday school, and helps wherever she is needed.

Lizzy opens the spare rooms of her home to visiting evangelists and their families as well as to furloughing missionaries and others needing temporary lodging. She provides meals, linens, and whatever might make her guests comfortable, all at her own expense.

Lizzy is getting on in years now, and caring for houseguests is becoming more difficult for her. I asked her recently whether it might not be time to turn this responsibility over to someone else.

"Who?" she asked.

I could not answer that. Very few people are willing to open their homes. Those who do are often under-appreciated.

—Albert J. Schneider.

Golden Text Illuminated

"He ordained twelve, that they should be with him, and that he might send them forth to preach" (Mark 3:14).

Jesus chose twelve men. Luke 6:12-13 tells us that He had spent the night on a mountain in prayer, communing with His Father before He made His choices. Jesus habitually spent time alone in prayer seeking His Father's will—especially when there were important decisions to be made. Leaders should always be chosen with care and much consultation with God, but this was a particularly important time.

The men Jesus chose would have the important job of carrying the gospel to all the known world. These men would be, in a sense, the creators of the New Testament church. They would also have to endure a time of incredible persecution. Walter W. Wessel wrote, "It was a strange group of men our Lord chose to be his disciples. Four of them were fishermen, one a hated tax collector, another a member of a radical and violent political party. Of six of them we know practically nothing. All were laymen. There was not a preacher or an expert in the Scriptures in the lot. Yet it was with these men that Jesus established his church and disseminated his Good News to the end of the earth" (Gaebelein, ed., *The Expositor's Bible Commentary,* Zondervan).

All of Jesus' choices were right, even though one of the men chosen was Judas Iscariot, who would betray Him. Jesus did not make a mistake; He knew (perhaps His Father had shown Him) that Judas was necessary to fulfill prophecy and to bring about the terrible final events of Jesus' life. So Judas became one of the Twelve.

That twelve were chosen is also significant. There had been twelve tribes of Israel in the old covenant; now there would be twelve apostles in the new covenant. The beginnings of the new church would have the symbolism of the Old Testament. The Jews would recognize this even as they resisted the truth. The number was significant enough that after Judas betrayed Christ and hanged himself, the disciples got together and chose Matthias to replace him and complete the number again (cf. Acts 1:15-26).

The Twelve would "be with him." Jesus needed close friends. With such large crowds milling around Him all the time, He needed help to keep things under control. More than that, He needed support: people to see to His needs and protect His space when necessary, people to share His heart with (even if they did not always understand).

The Twelve were more than just friends and followers. He "ordained" them. He called them apostles, literally "sent ones." He "ordained" them "that he might send them forth to preach." Jesus was going to take special time with these twelve men. He was going to teach them all they needed to know so that they could spread the gospel to all the world. In Mark 3:15 we find out that He also gave them power to heal diseases and to cast out demons. These men were going to be great leaders, teachers, and evangelists (all except Judas, of course).

The hope for all of us is this: that ordinary men and women who spend time with Jesus, give themselves totally to God for His service, and are filled with the Holy Spirit can do extraordinary things, can see miraculous things happen, and can change the world! If Jesus has called you into His salvation, you are His disciple. Do great things for Him!
—Julie Barnhart.

Heart of the Lesson

One of the most important decisions Jesus made was the choosing of His twelve disciples, whom He called His apostles. This was vitally important because they would be His instruments to carry on His work after He returned to heaven.

1. Choosing the right companions (Mark 3:13-19). The Word of God makes it clear that we need to be very careful in choosing our friends. Some very salient points about friends are made in the book of Proverbs (17:17; 22:24; 27:6, 17). The right friends stay with us through adversity, reprove us when we need it, and sharpen us in our spiritual effectiveness for the Lord.

Paul also stressed the importance of having godly companions, saying, "Be not deceived: evil communications (companions) corrupt good manners (character)" (I Cor. 15:33). We all want our children to find good friends because we know that if they get in with the wrong crowd, they might get into trouble. God wants His children to follow the same pattern.

Notice also that when Jesus chose His twelve close companions, He sent them out to preach "and to cast out devils (demons)" (Mark 3:15). Judas Iscariot is named among the Twelve (vs. 19). Did he who would later betray Christ also cast out demons? It would appear so.

What we must remember is that even something as important as exorcism is not proof that someone is a genuine believer. Jesus made that clear in Matthew 7:22-23: "Many will say to me in that day, Lord, Lord, have we not prophesied in thy name? and in thy name have cast out devils? and in thy name done many wonderful works? And then will I profess unto them, I never knew you." People may do great things in God's name, but that does not demonstrate a true relationship with Him.

2. Depending on the right companions (Mark 6:6b-13). When we choose the right friends, we will come to depend on them. That is the nature of friendships, and that is why it is so important to choose godly friends from the beginning. Jesus sent His friends out to proclaim His message to those in Israel. He gave them very specific instructions. They obeyed, and God blessed their ministry with great results.

This should encourage us to be the kind of friend God wants us to be. A friend is someone who can be counted on. Are we that kind of friend? Jesus is. Without a doubt, He is always the kind of friend we can depend on.

Abraham was called the friend of God (Jas. 2:23). God spoke to Moses "as a man speaketh unto his friend" (Ex. 33:11). "Yes," you might say, "but these were great heroes of the faith! I could never do what they did." Perhaps not—but you too can be the friend of God. He has made it possible for you to have a living relationship with Him, and that relationship is one of friend to friend.

We also can see that God blessed the disciples' ministry. There are times when we labor for God and seem to see no results. You might have a teenager who rebels against your desire to lead him in serving God. Take heart; God is in control. Whatever God calls us to do, He will show Himself faithful in the results, whatever they may be. We can count on it.

—John Haynes.

World Missions

Jesus gathered ordinary people around Him to help Him with His ministry on earth. He did not seek out the wisest ones or only the wealthy. He sought out men who were ordinary. Some may have been plain, but all of them were willing to give up all they had to serve and help Jesus.

Why do you think Jesus wanted twelve men? Could His ministry have been effective with just six? Later on in His ministry, Jesus had the disciples go out in pairs. Why did He not send them all out separately? He definitely did not need them to fulfill His earthly purpose; yet He chose each one for his uniqueness, and each helped Him spread His message.

This week's golden text points to Jesus' plan for His disciples. Mark 3:14 says, "He ordained twelve, that they should be with him." Part of the answer is that Jesus wanted the companionship of these men.

Each of them had a particular part in Jesus' ministry on earth. Each of them had a special talent or attribute that helped Jesus in His earthly ministry. Each had a purpose in the earthly ministry of our Lord—even Judas.

If you take a look at missionary endeavors in this century, it is rare to find missionaries trying to accomplish their job by themselves. For some it would have been completely impossible.

For example, some missionaries are required to go into the jungles of a tropical area. Without capable and skilled airplane pilots, they would never be able to reach their mission field destination.

Some missionaries are not allowed to enter their mission field without the companionship and help of another missionary couple. Many missionaries are required or encouraged to work in teams.

Why is this? Being on the mission field can be tiring, especially when the missionary is in a region that is secluded and isolated from his own country and his own people. Many missionaries would tire or become easily discouraged without other missionaries close by to lend a hand or give a needed break from the work they are involved in.

Missionaries are not an isolated people serving God. They require the people back in their home countries to pray and to support them financially to free them up to do their jobs.

Some missionaries need other couples to educate and care for their children. Some mission fields are not child friendly, and the mission board gives families the option to put their children in boarding school to help with their care.

Missionaries also need fully functional mission boards equipped with many people who can help manage their financial support. They need help sending out mission update letters and a staff that is willing to help them stateside with problems that may arise.

Jesus chose men to help complete His earthly ministry. There could have been many reasons for this, but the fact is that each man had an important purpose to fulfill as a disciple of Jesus.

God has given us other believers for encouragement. He has also given us Christian friends to pray for our needs and to keep us accountable in our Christian walk. His example teaches us that He never intended us to serve alone.

—Elizabeth Wehman.

The Jewish Aspect

The biblical account of the calling and preparation of the disciples is an absorbing one. Mark emphasized that the Lord called them to the mountain, "and they came unto him" (Mark 3:13). Luke added the information that the calling came after the Lord "continued all night in prayer to God" (Luke 6:12).

The Pharisees were disciple-makers, but they did not call men to revival or to a new relationship with God but rather to the narrow strictures of Pharisaism. Amid a long list of woes pronounced on that movement, Jesus observed bitterly, "Ye compass sea and land to make one proselyte, and when he is made, ye make him twofold more the child of hell than yourselves" (Matt. 23:15).

In terms of the rigors of Pharisaism, it was a difficult life. Fasting, prayer, and tithing were demanding, but the disciple could realize a degree of influence in religious and national affairs and apparently some ill-gotten gain (Matt. 23:14). Few Pharisees had the teachable spirit of Nicodemus or Paul.

Rabbi William B. Silverman wrote, "Despite a period in history when the Pharisees attempted to make converts from paganism to a belief in a God of morality, Judaism has not sought proselytes" (The Sages Speak: Rabbinic Wisdom and Jewish Values, Aronson).

Judaism does not seek proselytes, but it does attract them. At Rabbi Silverman's invitation I addressed about one hundred Gentile proselytes in a Sunday synagogue service. They responded to a gospel presentation with more hostility than one would receive from one hundred Jewish people.

The proselytes were attracted to Judaism by the beauty of its rituals. In private conversations I found those with former religious lives had attended churches with no gospel testimony. Many were from families with no spiritual roots at all. Some implied that Judaism was merely a kind of fad for them.

Judaism has a problem with accepting proselytes. The very existence of the Jews' religion, to give it Paul's name (cf. Gal. 1:13-14), depends on maintaining a core of Jews born to that ancient people. Judaism must have Jewish families at its heart. Recent studies show that a majority of Jews marry non-Jews.

Reform Judaism, the liberal wing of the faith, is subject to proselytism from Orthodox groups. A Jewish friend, Sidney, was devoted to his Jewish heritage but was very lax about any kind of religious practice. A group of Hasidic Jews, ultra-Orthodox in their brand of Judaism, convinced Sidney to wear phylacteries (two small boxes filled with Scripture from the Old Testament that are secured by leather thongs). Used in prayer, one box is tied to the forehead while a second box is placed on the inside of the left bicep. The thongs are wound around the head and down the arm to the middle and ring finger. The worshipper is holding the Word of God against the brain and the heart.

Sidney went along with this for a few days, but when it became too much trouble for him, he abandoned the practice. It was a curiosity to talk about for a few days, and then he went on to some other fragment of his Jewish past.

—Lyle P. Murphy.

Guiding the Superintendent

There are two phases in being a disciple of Jesus. There is the "being" stage, and there is the "doing" stage. Jesus called the Twelve to Him to be with Him. They had to be with Jesus in order to learn the ways and mind of Jesus. They were then to put what they had learned into practice. In this week's lesson, that is what the apostles were called to do. They were to take what Jesus had given them and apply it in ministry to others.

We believers today must first be with Jesus in order to become like Him (cf. John 15:5). In time, Jesus will call us to do a work. When we are ready, He will guide us into the proper good works that He has prepared for us (Eph. 2:10).

DEVOTIONAL OUTLINE

1. Calling the Twelve (Mark 3:13-19). After spending all night in prayer (Luke 6:12-13), Jesus chose those whom He would appoint as apostles. These men were to be with Him not only to learn but also to help Him in preaching the gospel.

2. Instructing the Twelve (Mark 6:6b-11). Jesus prepared His disciples to preach the gospel in the surrounding villages. They had the message. He gave them power over the unclean spirits and then gave them instructions concerning their provisions.

Jesus told the apostles that they were to take no provisions for their journey. This was a lesson in total dependence on their Heavenly Father. Jesus wanted to teach the apostles that money and possessions are never to be motivations for or hindrances to the spreading of the gospel.

Jesus also made it clear in His instructions how important their message was. The message was so important that acceptance or rejection of it would have consequences in the day of judgment.

3. Sending the Twelve (Mark 6:12-13). The Twelve were sent out on a prosperous mission. The gospel was preached, unclean spirits were cast out, and sick people were made well. We can be sure that their daily needs also were met.

AGE-GROUP EMPHASES

Children: Children are very trusting and easily get excited about things. Now is the time to get the child's faith fixed completely on the Lord.

Take this opportunity to impress upon them the truth that when we follow the Lord, He will take care of our needs (Matt. 6:33). Help them see that just as they trust their parents to take care of their needs, so they can trust their Heavenly Father to take care of their needs as well.

Youths: Encourage the youths to live out this lesson in a practical way, understanding that trusting the Father to provide for their needs is not just a first-century ideal. Challenge them to organize a day of evangelism or a day-long work project in another city. Have them look to the Lord as they plan. Exhort them to pray and ask the Lord to provide for their needs.

Adults: Urge the adults to focus on a ministry of giving and serving in order to proclaim the gospel. In addition, guide them to understand that those who refuse to hear or receive them are not to be hassled but left alone.

There are times when people have driven unbelievers far from Jesus by their constant pressure. Christians must learn to trust in the Lord and leave alone those who will not listen to the gospel. As you treat other people well, they will see your good works. Some may ultimately glorify God (Matt. 5:16).

—*David L. Schmidt*

SCRIPTURE LESSON TEXT

MATT. 13:24 Another parable put he forth unto them, saying, The kingdom of heaven is likened unto a man which sowed good seed in his field:

25 But while men slept, his enemy came and sowed tares among the wheat, and went his way.

26 But when the blade was sprung up, and brought forth fruit, then appeared the tares also.

27 So the servants of the householder came and said unto him, Sir, didst not thou sow good seed in thy field? from whence then hath it tares?

28 He said unto them, An enemy hath done this. The servants said unto him, Wilt thou then that we go and gather them up?

29 But he said, Nay; lest while ye gather up the tares, ye root up also the wheat with them.

30 Let both grow together until the harvest: and in the time of harvest I will say to the reapers, Gather ye together first the tares, and bind them in bundles to burn them: but gather the wheat into my barn.

31 Another parable put he forth unto them, saying, The kingdom of heaven is like to a grain of mustard seed, which a man took, and sowed in his field:

32 Which indeed is the least of all seeds: but when it is grown, it is the greatest among herbs, and becometh a tree, so that the birds of the air come and lodge in the branches thereof.

33 Another parable spake he unto them; The kingdom of heaven is like unto leaven, which a woman took, and hid in three measures of meal, till the whole was leavened.

NOTES

Growing God's Kingdom

Lesson Text: Matthew 13:24-33

Related Scriptures: Daniel 2:24-47; Matthew 13:36-43;
Mark 4:26-32; Luke 13:18-21

TIME: A.D. 28   PLACE: by the Sea of Galilee

GOLDEN TEXT—"Let both grow together until the harvest: and in the time of harvest I will say to the reapers, Gather ye together first the tares, and bind them in bundles to burn them: but gather the wheat into my barn" (Matthew 13:30).

Introduction

In spite of the ever-increasing hold of modern technology on people's attention, old-fashioned storytelling remains quite popular. Whether it is the bedtime story, storytime at the local library, or the various storytelling festivals that attract adults, this time-tested means of communication is alive and well.

While Christ used a variety of communication methods, the parable—often described as an earthly story with a heavenly meaning—was His most common one.

While both the disciples and the multitudes were intrigued by the stories that fell from the lips of the Master Teacher, that did not mean they always understood His teaching. On more than one occasion, those closest to the Saviour inquired privately about the meaning of a particular parable. By their very nature, parables had the ability to either reveal or conceal the truth.

LESSON OUTLINE

I. **PARABLE OF THE TARES—Matt. 13:24-30**

II. **PARABLE OF THE MUSTARD SEED—Matt. 13:31-32**

III. **PARABLE OF THE LEAVEN—Matt. 13:33**

Exposition: Verse by Verse

PARABLE OF THE TARES

MATT. 13:24 Another parable put he forth unto them, saying, The kingdom of heaven is likened unto a man which sowed good seed in his field:

25 But while men slept, his enemy came and sowed tares among the wheat, and went his way.

26 But when the blade was sprung up, and brought forth fruit, then appeared the tares also.

27 So the servants of the householder came and said unto him, Sir, didst not thou sow good seed in thy field? from whence then hath it tares?

28 He said unto them, An enemy

hath done this. The servants said unto him, Wilt thou then that we go and gather them up?

29 But he said, Nay; lest while ye gather up the tares, ye root up also the wheat with them.

30 Let both grow together until the harvest: and in the time of harvest I will say to the reapers, Gather ye together first the tares, and bind them in bundles to burn them: but gather the wheat into my barn.

Good seed (Matt. 13:24). Bible scholars believe that Matthew may have arranged material according to theme or topic. Some think he did this in Matthew 13, which contains seven parables. While that is possible, it seems more likely that on this particular occasion Christ delivered an entire sermon made up exclusively of parables. Like any preacher, the Lord could use the same stories in different settings, depending on His goals or the needs of His listeners.

{As Matthew 13 opens, the multitude was so large by the Sea of Galilee that Jesus got into a boat and taught the people as they stood on the shore (vss. 1-2). Opening with what has become one of His best-known stories, the parable of the sower, Christ reminded His hearers that not all those who hear come to genuine faith.}^{Q1} Quoting Isaiah 6:9, Jesus said, "By hearing ye shall hear, and shall not understand; and seeing ye shall see, and shall not perceive" (Matt. 13:14). While there may be a mixed response when the gospel is preached, it is still necessary to hear God's Word before faith can spring forth (Rom. 10:17).

After giving and interpreting the parable of the sower (Matt. 13:3-9; 18-23), Jesus proceeded to tell the parable of the tares. All the parables of this chapter are illustrations of Christ's kingdom. {Matthew is the only one of the four Gospels to use the expression "kingdom of heaven." Parallel passages in the other Gospels use the term "kingdom of God." Since Matthew was addressing a largely Jewish readership, he likely avoided the use of God's name, as was customary among the Jews. While there are debates concerning the precise definition of "kingdom of heaven" or "kingdom of God," it is probably best to think in terms of God's rule, whether on earth or in heaven, either in the present or in the future.}^{Q2} Either way, the parables of the kingdom reveal much about God's sovereignty, Christ's mission, and the nature of His kingdom during the present time between His first and second comings.

{As the parable of the sower depicted different soils representing different responses to the gospel, the parable of the tares assures us that Christ alone sows good seed (Matt. 13:37) in the field, which is the world at large. In this case, according to Jesus' own explanation, "the good seed are the children of the kingdom; but the tares are the children of the wicked one" (vs. 38).}^{Q3}

Unwanted growth (Matt. 13:25-26). {The tares sown by the enemy were actually weeds, probably darnel, which resembles wheat and is not easily detected at first.}^{Q4} "We must beware of Satan's counterfeits. He has counterfeit Christians (2 Cor. 11:26) who believe a counterfeit Gospel (Gal. 1:6-9). He encourages a counterfeit righteousness (Rom. 10:1-3), and even has a counterfeit church (Rev. 2:9). At the end of the age, he will produce a counterfeit Christ (2 Thess. 2:1-12)" (Wiersbe, *The Bible Exposition Commentary,* Cook).

{The enemy sowed the tares at night,}^{Q4} which is typical of Satan's strategy. His work is mostly covert, and by the time it becomes evident that he is behind an evil deed, the damage has already occurred and reversing the consequences of his work is difficult, if not impossible.

As described in the parable, once the tares became evident, it was almost harvesttime. As with all parables, the details should not be pressed. To be sure, some of the works of Satan and his helpers are easily and quickly seen for what they are. But the point of this parable is that this is not always true. If false teachers were immediately recognized, they would never gain a foothold in people's lives or in the churches they infiltrate. As Jesus warned, "Beware of false prophets, which come to you in sheep's clothing, but inwardly they are ravening wolves" (Matt. 7:15).

{As we have noted, Jesus identified the tares as the children of the evil one. They are false Christians.}Q5 "Satan cannot uproot the plants (true Christians), so he plants counterfeit Christians in their midst. In this parable, the good seed is not the Word of God. It represents people converted through trusting the Word. The field is not human hearts; the field is the world. Christ is sowing true believers in various places that they might bear fruit (John 12:23-26). But, wherever Christ sows a true Christian, Satan comes and sows a counterfeit" (Wiersbe).

Overreaction (Matt. 13:27-28). Discovering that tares had been sown among the wheat, the servants of the owner approached him concerning the seed he had sown in his field. Assuming good seed had been sown, the servants asked an obvious question: "Whence then hath it tares?"

Knowing that good seed had originally been sown in his field, the owner realized that some enemy was responsible. Apparently, the business practices of ancient Israel were no different from what sometimes occurs today. That a company or businessman attempts to steal trade secrets or sabotage the competition is nothing new. In the scenario depicted in this parable, someone may have had a grudge against the landowner and simply wanted to see his crop fail.

Since the tares represented a danger to the entire crop, the servants suggested that they quickly uproot the tares that had been sown. While this might seem a reasonable suggestion, it could actually have done more harm than good.

You can probably imagine similar situations in both families and churches in which quick action might result in more harm than good. This, of course, does not mean we should be content to allow evil to grow and flourish in our world. But forcibly trying to uproot evil can sometimes be counterproductive to the ultimate goals of the gospel. "Our task is not to pull up the false, but to plant the true. (This does not refer to discipline within the local church.) We are not detectives but evangelists! We must oppose Satan and expose his lies. But we must also sow the Word of God and bear fruit in the place where He has planted us" (Wiersbe).

Wise counsel (Matt. 13:29-30). {The owner wisely told his servants that in trying to rid the field of the tares, the wheat would likely be endangered.}Q6 Until harvesttime, when the two were more easily distinguished, the wheat and tares were to be permitted to grow side by side in the field. At that time, the tares could be gathered and burned and the wheat stored in the farmer's barn.

{As Jesus later interpreted the parable, both the wheat and the tares, that is, both the righteous and the wicked, will continue to the end of the age. At that time, judgment will fall on the wicked (Matt. 13:39-43). As for the righteous, they will be rewarded by the Father.}Q7 Scripture affirms over and over that judgment is coming (cf. II Thess. 1:7-9; II Pet. 3:10-13; Rev. 20:11-15).

PARABLE OF THE MUSTARD SEED

31 Another parable put he forth unto them, saying, The kingdom of heaven is like to a grain of mustard

seed, which a man took, and sowed in his field:

32 Which indeed is the least of all seeds: but when it is grown, it is the greatest among herbs, and becometh a tree, so that the birds of the air come and lodge in the branches thereof.

Small seed (Matt. 13:31). While Christ spoke frequently in parables, this was not unique, for parables were also used in the Old Testament (cf. Isa. 5:1-7). The Greek *parobolē* literally means "that which is cast beside"; hence, it is a comparison. The Hebrew word rendered "parable" had a wider meaning and could be understood as a proverb, riddle, or wise saying.

When we look at Jesus' parables, we find that some seem to stress just one point, whereas others are more allegorical, as with the parable of the sower and the parable of the tares. Since these two parables were interpreted point by point by Christ, it is sometimes assumed that each point of a parable has some particular meaning. This, however, is not necessarily true. During the early centuries of the church, not only did some attempt to find hidden meanings in the parables, but they also sought to do this with otherwise plain passages of the Bible. Such an approach ignores the original context and can lead to false and fanciful interpretations.

Once again, the purpose of the parable was to illustrate something about the kingdom of heaven. In this case, God's kingdom "is like to a grain of mustard seed" (Matt. 13:31). Other ancient Jewish literature indicates that the mustard seed was frequently used proverbially. "The point of comparison is not the seed in itself, but what happens when it is sown" (France, *Matthew,* InterVarsity).

Large tree (Matt. 13:32). Technically, there are other seeds smaller than the mustard seed, but such seeds were unknown to people in that part of the world. In spite of its small beginnings, the mustard seed grew to become the "greatest among herbs" and could even be described as a tree. While modern horticulture distinguishes between shrubs and trees, ancient peoples did not. So large was the mustard plant that birds could actually nest in it.

{Whether there is any significance to the birds in the parable is uncertain}[Q8] This could just be coloring in the parable, that is, something that enhances the total word picture Christ was painting without having any particular interpretative significance.

{On the other hand, there are some passages in the Old Testament in which such imagery did have significance. In Ezekiel 31, the Assyrians were described as a cedar of Lebanon (vs. 3) with many birds and beasts finding shelter therein (vs. 6). This presumably refers to people, not animals. A similar passage is found in Daniel 4. In this case, King Nebuchadnezzar had a dream of a large tree with abundant fruit. Birds of the air also dwelled in its branches (vss. 10-12). Interpreted by Daniel (vss. 19-22), the tree represented the king and his worldwide dominion. The birds represented nations.}[Q8]

Consequently, the birds in the Lord's parable may in fact depict both the preaching of the gospel to all nations (Matt. 28:19-20; Mark 16:15-16) and the eventual victory of Christ's kingdom. While the New Testament depicts the end of the current age as a time of great apostasy (cf. Matt. 24), this will not be the final word for earth, for Christ will return as conquering King (Rev. 19:11-21).

{Although the beginnings of Christ's kingdom appear to be small and insignificant, like the mustard seed, it is destined for greatness and glory.}[Q9] The fact that the Jews of Jesus' day rejected Him (John 1:10-11) does not mean that the plans and purposes of God are forever thwarted (Rom. 11:1-5). Gentiles have been grafted into the natural tree (vs. 17), enjoying rich kingdom privileges.

PARABLE OF THE LEAVEN

33 Another parable spake he unto them; The kingdom of heaven is like unto leaven, which a woman took, and hid in three measures of meal, till the whole was leavened.

{In some ways, the meaning of the parable of the mustard seed and the parable of the leaven is the same. The two parables might be summarized with the phrase "small beginnings; great results." There are, however, some differences between them.

Regarding the mustard seed, once planted, the growth would be evident. The seed, in fact, germinates quickly and grows rapidly. The kingdom's growth would be visible to all.

In the case of leaven, or yeast, the work is hidden. Of course, in time the work of the yeast does become evident as the dough rises.}[Q10] "If there is a distinction between this parable and the last one, it is that the mustard seed suggests extensive growth and the yeast intensive transformation" (Barker and Kohlenberger, eds., *The Expositor's Bible Commentary, Abridged,* Zondervan).

Those who bake bread know that the amount of yeast used in a batch of dough is relatively small compared to the amount of dough into which it is mixed. "*Three measures of meal* would be about 40 litres, which would make enough bread for a meal for 100 people, a remarkable baking for an ordinary *woman,* but it makes the point vividly" (France).

Since leaven is frequently used in the Scriptures as a symbol for the spread of evil (Matt. 16:6, 11-12; I Cor. 5:7-8; Gal. 5:8-9), some have theorized that this was the meaning Christ intended in this parable. But just as evil can spread undetected for a time, so can God's kingdom. Over time, both become evident. "The nature of yeast is such that once the process of leavening begins, it is impossible to stop. Perhaps Jesus was implying that those who profess to belong to the kingdom would grow in numbers and nothing would be able to stop their advance. This idea . . . makes sense in the flow of these parables" (Walvoord and Zuck, eds., *The Bible Knowledge Commentary,* Cook).

—John Alva Owston.

QUESTIONS

1. What preceded the parable of the tares?
2. Are "kingdom of heaven" and "kingdom of God" the same or different? Explain.
3. What are some differences between the parable of the sower and the parable of the tares?
4. What were tares? How did they get into the field in Jesus' parable?
5. What do the tares represent? Where might we see tares today?
6. What dangers were involved in uprooting the tares? How can this be applied today?
7. What point was Jesus making with the parable of the tares?
8. What interpretations have been given concerning the birds in the mustard plant?
9. What was the main point of the parable of the mustard seed?
10. How is the parable of the leaven both different from and similar to the mustard seed parable?

—John Alva Owston.

Preparing to Teach the Lesson

Today we will study three parables the Lord Jesus taught to His followers and consider what they teach us. Please understand that it is wise not to force every detail of any parable to try to get some significant meaning where there is no such meaning! This is a trap many have fallen into, but we can avoid it by studying the Scriptures and refusing to speculate where God has not specifically spoken.

In the case of the first parable we will study, the Lord Jesus gives the meaning of the significant elements of the parable in the verses that follow our lesson text for the week.

TODAY'S AIM

Facts: to learn some basic truths about the present development of God's kingdom.

Principle: to expect that many people who do not truly know the Lord will profess faith in Him.

Application: to acknowledge our limited understanding of people's hearts and trust the Lord to judge them perfectly.

INTRODUCING THE LESSON

The Lord Jesus sometimes taught in parables, which are stories that teach a spiritual truth without naming names or mentioning specific deeds by specific people. Parables are extended similies. In introducing a parable, the Lord would often begin with, "The kingdom of heaven is like—" This refers, then, to an idea, a similarity between the facts and events found in the parable and the truth or reality to which the parable points. Some parables offer practical instruction for daily living, while others are prophetic and give us insight into the plan of God for the future.

DEVELOPING THE LESSON

1. The parable of the wheat and the tares (Matt. 13:24-30). Here, the Lord Jesus began with, "The kingdom of heaven is likened unto—" His followers understood that He was teaching about the collection of believers on earth in the present era.

We are not required to judge people and declare that some are "not part of us." The Lord knows those who are His, and He has a plan in place to separate believers from unbelievers when the time is right. Well-meaning people may want to root out the unbelievers, but the Lord Jesus indicated that in so doing, we could uproot the believers. We could hurt the church of God with uninformed and unwise actions. While we should preach righteous living and seek purity, we must be aware of our own fallibility. Like the weeds, or tares, in the wheatfield, there will be unbelievers in our midst who are indistinguishable from true Christians. Only the Lord perfectly knows their hearts.

We must remember that the day is coming when the Lord Jesus will judge the world in righteousness. Until then, it is not required of us to try to separate the wheat from the tares—the true believers from mere professing Christians. We can, however, discern the difference between truth and error and not follow or be influenced by false teaching.

2. The parable of the grain of mustard seed (Matt. 13:31-32). Here, the Lord Jesus said that the kingdom of heaven is like a tiny mustard seed that grows into a large plant. Indeed, the kingdom, as seen in the Christian church, has grown from a very small beginning to include millions of people through the years.

Some have suggested that the birds represent something evil, perhaps false believers, but this may be an overreach. The point is that from the smallest sowing of the truth, a large number of believers would grow. Our small, seemingly feeble attempts to live for the Lord may be used by Him to do something greater than we could ever imagine. The kingdom of heaven is His to build as He pleases. It does not depend ultimately on human efforts, although He certainly can use human efforts to carry out His will.

3. The parable of the leaven (Matt. 13:33). In this parable, some have suggested that the leaven represents evil, and the Lord Jesus did warn His disciples to "beware of the leaven of the Pharisees and of the Sadducees" (16:6). He went on to explain that He was warning about their doctrine, or teaching.

But here He said, "The kingdom of heaven is like unto leaven" (13:33), so leaven in this case does not appear to mean anything evil. It refers, rather, to the growth and permeation of the gospel in a church or even in society as a whole.

Some of us can remember a time when the ordinary person on the street believed in being honest, not stealing, and honoring and respecting others. There have been times in history when the common attitude of society reflected the values of the Ten Commandments and the teachings of the Lord Jesus. His Word has resulted in respect for women and children more than have all the laws and pronouncements of man. Believing God's Word (or at least following it at a distance) has ennobled the human race more than any other factor or collection of factors. Rebelling against His Word has resulted in tragedy and moral decay.

ILLUSTRATING THE LESSON

Only God knows what is in each person's heart. He will build His kingdom as He sees fit.

THE LORD IS JUST

GOD'S KINGDOM

HE WILL GATHER

CONCLUDING THE LESSON

We can learn much from the parables of the Lord Jesus, but we may need instruction as to what the parables mean and how to use the information in daily life. Here we have the advantage of the Lord Jesus' explanation in the verses following our lesson text for this week. He gives the meaning of all the elements of the first parable and the significant teaching of the parable as a whole (Matt. 13:37-43).

All the elements of the parables were ideas and things known in the experiences of common people. The Lord then put these elements together in different ways and drew the people into His story. However, even His disciples, who were with Him constantly and heard His teaching, had to ask what the parables meant. They knew He was giving out new information, but they were not sure what it meant. Where we can, we should let the Scriptures explain themselves. Where we are not sure of their meaning, we may have to leave it with the Lord and seek more insight.

ANTICIPATING THE NEXT LESSON

Our next lesson explores the Lord's model prayer from Luke 11.

—*Brian D. Doud.*

PRACTICAL POINTS

1. Sometimes our enemies do everything they can to ruin our good work (Matt. 13:24-26).
2. It is important to seek counsel rather than to rush forward and make hasty decisions (vs. 27).
3. Choosing to wait rather than immediately reacting is a sign of wisdom (vss. 28-29).
4. At the appointed time, those who do not belong to God will be permanently separated from those who do (vs. 30).
5. God can cause those who seem insignificant to become people of importance (vss. 31-32).
6. Seemingly small acts can have enormous results (vs. 33).

—*Charity G. Carter.*

RESEARCH AND DISCUSSION

1. What are some modern-day examples of good seed that people of God sow (Matt. 13:24)?
2. Why were the men not punished for the growth of tares (vs. 25)? Does neglect enable the enemy to plant weeds among the crops?
3. Why did the owner of the crops not seem surprised about the maliciousness (vss. 27-30)?
4. What should we do when we think we discern that someone is not a genuine Christian (a tare among the wheat)?
5. In what ways do people find shelter in the kingdom of God (vss. 31-32)? Are all such people necessarily genuine believers?

—*Charity G. Carter.*

ILLUSTRATED HIGH POINTS

Ye root up also the wheat (Matt. 13:29)

"Don't throw out the baby with the bathwater" comes from a German expression simply meaning that although the dirty water needs to be tossed, a person should be sure to remove the tender baby first.

The enemy has certainly planted false Christians within the church ranks, but rashly tossing them out might cause harm to new believers in our midst—better to pray for wisdom and let God sort it out.

Hid in three measures of meal (vs. 33)

I recently saw a humorous sign that read, "Let's eat Grandma," followed by, "Let's eat, Grandma." It ended with the punch line "Punctuation saves lives." It reminded me of the common traffic signs that read, "Slow Men Working." Are they really that slow? If they are really such dawdlers, how do they keep their jobs? Of course, we know it means, "Slow, Men Working."

In biblical days, three measures of meal were commonly used to prepare a loaf. Leaven is a tiny but potent ingredient hidden in the dough as it is kneaded and left to slowly rise one or two times.

The Bible tells us that every believer is indwelled by the Holy Spirit (cf. John 14:23; Rom. 8:9). This indwelling has the power to lead us into God's glory (Eph. 3:16-19; Col. 1:27). However, it does not happen overnight, but through a slow, methodical process. The Father, the Son, and the Holy Spirit can seem to us like "Slow Men Working." And if we become impatient with the process, we can insert that comma and say instead, "Slow down, God is at work."

—*Therese Greenberg.*

Golden Text Illuminated

"Let both grow together until the harvest: and in the time of harvest I will say to the reapers, Gather ye together first the tares, and bind them in bundles to burn them: but gather the wheat into my barn" (Matthew 13:30).

Some organic farmers have begun "flame weeding" their cornfields. A tractor pulls an implement that shoots flames along the ground through rows of knee-high corn. It withers the weeds without harming the crop. In the parable of the wheat and the tares, Jesus also speaks of burning up weeds, but this happens only at the harvest. Rather than immediately eradicating the tares from His crop, the Lord deems it better to let them grow up among the wheat. This is a truly remarkable teaching, since it signals Jesus' intention to let evil people remain in the world along with His true children. Only at the end of the age will the evil people be judged (Matt. 13:40).

So why does God let the tares remain? Because the uprooting of evildoers involves judgment upon the world. If God were to visit His righteous judgment on the world before believers have matured and produced their fruit, God's purpose and plan would be thwarted by His own judgment. God's wisdom therefore dictates that He forestall any such judgment on the world until the full measure of His elect is complete. Then both the wicked and the righteous can be uprooted from the world without harming God's plan. The righteous will then be gathered in safely, and the wicked will be judged.

Jesus makes it clear that this parable is about the world at large, not about the church. God's servants have no authority to eliminate evil people from the world. They can preach the gospel to them and remind, admonish, and rebuke them about their evil behaviors, and pray for their conversion and reform, but as

Paul wrote, "We wrestle not against flesh and blood, but against principalities, against powers, against the rulers of the darkness of this world, against spiritual wickedness in high places" (Eph. 6:12). People are not our real enemies. Our true enemies are the spiritual forces behind people who do evil; and to combat those enemies, we have spiritual weapons that are abundantly powerful to achieve victory (cf. Matt. 16:18; II Cor. 10:3-5).

Within the church, Christ has indeed given us the authority and the means to uproot the tares among us through the process of church discipline (cf. Matt. 18:15-17; I Cor. 5:3-5). The church has a mandate from Christ to keep itself pure from those who, by their behavior, have revealed themselves to be false (vss. 6-8; Rom. 16:17; Titus 3:10).

False Christians will also one day be judged—thrown into the fire (II Cor. 11:15; II Pet. 2:3). And their punishment will be the greater for having heard the truth but choosing to pervert it instead of truly believing it (cf. Matt. 11:23-24).

Our golden text ends on an encouraging note, reminding us of the great ingathering of the true servants in God's kingdom. These have ears that truly hear and heed the gospel (Matt. 13:11-12, 16). Instead of being drawn away from Christ by the destructive heresies of false teachers, they hold on to the truth and faithfully serve in Christ's kingdom (Eph. 4:1; I Thess. 2:12). They learn to earnestly contend for the true faith against all counterfeits (Phil. 1:27; Jude 1:3).

Praise God for His great and wise plan that resolves all things justly and with finality!

—*Todd Williams.*

Heart of the Lesson

"What word or phrase would you use to absolutely capture the essence of the teaching and ministry of Jesus?" This was the question New Testament scholar Gordon Fee asked a class of forty seminary students during a course on the life and teaching of Jesus. Out of forty students, Fee recalls, only three gave the answer he was looking for. Most students gave answers such as "love" or "forgiveness." The best answer, however, is "the kingdom of God" (or kingdom of heaven). The abiding theme in the teaching of Jesus is the kingdom of heaven (cf. Matt. 4:17; 5:3, 10; 7:21; 8:11; 10:7; 13:11).

The start of Jesus' ministry (heralded by John the Baptist) marked the arrival of the kingdom of God (Mark 1:14–15). But what does the kingdom of God look like? What does it entail? Who are the members of this kingdom? Throughout His ministry, Jesus would teach on various aspects of God's kingdom. In this week's lesson, Jesus gives three parables that describe key features of this heavenly kingdom.

1. Two kingdoms in one land (Matt. 13:24-30). In the first parable, a sower planted good seed in his field, only to have an enemy contaminate the wheat by planting weeds in the same field. Jesus later explained that the field represented the world, the good seed were children of the kingdom, and the weeds were children of the evil one (vss. 36–43). The delay in removing the weeds was to prevent collateral damage to the wheat. The main point of Jesus' parable is that the kingdom of heaven is not isolated from the evil of this world; both will exist together until the end of this present age.

2. The growing and expanding kingdom (Matt. 13:31-33). The next two parables illustrate the growing and expanding nature of the kingdom of heaven. In the first, Jesus used the analogy of a very small grain of mustard seed that grows into an extremely large plant towering more than ten feet high. The inference is that although the kingdom will start small, it shall not remain small.

In the short parable of the leavened bread, Jesus described a woman mixing in a small amount of yeast (leaven) with about a bushel of flour. The yeast worked its way into the dough until the entire batch was leavened. The implication here is that the kingdom shall expand and have a far-reaching impact.

After Jesus' resurrection, there were about 120 disciples (Acts 1:12–15). What started with a few dozen followers of Jesus has spread and grown into many multitudes of Christians worldwide. The Christian faith consists of people from numerous cultural traditions, diverse ethnicities, and different nationalities, speaking a myriad of languages and holding various occupations.

Out of about 7,000 active languages, over 2,900 have at least one book of the Bible in their native tongue. Over the past decade, thousands of churches have been planted in places such as India, China, Africa, Europe, and Latin America, with many new converts (Garrison, *Church Planting Movements,* WIGTake Resources). As Christians we should be encouraged to know that although we live in a fallen world, the kingdom of God is still growing and expanding. The ultimate culmination of the kingdom of heaven, however, will come at the end of this age.

—*Armondo L. Jackson.*

World Missions

In Jesus' parable of the wheat and tares, He emphasized that evil can infiltrate the good. But He added the promise that He will separate the two at the proper time. Truth and deception, integrity and dishonesty, loyalty and treason can all grow together. Missionary families encounter "wheat and tares," particularly during their first year of ministry. They learn to trust God to show them what to do, where to go, and whom to believe.

Brad and Ellie visited our church after they had completed their first year working in a growing mission church in Uruguay. They presented their four children, including their three-month-old baby, who had been born on the mission field. Brad, whom the mission church congregation had affectionately nicknamed "Rojo" because of his flaming red hair, began his report with an incident at the airport. Upon landing in Montevideo, the family was to meet a member of the mission church, who would transport them to their new home, Santa Lucia, approximately thirty-five miles north.

As the family scanned the lines of people waiting for travelers, they spotted a friendly-looking man coming toward them with a broad smile on his face. He shook Brad's hand, speaking rapid-fire Spanish greetings. Brad could not keep up with the monologue and stumbled through his attempts to respond.

During this awkward exchange, Ellie tapped Brad on the elbow and pointed to a lone man holding a sign with their last name on it. Brad gathered up his family and walked over to the man, who spoke fluent English. This man, Paulo, explained to Brad and Ellie that the other man may have been a con man, one of many who prey on tourists, or a taxi driver who would have charged exorbitant prices. Among the wheat (Paulo), there was a tare (the stranger).

One of Ellie's stories involved a trip to a butcher shop in Santa Lucia. A woman from the mission church accompanied Ellie on her first few trips to the market. Ellie was grateful for the supervision, particularly since her communication was limited to a few phrases and her Spanish/English dictionary.

One day Ellie was feeling confident in her ability to shop alone, so off to the butcher she went. She was amazed at the price the clerk quoted for the meat, triple what she had paid before. She noticed right away that the discrepancy was not with the pricing but with the clerk. This clerk, aware of Ellie's broken Spanish, was attempting to overcharge her. Ellie had encountered another tare.

Jesus told His listeners that the enemy planted the tares among the wheat. Those who work in the field should wait and trust God to reveal the wheat and the tares. Brad and Ellie learned that God will expose the tares and send them wheat. Their job is to work in the field, the mission church in Santa Lucia.

As we answer God's calls to action in our lives, we should focus on the work God gives us to do. There will be wheat—true brothers and sisters sent to help—and tares—insincere people with deceitful motives. Trusting God will yield clarity, insure success, and bring kingdom results in our lives.

—*Beverly Medley Jones.*

The Jewish Aspect

"Ultra-Orthodox Jews Defend Right to Kaporos, Ritual Chicken Slaughter, for Yom Kippur," an October 2014 headline reads. The article goes on to state, "Believers grab hold of a live chicken and swing the clucking animal three times around their heads, symbolically asking God to transfer their sins to the birds" (Huffingtonpost.com). Yom Kippur, or the Day of Atonement, is one of the most important Jewish holidays. It is a day established to bring about reconciliation between the people and God.

In this week's lesson, we see Jesus teaching about the kingdom of heaven by presenting a parable about the final harvest, or final judgment. In Judaism, the festival of Yom Kippur centers around judgment. It is believed that on this day the judgment of the individual is sealed for the year.

In the month of Tishri, which correlates to September or October on our calendar, the High Holidays, or the "Days of Awe," occur. During this period, Jews are encouraged to assess their lives. Tradition teaches that during these ten days, God decides who should live and who should die in the coming year.

Rosh Hashanah (New Year's), a two-day holiday that is also known as "Trumpets," begins the ten-day period. The holiday is called "Trumpets" because of the blasts of the shofar, which play a dominant role in the holiday. The shofar is blown in the synagogue one hundred times on each of the two days.

Jewish philosophers describe the holiday as a time to "wake up" and repent. Rosh Hashanah begins the period of reflection and introspection.

Jewish folklore teaches that during the Days of Awe, God writes down the names of all who will live in the coming year. The names of those who are clearly righteous are inscribed in the Book of Life. The names of those who are clearly wicked are written in the Book of Death. All others are *beinonim,* or in the middle. Their fate is decided between Rosh Hashanah and Yom Kippur.

During the ten days, religious Jews take care to repent and do deeds that would get their names inscribed in the Book of Life. Confession, a major part of repentance, is one step believed necessary for forgiveness. If a person sins against God, he must verbally confess the sin before God. If his sin is against man, then he must go to the offended person and ask forgiveness from that one. Repentance remains incomplete until he confesses and then resolves to not do the act again.

Yom Kippur, a solemn fast day, sets as its goal total reconciliation. Because of this, Yom Kippur has the longest synagogue service, usually lasting from morning till nightfall, with short breaks during the day (Telushkin, *Jewish Literacy,* William Morrow).

The final part of Yom Kippur observance focuses on the "shutting of the gates." Since Jewish tradition sees Yom Kippur as the day that the gates of heaven close, intense repentance must be done before the final service ends. Repentance is necessary for the individual so that he will be admitted into God's presence, or added to the Book of Life, before the gates are closed, or the final service has ended.

Some Christians see prophetic significance in Israel's feasts. They connect the rapture, followed by seven years of tribulation, and finally the final judgment, with Rosh Hashanah, which comes with a blast of the trumpet, then seven days of repentance, and finally Yom Kippur.

—Robin Fitzgerald.

Guiding the Superintendent

We all like to see good triumph over evil. There is a reason most stories end with the good guy winning over the bad guy. If we are to determine what is truly good, however, we must seek God. Our vision, even of what we call good, is skewed by our own experiences and our own perceptions. In a political debate, for instance, each side will argue for whatever cause they deem most valid. Only God can see a picture in its entirety and make a totally unerring determination of what is truly good.

Often, even when we believe we are doing something good, our motives are not what they should be. There is a great emphasis on motives throughout the Bible. God's understanding of our good deeds is much greater than ours. He is able to separate the genuine from the false in our faith walk.

Ever since the Fall, we have been faced with an enemy who makes every effort to break our fellowship with God. In this week's lesson, Jesus gives us a picture of a wheat field that has been defiled with weeds by the enemy. The challenge for us remains in figuring out exactly what the weeds are in our faith and in our lives. While some of the weeds will be obvious, only God can uncover many of the others.

DEVOTIONAL OUTLINE

1. The wheat and the tares (Matt. 13:24-30). The servants alerted the master that the field had been sown with weeds. It is interesting that the master would tell them not to dig out the weeds. It may be because the weeds so closely resembled wheat that the servants would not be able to distinguish one from the other. Perhaps that is why the master said that while pulling weeds they might accidentally pull up the wheat. After the harvesttime, the tares would be gathered and burned, ending their pernicious influence and causing divine justice to prevail. Conversely, the wheat would be stored in the master's barn. God's Word will certainly yield fruit for His coming kingdom.

2. Tiny mustard seed (Matt. 13:31-32). Jesus stated that the mighty kingdom begins with something as small as the tiniest of seeds. Clearly God is able to do great works, but these works often begin as something as small as a mustard seed that grows into a great plant.

3. Leaven in meal (Matt. 13:33). Leaven is often used in the Bible to represent evil. But in this instance Jesus compared the kingdom to the transforming power of leaven hidden in the meal. Much in the same way, God's kingdom is alive and growing but often very much hidden in the world.

AGE-GROUP EMPHASES

Children: It is important for children to learn the parables early on so that they may begin to think about all the different meanings they hold. They should know that adults continue to find many hidden treasures in these earthly analogies that hold heavenly meaning.

Youths: This is a good time in a person's life to begin to weigh the impact his mustard seed of faith will eventually have on God's kingdom.

Adults: Adults should continue to learn not to place too much emphasis on what good we do but to focus on God's mysterious working in our hearts. After all, we live in a fallen world, with indwelling sin and an enemy who seeks to destroy us. Without God, we would hopelessly lose our way. He offers us His righteousness, His sacrifice, and His salvation.

—*Paulette L. LeBlanc.*

SCRIPTURE LESSON TEXT

LUKE 11:1 And it came to pass, that, as he was praying in a certain place, when he ceased, one of his disciples said unto him, Lord, teach us to pray, as John also taught his disciples.

2 And he said unto them, When ye pray, say, Our Father which art in heaven, Hallowed be thy name. Thy kingdom come. Thy will be done, as in heaven, so in earth.

3 Give us day by day our daily bread.

4 And forgive us our sins; for we also forgive every one that is indebted to us. And lead us not into temptation; but deliver us from evil.

5 And he said unto them, Which of you shall have a friend, and shall go unto him at midnight, and say unto him, Friend, lend me three loaves;

6 For a friend of mine in his journey is come to me, and I have nothing to set before him?

7 And he from within shall answer and say, Trouble me not: the door is now shut, and my children are with me in bed; I cannot rise and give thee.

8 I say unto you, Though he will not rise and give him, because he is his friend, yet because of his importunity he will rise and give him as many as he needeth.

9 And I say unto you, Ask, and it shall be given you; seek, and ye shall find; knock, and it shall be opened unto you.

10 For every one that asketh receiveth; and he that seeketh findeth; and to him that knocketh it shall be opened.

11 If a son shall ask bread of any of you that is a father, will he give him a stone? or if *he ask* a fish, will he for a fish give him a serpent?

12 Or if he shall ask an egg, will he offer him a scorpion?

13 If ye then, being evil, know how to give good gifts unto your children: how much more shall *your* heavenly Father give the Holy Spirit to them that ask him?

NOTES

Praying to God

Lesson Text: Luke 11:1-13

Related Scriptures: Exodus 16:15-22; Matthew 6:5-15;
Romans 8:14-17, 26-27; I John 1:5-10

TIME: A.D. 29   PLACE: Judea

GOLDEN TEXT—"When ye pray, say, Our Father which art in heaven, Hallowed be thy name. Thy kingdom come. Thy will be done, as in heaven, so in earth" (Luke 11:2).

Introduction

Prayer is universal. Every religion practices prayer in some form. Much of it is meaningless repetition (cf. Matt. 6:7). Some of it is empty meditation.

Even within Christendom, "many ideas concerning prayer exist. For some, it is a recitation of religious platitudes or exercises. For others, it is a mysterious technique for extracting benevolences from the Almighty in times of desperate need. It is considered by still others as a psychological exercise restoring poise and peace of mind to troubled souls" (French, *The Principles and Practice of Prayer,* Great Commission Prayer League).

While anyone who believes in God is naturally inclined to pray, the many divergent ideas about prayer demonstrate how important it is to learn what prayer is and how we are to pray. Most people learn to pray by observing others in their families and churches. But if we are to learn the distinctive qualities of Christian prayer, we must look first to Jesus Christ.

LESSON OUTLINE

I. **NEED FOR PRAYER—Luke 11:1**

II. **PATTERN FOR PRAYER— Luke 11:2-4**

III. **PERSISTENCE IN PRAYER— Luke 11:5-8**

IV. **FOUNDATION FOR PRAYER— Luke 11:9-13**

Exposition: Verse by Verse

NEED FOR PRAYER

LUKE 11:1 And it came to pass, that, as he was praying in a certain place, when he ceased, one of his disciples said unto him, Lord, teach us to pray, as John also taught his disciples.

As Jewish men, the disciples were very familiar with traditional Jewish prayers. No doubt they had said those prayers often. Yet as they had followed and observed Jesus, they recognized something very different in His prayers. {After watching Jesus pray somewhere, probably in the third year of His public ministry, one of the Lord's disciples asked Him to teach them to pray. Jesus' prayers made the disciples aware of their own inadequacies when it came to prayer. They knew the importance of prayer, but they did not know how to address the God they now personally knew.

The disciples also knew that John the Baptist had taught his disciples to pray; they wanted Jesus to teach *them* how to really pray.}[Q1]

PATTERN FOR PRAYER

2 And he said unto them, When ye pray, say, Our Father which art in heaven, Hallowed be thy name. Thy kingdom come. Thy will be done, as in heaven, so in earth.

3 Give us day by day our daily bread.

4 And forgive us our sins; for we also forgive every one that is indebted to us. And lead us not into temptation; but deliver us from evil.

Worshipping God (Luke 11:2a). In responding to His disciple's question, Jesus presented what is commonly called the Lord's Prayer. It answers *how* we are to pray and the general subjects that we should pursue. As such, it is a model for our prayers.

When we pray, we are to acknowledge God as our Father. This is not a form of address commonly used in the Old Testament, but with Jesus it becomes the standard way of addressing God.

{The title "Father" suggests relationship. God is not unknowable. We can relate to Him in a personal way.}[Q2] Indeed, only those who know Him personally can address God in this way. Jesus addressed God as His Father, and He told His followers to address God the same way.

All prayer should involve worship, and worship means recognizing the unique character and attributes of God. Not only is God to be addressed as our Father, but He is also to be acknowledged as transcendent and sovereign. The fact that He is in heaven suggests that He is far above us—beyond our full comprehension. He is not one of us; He is above us as sovereign Lord. Yet at the same time, He is approachable as our Father. What a blessing it is to know that the mighty God can be known and loved and trusted!

{We approach God as Father, but He is to be acknowledged as perfectly holy. "Hallowed" means "treated as holy." "Name" speaks of the Person and character of God. Thus, in prayer we are to worship God as the Holy One.}[Q3] We are to hold Him in the highest regard as the One who is wholly separated from sin.

The opening words of Jesus' model prayer instruct us to praise God. In doing this, we remind ourselves of whom we are addressing when we pray.

Desiring God's will (Luke 11:2b). Prayer involves praise and worship, but it also involves petition—asking God for things. {Particularly, Jesus said we are to ask for God's will to be done. This is to be our highest desire, and it precedes all other requests.}[Q4]

Our desire and prayer must be that God's desire will be accomplished on earth as it is in heaven—that is, willingly, perfectly, and completely. While it is to be our prayer that this will be done in any given situation right now, we recognize that His will shall be fully manifest on this earth only when Christ comes again, this time in majesty and power. That means we are to pray for the coming of His glorious and triumphant kingdom to earth (cf. Rev. 20:4).

{We thus should be praying for Christ to return. In fact, that is the essence of the last prayer recorded in the Bible (cf. Rev. 22:20). Our time here on earth is to be an active cooperation with God to prayerfully hasten Christ's return (II Pet. 3:12). We are to pray for His return because of our desire to see His will perfectly fulfilled.}[Q5]

Our prayers are to be characterized by an overwhelming desire to see God's will done. While we do not always know what is best in a particular situation, we can—and should—pray for His will to be done, for His will is always best.

Making our requests (Luke 11:3). Jesus' model prayer also instructs us to ask God to meet our physical needs. We are to ask Him to "give us day by day our daily bread." "Bread" stands for all food and here suggests more broadly all the physical and material provisions we need for daily life.

Such a prayer for God's daily provision might seem irrelevant to people who never lack such things. However, to pray this way is to acknowledge our dependence upon the Lord for everything we have. Ultimately, He is the one who provides the health and ability to obtain the things we need. And the prosperity and health we enjoy can quickly disappear.

Seeking forgiveness (Luke 11:4). Prayer also involves asking God to meet our spiritual needs. This is a model prayer for God's children, those who can call Him "Father." Thus, this request does not involve salvation, which God's children already possess, but rather our relationship with the Father. Daily sins require daily forgiveness to restore us to a position of communion with God. Thus, on the basis of Christ's atonement, we are to ask for God's forgiveness whenever we sin.

Our sins, like those of others, are viewed as debts. They are debts that cannot be paid off; they must be forgiven.

{God's forgiveness of us is tied to our forgiveness of others—those who are in our debt. This does not mean that we earn God's forgiveness by forgiving others, for God's forgiveness is by grace. But if we refuse to forgive others, we are in fact sinning ourselves and cannot be in a right relationship with God. If we desire God's forgiveness, we must be willing to forgive others (cf. Col. 3:13).}[Q6]

The final petition set forth in Jesus' model prayer is "Lead us not into temptation; but deliver us from evil" (Luke 11:4). This request is difficult to understand. If we take "temptation" to mean temptation to do evil, we would be asking God not to do something that is already impossible for Him (Jas. 1:13). If we understand the term to mean testing, as it often does, we would be asking God to keep us from something He sometimes wants us to endure.

{It is probably best to take this request as a "plea that God, in his providence, will spare the supplicant from needless temptations" (Pfeiffer and Harrison, eds., *The Wycliffe Bible Commentary,* Moody). Our words and actions sometimes put us in situations where temptation can overwhelm us. We are to pray that God will spare us from this.}[Q7]

"Evil" in Luke 11:4 is almost certainly a reference to Satan, the evil one. We are to pray that God will spare us from the devil, that is, deliver us out of his hands. Thus, the one praying recognizes his "helplessness before the Devil whom Jesus alone could vanquish . . . [and] delights to trust the heavenly Father for deliverance from the Devil's strength and wiles" (Gaebelein, ed., *The Expositor's Bible Commentary,* Zondervan).

The Lord's Prayer is not a prayer Jesus would pray Himself, for He did not need forgiveness. Rather, He offered this prayer as a model for us. It is not a prayer we are required to repeat endlessly but one that should be reflected in our own personal prayers. We are to recognize God for who He is, we are to recognize His will as supreme, and we are to recognize Him as the true source for meeting our physical and spiritual needs. These are the things we are to pray about and pray for.

PERSISTENCE IN PRAYER

5 And he said unto them, Which of you shall have a friend, and shall go unto him at midnight, and say unto him, Friend, lend me three loaves;

6 For a friend of mine in his journey is come to me, and I have nothing to set before him?

7 And he from within shall answer and say, Trouble me not: the door is now shut, and my children are with me in bed; I cannot rise and give thee.

8 I say unto you, Though he will not rise and give him, because he is his friend, yet because of his importunity he will rise and give him as many as he needeth.

Simple request (Luke 11:5-6). Jesus not only taught the disciples how to pray; He also encouraged them to pray and to pray with persistence. He did so through a parable.

Jesus told of a man who was unprepared for a guest who arrived unexpectedly late at night. Travel in that day was often done at night to avoid the heat of the day. Travelers had few options for lodging and were seldom able to alert friends in advance of their arrival.

Hospitality was a sacred duty, and people depended on one another for lodging while traveling. They tried to be ready for unexpected guests, but Jesus described a man who was unprepared and had no food for his late-arriving friend. So he went to a neighbor and asked for three loaves of bread.

Repeated request (Luke 11:7-8). The friend was reluctant to get out of bed and give his neighbor the loaves he requested. It was an inconvenience to get up and disturb the whole family, who slept together in a one-room house. Jesus noted, however, that the man in bed would finally grant the request—not out of friendship but because of his friend's "importunity," or persistence, in asking for the bread.

We must not be distracted by details that simply fill in the story. Neither the loaves nor the individuals involved are symbolic. {The parable has one simple point: persistence pays off.}[Q8] Even an earthly friend will extend help to us when we persistently seek it.

FOUNDATION FOR PRAYER

9 And I say unto you, Ask, and it shall be given you; seek, and ye shall find; knock, and it shall be opened unto you.

10 For every one that asketh receiveth; and he that seeketh findeth; and to him that knocketh it shall be opened.

11 If a son shall ask bread of any of you that is a father, will he give him a stone? or if he ask a fish, will he for a fish give him a serpent?

12 Or if he shall ask an egg, will he offer him a scorpion?

13 If ye then, being evil, know how to give good gifts unto your children: how much more shall your heavenly Father give the Holy Spirit to them that ask him?

A habitual practice (Luke 11:9-10). These verses contain the application of Jesus' parable. The three commands in verse 9 are parallel, but there is an increasing intensity with each one. "Ask" is a term that describes a humble request of a superior. "Seek" adds the idea of effort, and "knock" adds the thought of repetition, since one never knocks only once. In fact, the tenses of all the verbs indicate continuing action and thus persistence.

{Verse 10 repeats the statements of verse 9 but adds that everyone who persistently prays in this way will be satisfied.}[Q9]

An earthly illustration (Luke 11:11-12). Here Jesus drew a contrast between people and God—a contrast that is implied in His previous parable (vss. 5-8). He said that fathers will surely give their children good things when they ask for them. They will not give their children harmful things (stone, serpent, scorpion) rather than the good things they request (bread, fish, egg).

A loving Father (Luke 11:13). {Jesus' argument was from the lesser to the greater. If earthly fathers—who are sinners (cf. Matt. 7:11)—desire to give the best to their children, how much more will God give good things to His children? He does this not because He is annoyed by our requests but because He is our loving Heavenly Father.}[Q10]

While the parallel passage in Matthew 7 speaks of God giving "good gifts," here the greatest gift, the Holy Spirit, is the good thing God gives. The Spirit's power is in view here. This is what we need in every situation that calls for prayer. We often pray for deliverance, strength, or understanding. What we are really praying for is the Spirit's power, for He gives strength and understanding to endure and triumph in any circumstance.

The point of Jesus' teaching is that God is willing to answer our prayers. Persistence is important and needed, but the reason we are to be persistent in prayer is that God is always willing to answer.

But why be persistent if God knows our needs and is willing to answer? The purpose of persistent prayer is not to convince God or to wear down His resistance. Rather, it is for our sake. Persistence reveals to us the true nature of our prayers. Sometimes we are not persistent because we are not very serious. Leon Morris wrote, "If we do not want what we are asking for enough to be persistent, we do not want it very much" (*Luke,* InterVarsity).

God is not a vending machine that automatically gives us what we want when we insert the right prayer. He is a person, and if we want His will and His best, we must approach Him with earnest faith and persistence.

—*Jarl K. Waggoner.*

QUESTIONS

1. Why did the disciple want Jesus to teach them all how to pray?
2. What is suggested by addressing God as "our Father" (Luke 11:2)?
3. What does "hallowed" mean? How do we hallow God's name?
4. What request in Jesus' model prayer precedes all others?
5. What should motivate us to pray for Christ's imminent return?
6. In what way is God's forgiveness of us tied to our forgiveness of others?
7. What is meant by the plea to "lead us not into temptation" (vs. 4)?
8. What point was Jesus' parable teaching?
9. What promise is given to one who is persistent in prayer?
10. How did Jesus underscore God's willingness to answer prayer?

—*Jarl K. Waggoner.*

Preparing to Teach the Lesson

The subject of prayer is one that needs continual attention in our churches. If we are honest with ourselves, we have to admit that most of us fall short in obeying the Scripture's instruction to "pray without ceasing" (I Thess. 5:17).

Because of the importance of prayer, studying the principles and practice of prayer is an appropriate way to spend the summer. Help your learners make this a summer of prayer.

TODAY'S AIM

Facts: to review the Lord's model for prayer.

Principle: to understand the importance of regular prayer.

Application: to commit to more focused, intentional, and persistent prayer.

INTRODUCING THE LESSON

Midsummer is a time of recreation and outdoor activity. It may be difficult for your students to make time for prayer to God and meditation on His Word when there are so many temptations to do other things that seem to offer greater enjoyment and entertainment.

Remind your students that investing time in prayer is actually much more rewarding than the many summer activities that compete for their attention. Time spent in prayer is what will make how they spend their summer more meaningful. It will help to align their own desires with God's desires for not only their summer, but for their entire lives.

DEVELOPING THE LESSON

1. Our model for prayer (Luke 11:1-4). Jesus' disciples often observed Him praying. From His example, the disciples sensed the importance of prayer. So on a certain day when Jesus had finished praying, one of His disciples said, "Lord, teach us to pray." That request led to the Lord's instruction on what to include in our prayers in verses 2-4:

- "Our Father which art in heaven." Address God as Father in our prayers.
- "Hallowed be thy name." Exalt God's Person and name as holy.
- "Thy kingdom come." Look for and live in the light of God's coming kingdom.
- "Thy will be done, as in heaven, so in earth." Pray for the Lord's will to be done in all situations.
- "Give us day by day our daily bread." Ask the Lord to meet our needs.
- "And forgive us our sins; for we also forgive every one that is indebted to us." Confess our sins, and forgive others.
- "And lead us not into temptation; but deliver us from evil." Pray for the Lord's deliverance from temptation and sin.

If we include these elements in our prayers, we are following the model the Lord set for us.

2. An encouragement for prayer (Luke 11:5-8). After establishing the model prayer, our Lord used an illustration to encourage persistent prayer.

The illustration involved a person who had an unexpected houseguest but no food to give him. The person went to his friend to ask for three loaves of bread even though it was midnight. The friend replied that he could not do so because of the late hour and because he and his children were already in bed.

The Lord then drove home the illustration: "Though he will not rise and give him, because he is his friend, yet because of his importunity he will rise and give him as many as he needeth" (Luke 11:8).

The man already in bed would give his friend bread not because of their friendship but because of his friend's persistence. He refused to stop asking!

3. The invitation to pray (Luke 11:9-13). Following the illustration, the Lord issued an invitation to pray and gave assurance of answered prayer. His invitation took the form of three words—"ask," "seek," and "knock."

If we ask in prayer, the Lord will give us what is best. If we seek something from the Lord, we will find it. If we knock on a door in prayer, the Lord will open that door to us.

The force of these words is not "Ask once, and see what the Lord will do." The thought is to keep on asking, seeking, and knocking. We should never give up.

We should, of course, understand that the Lord does not give us everything we ask for; but these instructions in Luke 11:9, repeated in verse 10, show us what our part in prayer should be.

Jesus concluded His instruction with another illustration to show how eager God is to answer our prayers. The three questions of Luke 11:11-12 all have the same answer: a good father would never respond to his son's request in a cruel manner. If your son asks for food, you would never think of giving him a stone, a serpent, or a scorpion. A good father gives his children what is good for them, not something harmful.

Since we mere human fathers desire to give good gifts to our children, how much more shall our Heavenly Father give us the Holy Spirit, from whom are bestowed all the greatest treasures of heaven?

In these verses, the Lord tells us how to pray, invites us to pray, and urges us to pray more persistently.

ILLUSTRATING THE LESSON

Let us commit to a more consistent and persistent prayer life this summer.

IGNORE THE DISTRACTIONS

TV
RECREATION
WORK
PLEASURE

KEEP ON PRAYING!

CONCLUDING THE LESSON

This summer, we have the opportunity to renew our commitment to prayer. The key to a persistent prayer life is making prayer a daily habit. Someone once said that we need to do something thirty times for it to become a habit. In other words, we need to do it for a month.

What would help us be more regular and persistent in prayer? We can set a time for prayer and keep to that time each day. If we miss a day, we should not give up but pick up the next day.

We can also set a certain amount of time for prayer each day. Five minutes a day is usually not enough. Establish a goal and stick to it. We can also identify a certain place for prayer each day. These simple steps can help us make prayer a habit this year.

ANTICIPATING THE NEXT LESSON

Our next Bible study examines who God invites to partake in His great heavenly banquet.

—Don Anderson.

PRACTICAL POINTS

1. Like the disciples, we should look to Jesus' model of prayer (Luke 11:1).
2. We should start our prayers by giving reverence to God (vs. 2).
3. When we pray, we should ask God to provide for our needs (vs. 3).
4. Even though we know God will forgive us, we should pray for the strength to not sin (vs. 4).
5. We need to stay persistent in prayer, even when God has not yet answered our prayers (vss. 5-8).
6. Everyone who truly seeks God will find God (vss. 9-10).
7. If people can give good gifts, we can trust God to give us what is good for us (vss. 11-13).

—Stuart Olley.

RESEARCH AND DISCUSSION

1. Why did Jesus go to certain places to pray (Luke 11:1; cf. 6:12; 9:18)? How could doing that help us in our prayers?
2. What practical steps do you see in Jesus' example of prayer (Luke 11:2-4; cf. Matt. 6:9-13)?
3. What are the similarities between Jesus' example of the friend asking for bread and the parable of the persistent widow (Luke 11:5-8; cf. 18:1-8)?
4. How can obeying Jesus by being steadfast in prayer help us be more like Him (Luke 11:8; cf. II Pet. 1:5-11)?
5. What are the good things we should ask God for (Luke 11:11-13; cf. Jas. 1:5, 17)?

—Stuart Olley.

ILLUSTRATED HIGH POINTS

Our Father (Luke 11:2)

I learned to recite the Pledge of Allegiance and the Lord's Prayer in the first grade. I confess that I had no clue what they meant, and I do not recall anyone explaining the big words to a six-year-old.

In time, I began to understand the big words in the pledge. It took longer to begin to understand and appreciate the depth of the spiritual significance of the prayer.

Sadly, all too many simply recite the words of the Lord's Prayer without any relationship with God or understanding of the truth it contains.

Because of his importunity (vs. 8)

A book on prayer written in 1955 dealt with many subjects, one of which was "How to Pray with Persistence."

At the close of the chapter was a challenge to pray that the men in the Kremlin would repent and be converted in the interest of world peace. We now know that such prayers are always needed. Victories in a fallen world are rarely permanent. Question: Are we praying for the nations of the world?

Ask (vs. 9)

When we went to Ukraine on a short-term missions trip to teach in a Bible college, we were often given timely advice by the full-time missionaries and teachers. It was possible that a student might take us aside and ask for a gift of one hundred dollars since we were "rich" Americans. Now, most of us had that amount, but was it wise to help such a student? We were told to say no. The student would then say, "OK," and go on. He would not be offended by our refusal. In other words, there was no importunity in his request.

—David A. Hamburg.

Golden Text Illuminated

"When ye pray, say, Our Father which art in heaven, Hallowed be thy name. Thy kingdom come. Thy will be done, as in heaven, so in earth" (Luke 11:2).

It is past midnight, and I am awake, researching symptoms I have had today that might result in a trip to the hospital tomorrow. Many readers may be going through a similar crisis or just feeling the strain and difficulties of everyday life in this fallen world.

For any of the above, Jesus has given us a model prayer to pray, a model good for when we are rejoicing or when we are hurting, when we notice the many praiseworthy things around us or when we feel paralyzed by fear.

"Our Father." This is a perfect beginning that reminds us of several beautiful, reassuring truths.

1. God is Father, not some vague, aloof deity we must placate by gongs or incessant chanting or giving a bribe of some sort. We are His family.

2. God is our God, not merely a deity we have heard of who belongs to others but not to us.

3. When we call on God, it is as our loving Father, not only as King of kings or Lord of lords. How beautiful that of all the titles that are rightfully His, the one He wants us to use is the most intimate and loving.

"Which art in heaven." In this we not only recognize His high position of authority but also confess that He is separate from this sinful, sorrow-filled world we live in. Our Heavenly Father is holy, and His authority is above all others.

"Hallowed be thy name." We confess that God's name is holy to us and that our desire is for everyone to regard His name as holy. God's name deserves our reverence and eternal awe. Our words and our lives should manifest the desire that His name be lifted up, glorified, and honored above all.

"Thy kingdom come." In this phrase we look to the future with hope. His kingdom is coming! One day, all the things of this life will fall away, and we will be where we belong—where justice and righteousness reign, where all tears will be wiped away. As John wrote in Revelation, "Even so, come, Lord Jesus" (22:20). Amen!

"Thy will be done." These words are easy to say but sometimes difficult to actually mean. God knows what will draw us to Himself. If we truly believe that He loves us and wants what is best for us, we can say this phrase with confidence, even if it means that difficulties lie ahead.

"As in heaven, so in earth." In heaven, God's will is immediately and fully carried out—no questions, no hesitation, no fear. For us to pray for God's will to be done in the same way on earth requires not just a willing heart but obedience as well. We should be ready to do God's will immediately—the moment it is clear to us.

Jesus' model prayer displays both the depth of God's wisdom and the humility and simplicity of a true disciple. This combination of divine profundity and humble dependence upon God should be the definitive example for Christian prayer.

When we pray this prayer and truly believe it, we can rest without fear of what tomorrow may bring, knowing that our Heavenly Father loves us and wants what is best for us.

When we offer God this prayer, we offer ourselves. That is truly meaningful worship.

—Kimberly Rae.

Heart of the Lesson

1. The disciples' request to be taught to pray (Luke 11:1). It was common for rabbis to teach their disciples memorized prayers. John the Baptist taught his followers prayers. The Lord Jesus did not use formal prayers; He simply talked to His Heavenly Father. The disciples wanted a pattern or an example they could use.

2. The Lord Jesus' model prayer (Luke 11:2-4). The teaching of this model prayer is very clear. We start to pray, to address our God, by remembering who He is and who we are. He is our Father, and we are His children.

In the model prayer, we see "Thy kingdom come" (vs. 2). This is immediately followed by, "Thy will be done, as in heaven, so in earth." God's will is done instantly and perfectly in heaven, and our prayer is that it will also be done that way on earth and in our experience. In praying, we are to consciously place ourselves under His will.

We must come in a spirit of forgiveness toward everyone who has offended us. Our fellowship with our Heavenly Father will be broken by the sin of an unforgiving heart. If our fellowship with Him is not full and complete, our prayer may not be answered.

The model prayer includes a request not to be led into temptations or testings under which we would be likely to fall into sin. He may, though, bring some testings whereby we can be taught to trust and obey Him more fully. The Lord does not tempt us to do evil, but He does want us to learn to resist evil and do His will. In this regard, the Lord Jesus in His temptation in the wilderness provides our example. The Lord Jesus consistently quoted God's Word to refute the statements of Satan and thus demonstrate how we should handle such situations.

3. The Lord Jesus' teaching on prayer (Luke 11:5-13). The answer the Lord Jesus gave to the disciples' request to be taught to pray far exceeded all of their expectations. He began with a hypothetical situation with which they could identify. A need arises; an urgent request is made. Because of the urgency and insistency of the request, the friend being asked rises from bed and grants the request.

The teaching is about prayer by a true child of God and its answer by his Heavenly Father. It is not about a positive mental attitude or any similar programmed approach to life. It is about our continually asking, seeking, and knocking. The verb tenses here emphasize that. When we are constantly asking, He is constantly giving.

The Lord Jesus then gave a concluding example: fathers love to give good things, not bad things, to their children. They love to give them what they want.

The Lord Jesus was drawing here the strongest of contrasts. Our Heavenly Father is perfect and all-powerful. His gifts can be exceedingly abundant, far above anything that we ask for or think of (Eph. 3:20).

God has given us all things that pertain to life and godliness (II Pet. 1:3). With the Holy Spirit, we are given the fruit of the Spirit. We have the One who makes intercession (prays) "with groanings which cannot be uttered" (Rom. 8:26). He says the things too deep for words that we cannot say but are trying to say. What a powerful and precious answer to our prayers!

—*Brian D. Doud.*

World Missions

Christians are called to be a generous people. In Tertullian's *Apology*, written around A.D. 200, it is said that outsiders to the faith observed the early Christians' practice and remarked, "Look how they love one another!" The mark of Christianity is love. It started with our Heavenly Father and extends to His people. Our God loves us so much that He will deny us what is merely good so that we will attain to His best. Our God is a giving God who even gave His only Son to die for us.

This message of giving from a heart of love is at the very core of the Christian gospel. It works even for the benefit of those outside the faith in order to bring them into the fold of the redeemed. We know this is the heart of God because we have learned it from the Word of our Heavenly Father. This concept is foreign to many religions, in which God is so remote and distant that there is no way to reach up to have contact with Him. In Christianity, we have a God who actually came down and became one of us!

Bilquis Sheikh found this glorious truth for herself when she turned to God as her own Heavenly Father, a concept that she did not have when she was following her previous religion. You can read her story in the book *I Dared to Call Him Father* (Baker). In it she talks about how she could look to God as her personal, comforting Heavenly Father. The message of the gospel that our world needs to know is that God loves us so much that He sent His beloved Son to die for our sins. God raised Jesus from the dead and sent His Spirit to live in believers to prepare them for His kingdom. There is nothing more perfect than this!

If God is our Father, we can talk to Him every day. He is no longer distant and inaccessible but is always listening in eagerness for us to talk with Him. When our own children come home from school, we ask them all about their day. As human parents, we look to see whether they have any need for encouragement, especially if things are not going well for them. Our Heavenly Father is like that when we talk with Him and listen for His words of peace and comfort. He responds to us.

Some who are reading this lesson might have had bad experiences with earthly fathers, and the pain does not go away easily. Now is our opportunity to experience the divine love of the Heavenly Father, who will never let us down under any circumstances. We can be sure of that because He keeps His Word. We dare not forget that this Heavenly Father loved us so much that He sent Jesus to save us. He will not stop until He molds us into the image of Jesus, His Son, and makes us ready for heaven.

The world needs to know that when a sinner trusts in Christ, his sins are forgiven. His life is then to be a living sacrifice to God's service. God listens to our cries and understands our pain. The task of every Christian is to share this good news with the world, not keep it to ourselves. Jesus came to save the whole world, not just the people in our church. Every human being needs this good news. God listens when we call, and He is always there.

The church's mission is to tell the world that we have a Heavenly Father who loves us and is calling upon us to turn to Him.

—A. Koshy Muthalaly.

The Jewish Aspect

Daily life in a typical Jewish home in Jesus' day is clearly reflected in Luke 11:5-10. Jewish hospitality is illustrated in this parable.

A guest arrived at midnight, and the host immediately began to care for him. People in ancient times often traveled "by night to avoid the heat of daylight" (Pate, *Luke,* Moody). The host realized that he was out of bread. A woman typically baked the day's supply early in the morning. By midnight, it was all gone. The host went to a neighbor, greatly bothering him and his family, to borrow three loaves of bread.

Jewish culture had firmly established principles for hospitality. When Jesus told this parable, it would not have surprised His listeners. Jewish rabbis observed that the first time hospitality was shown in the Torah was in Genesis 18, "when Abraham invites the three wanderers from Mamre to relax while he brings them water and food" (Scheib, "Hospitality").

Rabbis taught that Abraham kept all four sides of his tent open so that guests could easily enter from any direction. Rabbis emphasized that Jethro "was particularly disappointed at being deprived of the opportunity to extend hospitality to Moses (Ex. 2:20)" ("Hospitality"). They taught that since Israel was a "stranger" in Egypt, they knew how to treat any stranger with proper hospitality (Lev. 19:34).

The Babylonian Talmud specifically asserted that "hospitality to wayfarers is greater than welcoming the presence of the *Shechinah*" (Shabbath 127*a*). Receiving guests into one's house was considered a great "mitzvah," a praiseworthy deed. It was even more praiseworthy when such hospitality was shown to the poor. Because of this emphasis on hospitality, rabbis developed instructions governing this practice. The apocryphal book of Ecclesiasticus, dated to around 180 B.C., gave instructions for a guest's manners (31:21-26) and condemned the person who took advantage of others while they were guests in their homes (29:23-28).

The host was obligated to never do anything that would make the guest feel awkward or unwelcome. He was to provide both lodging and food and always show a smiling face toward the guest. "Better, teaches the Midrash, to offer a guest but a little in a gracious tone than large portions obviously proffered grudgingly" ("Jewish Hospitality"). A host was never to appear to be miserable in front of a guest, nor was he to make a guest uncomfortable by observing him too closely. Parents taught their children to be hospitable. Whenever a child answered the door, he was to invite the guest to dine with the family.

The guest likewise had requirements. Most important, he was to be thankful for all that the host did and provided. He was to offer a prayer of blessing on the host after a meal and leave some food on his plate so as not to be seen as a glutton. A guest was to stay for only three days. Concerning this, the Jewish Midrash Tehillim 23:3 states, "On the day a guest arrives, a calf is slaughtered in his honor; the next day, a sheep, the third day, a fowl, and on the fourth day, he is served just beans" (Scheib).

Contemporary Jews still practice hospitality. They especially emphasize filling a guest's soul and spirit beyond physical needs.

—*R. Larry Overstreet.*

Guiding the Superintendent

Jesus was always a source of amazement to His disciples. They walked, talked, and lived with Him, but they never really understood Him. Somehow they saw that His prayer life made the difference. One day they asked Him to teach them to pray. Today we call the instructions He gave the Lord's Prayer.

Sadly, this prayer has become little more than a ritual routine for many people. Jesus never intended for this to happen. What Jesus was doing was giving people a set of guidelines for their prayers.

DEVOTIONAL OUTLINE

1. Pattern of prayer (Luke 11:1-4). All prayer should begin with God, not us. Our relationship with God should take the central place in prayer. Jesus emphasized three focuses: (1) that God's name be honored, (2) that God's kingdom be sought, and (3) that God's will be done.

The second part of Jesus' prayer focuses on daily needs (Luke 11:3-4). We are to trust in Him one day at a time. The focus should be on our needs, not our wants. We are to pray for the daily needs of our bodies. And we are to pray for our soul needs—for a life cleansed from sin. We are to pray that we do not succumb to temptation.

Instead of this being a memorized ritual to get us out of trouble, the Lord's Prayer should be a set of guidelines that covers our relationship with God.

2. Approach of prayer (Luke 11:5-13). Jesus enjoyed telling stories to drive home His point. This He did after He had taught about prayer. What follows are two illustrations that are used to encourage us to pray and not give up. God will answer in His own time and way.

Jesus' first example is a parable (vss. 5-10). It tells of a person who goes to a friend late at night for some supplies. At first the friend does not want to disturb his sleeping household to get up to help. But because of the person's persistence, the neighbor does finally get up and provide the food.

Jesus teaches by contrast here. Do not miss His point. God is just the opposite of the sleepy, unwilling neighbor. He is always willing and ready to answer our prayers.

Jesus' second example involves a loving father who desires to give his child what he requests (vss. 11-13). While the first example taught by contrast, this one teaches by comparison. Just as a loving father would not give his child a scorpion when the child wanted an egg, so God is not capricious in His giving. In fact, God desires to give even more than an earthly father does.

Jesus encourages us to pray, first for God's will and then for our daily needs. With His illustrations of the sleepy neighbor and the loving father, He assures us that He does desire to answer our prayers.

AGE-GROUP EMPHASES

Children: Using the first and second parts of the Lord's Prayer, have the children suggest what it means to pray that God would be first in their lives and then consider what their daily needs are.

Youths: Many teens have memorized the Lord's Prayer. Help them understand that it is not a ritual but a guideline for their prayers.

Adults: Adults will enjoy discussing the issue of persistence in prayer. Exactly what is this persistence?

—*Martin R. Dahlquist.*

SCRIPTURE LESSON TEXT

LUKE 14:7 And he put forth a parable to those which were bidden, when he marked how they chose out the chief rooms; saying unto them,

8 When thou art bidden of any *man* **to a wedding, sit not down in the highest room; lest a more honourable man than thou be bidden of him;**

9 And he that bade thee and him come and say to thee, Give this man place; and thou begin with shame to take the lowest room.

10 But when thou art bidden, go and sit down in the lowest room; that when he that bade thee cometh, he may say unto thee, Friend, go up higher: then shalt thou have worship in the presence of them that sit at meat with thee.

11 For whosoever exalteth himself shall be abased; and he that humbleth himself shall be exalted.

15 And when one of them that sat at meat with him heard these things, he said unto him, Blessed *is* **he that shall eat bread in the kingdom of God.**

16 Then said he unto him, A certain man made a great supper, and bade many:

17 And sent his servant at supper time to say to them that were bidden, Come; for all things are now ready.

18 And they all with one *consent* began to make excuse. The first said unto him, I have bought a piece of ground, and I must needs go and see it: I pray thee have me excused.

19 And another said, I have bought five yoke of oxen, and I go to prove them: I pray thee have me excused.

20 And another said, I have married a wife, and therefore I cannot come.

21 So that servant came, and shewed his lord these things. Then the master of the house being angry said to his servant, Go out quickly into the streets and lanes of the city, and bring in hither the poor, and the maimed, and the halt, and the blind.

22 And the servant said, Lord, it is done as thou hast commanded, and yet there is room.

23 And the lord said unto the servant, Go out into the highways and hedges, and compel *them* **to come in, that my house may be filled.**

24 For I say unto you, That none of those men which were bidden shall taste of my supper.

NOTES

Accept God's Invitation!

Lesson Text Luke 14:7-11, 15-24

Related Scriptures: Proverbs 25:6-7; Matthew 21:42-44; 22:1-14

TIME: A.D. 30   PLACE: Perea

GOLDEN TEXT—"And the lord said unto the servant, Go out into the highways and hedges, and compel them to come in, that my house may be filled" (Luke 14:23).

Introduction

The events recorded in Luke 14 took place at a banquet on the Sabbath Day in the home of one of the chief Pharisees (vs. 1). Among those gathered was a man with dropsy. Jesus looked around at the lawyers and Pharisees and asked, "Is it lawful to heal on the sabbath day?" (vs. 3).

Jesus' question put them on the spot, because it was allowable according to rabbinical interpretation to give medical treatment on a Sabbath if a life was endangered. Everyone kept silent. The man's life did not seem to be at stake, but the religious leaders did not want to appear indifferent to the man's suffering by insisting that he could not be healed on the Sabbath. In the face of their silence, Jesus healed the man and sent him away.

Jesus asked, "Which of you shall have an ass or an ox fallen into a pit, and will not straightway pull him out on the sabbath day?" (vs. 5). It was natural to rescue an animal that had fallen into a pit, no matter what day it was. Certainly they should not object to His helping a suffering human being.

LESSON OUTLINE

I. **ATTITUDES**—Luke 14:7-11

II. **OPPORTUNITIES**—Luke 14:15-20

III. **DECISIONS**—Luke 14:21-24

Exposition: Verse by Verse

ATTITUDES

LUKE 14:7 And he put forth a parable to those which were bidden, when he marked how they chose out the chief rooms; saying unto them,

8 When thou art bidden of any man to a wedding, sit not down in the highest room; lest a more honourable man than thou be bidden of him;

9 And he that bade thee and him come and say to thee, Give this man place; and thou begin with shame to take the lowest room.

10 But when thou art bidden, go and sit down in the lowest room; that when he that bade thee cometh, he may say unto thee, Friend, go up higher: then shalt thou have worship in the presence of them

that sit at meat with thee.

11 For whosoever exalteth himself shall be abased; and he that humbleth himself shall be exalted.

An observation (Luke 14:7). {Jesus had already observed that the people at the banquet had been acting to preserve their own interests. As they entered the room, they evidently had been scrambling for the places of honor at the banquet table.}[Q1] The most honored places were those closest to the host, and Jesus had seen the maneuvering taking place to get into those seats of honor. Apparently this was a rather important occasion, and everybody desired to be seen as being among those of special distinction.

Even though this was apparently a fairly serious occasion, it must have been almost comical to Jesus to watch the subtle attempts to get the best places without appearing too obvious. He knew that their values were completely misplaced and that there was a much better way to handle such a situation. The scene reminds us of a modern-day political scene, where everybody wants to be as close as possible to the main person at the event. Who has not witnessed the big, often pasted-on grin of the observer standing nearby?

There is going to be a good lesson for all of us here because of the natural propensity we have for self-promotion. One of the evidences of a self-centered person is that he goes out of his way to let others know how good, how talented, or how valuable he is. As Christians, it is far better to simply let others know our interests and then wait for the Lord to open doors instead of promoting ourselves. When God wants us involved in something, He will see to it that the people in charge learn of our abilities.

A wrong choice (Luke 14:8-9). Although Jesus was probably not at a wedding feast Himself, He used that as His illustration, perhaps trying in a more sensitive and subtle way to let the people know how foolish they had been in securing their seats. Maybe nothing would happen this time to change the seating arrangement, but Jesus wanted to warn them that their assumptions in their scramble for the more prestigious seats could possibly lead to their embarrassment. The instruction He gave them was simple and straightforward.

{Jesus said that when a person was invited to a wedding feast, he should not assume that he should go to the best seat, for the host might have invited someone more deserving of that place.}[Q2] When the guest arrived, the host would come to him and ask him to move to another seat farther away; this would prove to be a most embarrassing moment. The attempt at self-exaltation would turn into humiliation because of the public attention drawn to a person for the wrong reason.

We could compare this today to a banquet head table, where the host and main speaker usually sit. Often included at this table are others who hold certain positions of authority in an organization. When you have been invited to such a special occasion, it is never safe to assume that you should seat yourself at the head table unless you have specifically been told to do so. An attitude of pride can lead to humiliating situations and does not please the Lord.

A right choice (Luke 14:10-11). It is much safer for one to assume that he is simply one of the invited guests at the banquet and should sit wherever there is an open seat. Jesus said that one should go to the lowest place instead of the highest. If the host wants him to be in an honored position, he will come and invite the guest to sit in another seat. In the process it will be publicly noted that he deserves special recognition. Instead of being embarrassed, he will be properly exalted before the other attendees.

{Jesus then verbalized a very important life principle: "Whosoever exalteth himself shall be abased; and he that humbleth himself shall be exalted" (vs. 11).}Q3 The unsaved world cannot understand this principle. It happens because of God's control. The attitude of the world is to promote oneself and achieve recognition in order to be successful. God's desire is that we humble ourselves and let Him do the exalting if and whenever He sees fit. Self-exaltation will ultimately result in humiliation.

In the wedding feast situation, it was not the one who honored himself who was truly honored but the one the host honored. {In spiritual terms, it is not the one who exalts himself who is truly honored but rather the one whom God exalts.}Q4 As God's children, it is far better to humbly carry out whatever ministry He has allowed us, without seeking public acclaim. When we endeavor to exalt ourselves, we usually look foolish; but when God honors us in some way, we become a testimony to others of how He can use us effectively.

OPPORTUNITIES

15 And when one of them that sat at meat with him heard these things, he said unto him, Blessed is he that shall eat bread in the kingdom of God.

16 Then said he unto him, A certain man made a great supper, and bade many:

17 And sent his servant at supper time to say to them that were bidden, Come; for all things are now ready.

18 And they all with one consent began to make excuse. The first said unto him, I have bought a piece of ground, and I must needs go and see it: I pray thee have me excused.

19 And another said, I have bought five yoke of oxen, and I go to prove them: I pray thee have me excused.

20 And another said, I have married a wife, and therefore I cannot come.

Blessing (Luke 14:15). Jesus followed His teaching on humility with a teaching directed to those who host dinners (vss. 12-14). He told them that they should not limit their invitations to those who have the ability to reciprocate but should include those who are financially unable to do so. For this they would be blessed and rewarded by God Himself at the resurrection. {It was upon hearing this instruction that someone present spoke up with a pronouncement of blessing of his own.}Q5

{This particular guest did not really understand what Jesus had been teaching, and his statement sounds like a pious expression meant to impress Jesus.}Q6 He seems to have connected in his mind the idea of being honored and blessed at a feast with the presupposition that the prosperous people attending the present banquet had a lot to look forward to. There is a hint in his statement that he assumed every outwardly righteous Jew would automatically be in the future kingdom.

Such an understanding leads us to think that this man was one of the Pharisees. When Jesus mentioned the resurrection of the just (vs. 14), this man's mind went to the future kingdom. It may have been his understanding that when the Messiah came, He would deliver the Jews from the domination of the Roman Empire. Then they would live in peace and prosperity, without warfare and uncertainty. Undoubtedly he was convinced that all Israelites would be there enjoying kingdom blessings.

Invitations (Luke 14:16-17). {In this parable Jesus used the idea of a great supper to portray salvation, which results, of course, in becoming a part of God's kingdom. The invitations to the supper represent the invitation God has given to people to become part of His family through His Son,

Jesus.}[Q7] Since it was clear to Jesus that the man who had just spoken did not understand salvation, He specifically addressed him in response to his comment about eating in the kingdom.

In Jesus' parable a certain man planned a huge dinner party and sent invitations to everyone he wanted to attend. It was customary to invite people well in advance of the event, with an approximate starting time specified. When everything was ready, a servant went to tell those who had accepted the invitation that it was time for them to come. Apparently, everyone had accepted the invitation, so the plans had been made accordingly. At this point it would be extremely insulting to not show up for the event.

Throughout the Old Testament, announcements were made that the Messiah was coming and that the Jews should be getting ready for His arrival. The announcements were received and accepted gladly. No one knew the exact time of His arrival, but it was certainly good news that He was coming, for He would provide deliverance for His people. The people of Israel were expectant and ready—or so they thought.

Excuses (Luke 14:18-20). {As the servant went from person to person to let them know it was time for the dinner to begin, he received many excuses as to why they could not attend after all. Every excuse reeked of insincerity. Each person indicated a preoccupation with other things that they considered more important than the dinner.}[Q8] The first said he had bought a piece of ground and needed to go see it. The second said he had bought five yoke of oxen and needed to test them. The third said he could not come because he had just married.

It is easy to see these are nothing more than excuses. Who would buy a piece of property without having seen it first? We have heard of certain scams involving the sale of unusable property to unsuspecting buyers sight unseen,

but not many fall for that type of scheme. Likewise, who would invest in five yoke of oxen without knowing they were good, strong, and useful? As for the bridegroom, why did marriage suddenly prevent him from attending such an important function? The people's preoccupation with things they felt were more important reveals a lack of interest in fulfilling the commitment they had made when they accepted the initial invitation.

When the Messiah finally arrived in Israel, a large number of the people were so involved with their everyday lives that they were not interested in hearing what He had to say. They paid little or no attention to the message He proclaimed. They were simply too busy and too involved in their normal activities to make any changes at that time.

DECISIONS

21 So that servant came, and shewed his lord these things. Then the master of the house being angry said to his servant, Go out quickly into the streets and lanes of the city, and bring in hither the poor, and the maimed, and the halt, and the blind.

22 And the servant said, Lord, it is done as thou hast commanded, and yet there is room.

23 And the lord said unto the servant, Go out into the highways and hedges, and compel them to come in, that my house may be filled.

24 For I say unto you, That none of those men which were bidden shall taste of my supper.

New invitations (Luke 14:21-22). {When the servant returned and told his master about the excuses he had received, the master became angry and devised another plan. "Go out quickly into the streets and lanes of the city, and bring in hither the poor, and the maimed, and the halt, and the blind," he said.}[Q9] The dinner was ready, and time was now of the essence. If those invited were so unappreciative that they would offer terribly lame excuses for not coming, invitations would go to those who would respond eagerly and be grateful for them.

The master specified that the servant should go into the various areas of the city, both the broad streets and the narrow lanes, and invite the poor, maimed (crippled), halt (lame), and blind. The master had first invited those of higher class, but he now turned to others when his invitation was rejected. In the eyes of the Pharisees, these people were outcasts, much like the tax collectors.

In Israel it was the religious leaders who first rejected Jesus and eventually saw to His death. They had an opportunity to receive Him but refused. Jesus therefore turned to the common people with His invitation. Since the religious leaders showed no interest in spiritual truth, Jesus went directly to the people with His teaching. The Gospels indicate repeatedly that this was where He received His greatest response.

In Jesus' parable, the servant reported to his master that he had done as he was told. The people had responded and come, but there was still room left for many more.

Expansion and exclusions (Luke 14:23-24). Since there was still room in the dining hall, the master told his servant to expand the parameters of the invitation. Now he should go beyond the city limits out into the countryside and invite people on the highways or along the hedges that acted as fences. He was to speak urgently to them, compelling them to come so that the master's house would be full of people. Persuasion was required, for this group would not feel worthy of such an invitation and needed to know that they were welcome.

The master's concluding statement was a somber one: "For I say unto you, That none of those men which were bidden shall taste of my supper" (vs. 24). Those who had rejected his invitation would be excluded forever. Jesus' parable described His own offer of salvation for people to become part of the family of God. It remains true today that many reject the invitation while others accept it gladly.

{Just as the guest who pronounced the blessedness of those who eat in the kingdom of God did not understand how to get there himself, so there are many today who speak of God and heaven without an understanding of how to be sure of going to be with God after this life. We should willingly reach out with the good news to everyone we can. It is a message of utmost urgency.}Q10

—*Keith E. Eggert.*

QUESTIONS

1. What had Jesus observed as He watched the people coming in?
2. How did Jesus say they should act when attending such an event?
3. What principle did Jesus set forth regarding being exalted?
4. What lesson about self-exaltation can we learn from this?
5. What statement did one of the guests make to Jesus after this?
6. What was his understanding concerning the kingdom of heaven?
7. How did Jesus portray salvation in His parable?
8. What happened to the master in Jesus' parable after he invited a large group of guests to dinner?
9. What steps did he then take to fill his banquet hall with people?
10. How are many people today much like the Israelites of Jesus' day in their response to Him?

—*Keith E. Eggert.*

Preparing to Teach the Lesson

Our lesson this week reminds us of our obligation as Christians to do all we can to bring others to saving faith in Jesus Christ.

TODAY'S AIM

Facts: to show through the illustration of a wedding feast that we must do all we can to bring people to Jesus.

Principle: to stress that as Christians we are obligated to tell others about Jesus.

Application: to urge students to do everything they can to bring others to Jesus.

INTRODUCING THE LESSON

Once we have experienced something good, we naturally want to share it with others. One writer said that sharing the good news of salvation is like one beggar telling another where to find food.

DEVELOPING THE LESSON

1. Instruction on humility (Luke 14:7-11). Jesus was having a meal at the home of one of the leaders of the Pharisees. There He noticed that all the invitees were trying to get the best seats, the places of honor, so that they would be recognized.

Jesus responded by telling them that when they were invited to a feast, they should not choose the best seats. If they did and then somebody more important showed up, they would be asked to move down to a lower seat, and they would be disgraced.

Jesus advised His hearers that when they were invited to a meal, they should instead take a lower seat. Then the host might come to them and send them to a more prominent seat, and they would be honored in front of everyone present.

Jesus concluded by stating the general spiritual principle that the proud will be humbled and the humble will be honored.

The meaning of Jesus' illustration becomes clear when we understand that Eastern society was very hierarchical by nature, much more so than here in the West. Titles and dress codes that indicate power and status were unduly prized. In that kind of society, Jesus called on His hearers to do the untraditional and look to receiving their honor from God.

2. A share in the kingdom (Luke 14:15). One of those who sat at the table with Jesus responded by saying how wonderful it would be to eat bread in the kingdom of God. Eating bread was a sign of fellowship and being accepted. Hospitality in the Eastern culture was almost always denoted by sharing a meal together. This man assumed that he and the others present would also be present in God's kingdom. Jesus' story challenged the assumptions of this man and many others.

3. Lame excuses by the invitees (Luke 14:16-20). Jesus' story centered around another feast. The host sent out invitations to the feast. When the meal was ready, he sent out his servants to call the invitees to come. All of them made excuses, however. The excuses were frivolous ones and showed disrespect to the host, who had painstakingly arranged the meal for them.

One invitee said that he had just bought a field that had to be inspected. Another said that he had just bought five pair of oxen and had to test them. Another said that he had just been married and thus could not come.

In the Eastern world, the way a person responds to an invitation indicates the way he regards the host. Invitations are usually given in person and with great investment of time and effort. People take offense if they are not invited in person. This shows that the invitee is held in high regard. That respect is expected to be reciprocated.

Discuss what we do with invitations and how we usually respond. How does our response show our love and respect for the person who invited us? How did we respond to God when He invited us into His kingdom? Do we extend the same invitation to others so that they can come into His kingdom?

4. The call to invite all who would come and to fill the house (Luke 14:21-24). The host was angry when the servant reported that none of the invitees were coming to the meal. He ordered the servant to go out into the streets and invite the poor, the crippled, the lame, and the blind to his feast. These were people who were not normally invited to such feasts. When there was still room for more, the master told the servant to go out into the highways and along the hedges and invite everyone he could find to his feast.

Here we have a picture of the Jewish nation of Jesus' day that was privileged to hear the gospel first. When the nation as a whole rejected Christ, others were given the opportunity to receive the good news and experience it for themselves. Is it possible that in some of our lands today people assume that God accepts them simply because the gospel has become so commonplace while others in generally pagan countries are ready to receive the gospel with eagerness?

One lesson here is that as Christians, we are called to go out and share the gospel with all people. Some will not receive it, but we are to move on in the task of evangelism to others who will.

Jesus concluded by indicating that those who reject the gospel now may not be given another opportunity to respond in faith. Anyone can receive the gospel invitation and enjoy its blessings, but for some it soon may be too late if they do not take advantage of the offer when it is extended to them. Our task as Christians is to encourage all to receive Christ before it is too late.

ILLUSTRATING THE LESSON

We are called to go out and lovingly invite others into the kingdom by sharing the good news of Jesus as often as we can.

SHARE THE GOOD NEWS

CONCLUDING THE LESSON

Our lesson this week shows us how we as Christians, having experienced the good news of Jesus, are to go out and invite others into the kingdom of God. We want everyone to taste of the feast that is prepared for them by our Lord. We are to do this in a loving manner with all we meet.

ANTICIPATING THE NEXT LESSON

Our next lesson examines Jesus' story of the rich man and the beggar Lazarus from Luke 16.

—A. Koshy Muthalaly.

PRACTICAL POINTS

1. God honors those who do not seek honors from people (Luke 14:7-11).

2. God has chosen to use us as His ambassadors to invite the lost to salvation (vss. 15-17).

3. We should not be surprised if the gospel is met with excuses rather than joyous acceptance (vss. 18-20).

4. The despised and forgotten of the world are the objects of God's love (vss. 21-22).

5. We should make every effort to take the gospel to unbelievers, but ultimately they are responsible for how they respond (vss. 23-24).

—*Jarl K. Waggoner.*

RESEARCH AND DISCUSSION

1. How do you think Jesus would evaluate some of our social customs (Luke 14:8-11)?

2. How can we consciously develop a humble attitude without seeming self-righteous (vss. 10-11)?

3. How can people who are so mistaken about their own destiny be so sure of their acceptance by God (vs. 15)?

4. Why do people feel the need to offer excuses for rejecting Christ (vss. 18-20)?

5. What is the Christian's responsibility in bringing people to Christ (Luke 14:23; cf. 24:46-47; John 6:44)? Is there a sense in which we should "compel" people?

6. What aspects of God's character are revealed by the statements of the master in Luke 14:23-24?

—*Jarl K. Waggoner.*

ILLUSTRATED HIGH POINTS

He that humbleth himself (Luke 14:11)

As Jesus sat in the house of one of the chief Pharisees as an invited guest, He gave a parable. In that situation, the Lord's purpose was to teach humility. He clearly revealed His goal in Luke 14:11.

Though Christ is the Son of God and was destined to be acknowledged as the King of the universe, the whole tenor of His ministry demonstrated a humble spirit (cf. Phil. 2:7-8).

By telling the parable, Jesus was subtly pointing out what a person's sinful flesh can so easily make him do, namely, seek all the best for himself, including the best place at a festivity.

Most of us have, at one time or another in God's kingdom work, noticed that even Christian leaders can seek their own personal gain and self-aggrandizement by means of church politics, manipulation, and competition. That is not God's way of accomplishing His will.

Go out into the highways (vs. 23)

The Bible teaches very clearly that mankind apart from Christ is hopelessly lost in sin. In response to a statement made by a person at the feast (Luke 14:15), Jesus taught about those who are invited to enter the kingdom of God by faith. Sadly, many refuse God's invitation and offer various excuses. This, however, is no reason to cease offering the gospel invitation to people. We are to go into the "highways and hedges" (vs. 23) to take the gospel to people who are often overlooked.

One application of the Lord's teaching is the evangelistic efforts today among children. In our city, a work among the children of parents of all walks of life has been very successful. Hundreds of them have made professions of faith.

—*P. Fredrick Fogle.*

Golden Text Illuminated

"And the lord said unto the servant, Go out into the highways and hedges, and compel them to come in, that my house may be filled" (Luke 14:23).

The man was greatly loved by his family, and the man loved ice cream. So when he passed away, his family honored him by going to the local ice cream shop and paying the bill for everyone present. The customers were inspired and responded by collecting $700 to pay for everyone's ice cream the rest of the day!

Kindness and generosity naturally inspire gratefulness and more kindness. There is something wrong with a person who responds to graciousness with coldness and disdain. Sadly, this latter reaction came from every guest the rich man had invited to his banquet in Jesus' parable. Their rudeness, however, did not send the banquet host into despair; instead, he became even more generous than before.

This wealthy banquet host beautifully illustrates the abundant grace of God. Let us consider how this is true.

First, the host did not simply put up a sign offering to feed any passersby. He sent his servant out to *compel* people to come in. We see that is similar to God's behavior. As John 3:16 tells us, He sent His Son to the world to convince people to accept His kindness and mercy. At first, it might seem odd that people actually need any convincing. Are they not being offered a free pardon for all their sins? Yes, it seems that people should all jump at the opportunity! But Scripture makes us face reality: there are none who seek God (Rom. 3:11). Everyone chooses to go his own way (vs. 12). We must be convinced to accept God's mercy; otherwise, we would all reject God's offer just like those who declined to attend the banquet.

Second, note where the servant in the parable was sent: to the "highways and hedges." This indicates that the new group of guests would likely be common people and possibly poor. In fact, the word "hedges" may possibly hint at the idea that some of the people were homeless and had erected makeshift shelters against walls around vineyards and gardens. We cannot say that with great certainty, but we do know that the servant was not sent to ritzy neighborhoods. Likely, the affluent would have responded with the same indifference as the first guests.

We see here a parallel with what Jesus, God's Servant, did when He came to earth. He spent most of His time with common people (fishermen, tax collectors, etc.) and the poor and needy. The rich and powerful, on the other hand, usually gave Him the cold shoulder or even persecuted Him. Not surprisingly, it was those who were suffering and helpless who readily accepted His kindness. Throughout church history, this has been a clear pattern: not many powerful and popular people come to enjoy God's grace (I Cor. 1:18-31).

Finally, why was the banquet host so willing to invite common people and poor people to enjoy his feast? Because he wanted a full house. He was not stingy. Like God, he was so gracious that he wanted as many as possible to enjoy his lavish abundance. That is why the apostle Peter could say, "Whosoever shall call on the name of the Lord shall be saved" (Acts 2:21).

Today's golden text reminds us forcefully of the character of God's glorious kingdom. It is not built on cruelty and crushing power but rather on the abundant mercy and kindness found in Christ.

—*Todd Williams.*

Heart of the Lesson

Vacations are great times to get away with the family and visit relatives or see interesting historical sites. They can be fun and relaxing—if you know where you are going!

On the other hand, a vacation can be stressful and irritating if you do not follow the map. Being lost is not fun at all. In fact, it can even be dangerous if you end up in a violent part of the city or run out of gas out in the middle of nowhere! Our text talks about being lost in a worse way—forever!

1. Humility honored (Luke 14:7-11). Jesus explained how important it is to be humble with other people. Imagine yourself at a fancy dinner honoring an important guest. Think how embarrassing it would be if you sat down near the celebrity but the host asked you to move farther away. Jesus said it is much better to begin farther down the table and then have the host ask you to move up.

Jesus explained through this story that our place at God's table is totally dependent on Him. There is nothing we can do to improve our status with God; it is only through His grace and mercy that we are even seated at His table. We should be humbled by this truth.

In a practical sense, we can imitate God. Rather than spend time only with those in our close circle of friends, we should reach out to those around us who are in need and do not have the means to reciprocate. We are then being truly hospitable, not merely entertaining with the expectation of a return invitation.

2. People and their excuses (Luke 14:15-20). Jesus told a parable about a great feast. The host invited all his friends to come. All initially accepted the invitation, but when the time for the feast arrived, each one declined and offered an excuse. As most excuses are, these were flimsy. One said he had bought land and needed to look at it. Who would buy land without looking at it first? Another gave a similar excuse, saying he had bought oxen sight unseen. A third gave the excuse of being recently married. Obviously, these people did not really want to come to the feast.

3. God reaches out (Luke 14:21-24). As you can imagine, the host in Jesus' parable was angered by these excuses, taking them as personal insults. He ordered his servant to go out and invite the poor and disabled people of the area. These folks were grateful for the invitation and happily attended.

There was still room at the table, so the host told his servant to go out and urge anyone he saw to come to the feast. The host wanted every place filled.

If any of those who had given an excuse before was now willing to come, it was too late. They had refused before and now were to be excluded.

Jesus' parable has clear application for us today. God is the Host who invites all to come and be a part of His feast—that is, receive eternal life with Him. This is His greatest possible gift to each one.

When people hear about God's gift of salvation, they have the opportunity to accept it or reject it. He offers it freely now.

There will come a time, though, when God's invitation will be closed. When He decides it is time to "close the gate," it will be too late for those who have rejected Him.

What a compelling picture this is! This should motivate those of us who have already received God's salvation to bring the lost to Him, before it is too late.

—Judy Carlsen.

World Missions

Christians wince when the gospel is rejected—not because of a feeling of personal rejection but rather because the unbeliever does not fully realize that his eternal destiny hangs by a thread. God could well bring his life to a close before the night is over.

In the parable in this week's text, we are told that those initially invited to a great feast "all with one consent began to make excuse" (Luke 14:18). The invitation to the feast, representing the gospel invitation, offers great fulfillment to those who accept it. William M. Taylor, interpreting the parable in this way, suggested a blessing that includes a pardon for sin, favor with God, peace of conscience, and renewal of the heart (*Parables of Our Saviour*, Kregel).

We all know those who have refused the Lord's gracious invitation to come to faith in Christ. Speaking informally to university students, I was able to make the gospel clear without any overt rejection by any of my hearers. Later, one young woman rebuked me with the words, "Are you trying to say I am not going to heaven?" I replied that I had no knowledge of who would miss heaven. I simply said that there is only one way to get there—through the finished work of Christ on the cross. She turned on her heel and stalked off.

I was burdened for Clyde. I gave him the gospel a number of times, and he laughed it off. "I will be in hell with my friends," he said. "Hell is no place for anyone," I replied. At first he was at least cordial, but every presentation to him resulted in the same flouting of the grace of God. I believe he understood the gravity of his need, but he eventually refused to see me.

Caleb was an especially tragic example of the peril of rejection. He found the gospel absorbing. He was thoroughly convinced Jesus was the Messiah his Jewish people had long sought, but he steadfastly refused to ratify his convictions with a decision. He reassured me that when his Orthodox Jewish father passed away, he would leave Judaism for Jesus Christ.

On his deathbed, Caleb's father had him place his hand under his father's thigh in a very ancient custom. Solemnly the old man pressed Caleb to vow he would never leave the faith of his fathers. Caleb, out of devotion to his father, did so. Never again could I raise the claims of the Messiah. Caleb passed away, probably without trusting the Saviour.

Richard practiced a very shallow, perhaps even artificial, kind of Judaism. He carefully investigated the claims of Jesus as the Messiah and was generally convinced of the truth. Family wealth, security, and a respected place in the Jewish community, however, were his unexpressed reasons for passing up the invitation to the gospel feast.

Jesus made it clear that Christ rejecters will not have limitless opportunities to repent. The man in Jesus' parable said of those who rejected his invitation, "None of those men which were bidden shall taste of my supper" (Luke 14:24).

It is good to know that missionaries and other believers are out in the highways and hedges, inviting men and women to believe the glorious message of salvation. It is sad to recall those who have rejected the gospel, but the marriage supper of the Lamb in the last days will be very well attended (Rev. 19:6-9).

—*Lyle P. Murphy.*

85

The Jewish Aspect

A typical first-century Jewish marriage began with a yearlong betrothal period after formalizing the marriage contract. This provided the couple with time to prepare for the establishment of their home and financial independence.

On the day of the actual wedding, the properly dressed groom would go with his groomsmen to the home of his awaiting bride. Often he was preceded by a group of singers or musicians.

Upon arriving at the bride's home, the groom would bring her into the procession to take her to either his or his father's home. The procession would grow with the addition of the bride's attendant maidens and others who might join the celebration along the way. The joyous procession would make its way through the streets to the groom's home for the wedding feast.

All of the friends and neighbors were invited to the wedding feast. While the traditional Jewish wedding festivities normally lasted for seven days, the festivities could stretch to as much as two weeks.

The wedding feast was an incomparable celebration. The Talmud provides insight into some of the customs of the wedding celebration and the differing views of some of the early rabbis.

The wedding celebration was so important that the rabbis determined that even the study of the law was to be interrupted so that the newlyweds could be properly honored. Differing opinions among rabbis are found in one somewhat amusing example. Bearing in mind that beneath every activity was a code of proper conduct, some activities normally forbidden were permitted at weddings.

For example, according to the *halakhah,* or traditional Jewish teaching, it was forbidden for a man to gaze upon the face of a bride or any other married woman. This prohibition included the time of the wedding itself.

The Gemara, however, presents a conflicting view. According to one rabbi, it was permissible to look upon the bride's face for the entire seven days of the wedding celebration. Even more than this, the beauty of the bride was to be expounded and celebrated. Even if the bride was homely or disfigured in some way, some rabbinical schools advised that she should be praised for her beauty.

The reason for this was to inspire the husband's further appreciation for his new bride. As he saw others admiring the beauty of his wife, he would appreciate her even more.

Weddings were so important that if a wedding procession intercepted a funeral procession, the wedding party was given preference. The only person who took precedence over a wedding party was the king of Israel himself. The story is written that even King Agrippa once relinquished his privilege for a passing wedding party, to the praise of the rabbis.

The wedding celebration was of the highest priority in the community. Within this celebration, the focus of attention was on the bride and groom; therefore, if guests at the wedding feast were concerned with seeking the places of honor, their attention was improperly focused. Similarly, if other matters were more important than attendance at a feast, the difficulty lay with misplaced priorities.

--Carter Corbrey

Guiding the Superintendent

Many opinions exist concerning what the focus of the church should be in the twenty-first century. Many today stress the importance of biblical worship and discipleship, while others place their emphasis on healing and spiritual gifts.

In this week's lesson text Luke recorded two parables that Jesus proclaimed. Taken together, they remind believers what the primary focus of the church should be in the twenty-first century—conducting ourselves in such a manner that nothing prevents us from bringing the lost to saving faith in Jesus Christ.

DEVOTIONAL OUTLINE

1. The parable on status seeking (Luke 14:7-11). Jesus noticed how people actively sought out the seating places of honor at the formal dinner being held at "the house of one of the chief Pharisees" (vs. 1). Jesus related a parable about personal humility at a wedding celebration.

Jesus instructed the self-seeking guests not to seek out the important seats at the dinner table. Doing so was a potential cause for acute embarrassment, for a more prominent guest might arrive later, and the already-seated guest would draw everyone's attention when he had to move to a place of lower status.

In order to prevent such humiliation, Jesus taught His listeners to seek out the less prominent seats. This humble action could result in the guest being promoted to a more prominent, unoccupied seat.

2. The parable of the great banquet (Luke 14:15-24). One of the guests who had been listening closely to Jesus' wedding parable made a high-spirited statement that prompted Jesus to relate another parable about a "great supper."

This teaching story emphasized the gracious invitation to the feast. When the time of the banquet arrived, several of the invitees offered feeble excuses for their nonattendance. When the lord of the feast heard that his gracious invitation had been rejected, he sent his servant into the city to invite those who otherwise would never have had an opportunity to experience such a magnificent event.

When the "poor, and the maimed, and the halt, and the blind" (vs. 21) accepted the invitation and attended the banquet, the lord of the feast discovered that there was still room for more guests. He sent his servant out a second time to bring other strangers to join the festivities. Jesus then concluded His parable by stating the serious consequences for those who had rejected the gracious invitation.

AGE-GROUP EMPHASES

Children: You never know when the heart of a young child is ready to believe the gospel. Encourage your teachers to use this week's lesson text to tenderly invite their students to believe in the Lord Jesus Christ as their Saviour.

Youths: Teens no doubt have had many more opportunities than children to respond to the gospel. Encourage your teachers to invite their students to put their faith in the Lord Jesus Christ, noting the consequences of continued rejection.

Adults: It is not for us to know when the heart of an adult may have hardened to the message of the gospel. If you suspect there are any unsaved individuals in your adult classes, invite them to believe in the Lord Jesus Christ. Let Him break open the hardened heart by His marvelous grace.

—*Thomas R. Chmura.*

SCRIPTURE LESSON TEXT

LUKE 16:19 There was a certain rich man, which was clothed in purple and fine linen, and fared sumptuously every day:

20 And there was a certain beggar named Lazarus, which was laid at his gate, full of sores,

21 And desiring to be fed with the crumbs which fell from the rich man's table: moreover the dogs came and licked his sores.

22 And it came to pass, that the beggar died, and was carried by the angels into Abraham's bosom: the rich man also died, and was buried;

23 And in hell he lift up his eyes, being in torments, and seeth Abraham afar off, and Lazarus in his bosom.

24 And he cried and said, Father Abraham, have mercy on me, and send Lazarus, that he may dip the tip of his finger in water, and cool my tongue; for I am tormented in this flame.

25 But Abraham said, Son, remember that thou in thy lifetime receivedst thy good things, and likewise Lazarus evil things: but now he is comforted, and thou art tormented.

26 And beside all this, between us and you there is a great gulf fixed: so that they which would pass from hence to you cannot; neither can they pass to us, that *would come* from thence.

27 Then he said, I pray thee therefore, father, that thou wouldest send him to my father's house:

28 For I have five brethren; that he may testify unto them, lest they also come into this place of torment.

29 Abraham saith unto him, They have Moses and the prophets; let them hear them.

30 And he said, Nay, father Abraham: but if one went unto them from the dead, they will repent.

31 And he said unto him, If they hear not Moses and the prophets, neither will they be persuaded, though one rose from the dead.

NOTES

Abraham's Bosom - synonym for the hereafter. To go and be w/ the Fathers

Sheol - OT - Abode of the dead / Hebrew equivalent of the Greek Hades (unseen world)

A Warning for the Hard-Hearted

Lesson Text: Luke 16:19-31

Related Scriptures: Matthew 6:19-20;
Hebrews 3:7-19; Revelation 20:11-15; 21:5-8

TIME: A.D. 30   PLACE: probably Perea

GOLDEN TEXT—"Son, remember that thou in thy lifetime receivedst thy good things, and likewise Lazarus evil things: but now he is comforted, and thou art tormented" (Luke 16:25).

Introduction

Pollsters tell us that a high percentage of Americans believe in God; most of these people also believe in heaven. A significantly lower percentage believes in hell. As might be expected, though, those affirming the existence of hell usually do not believe they will go there!

Throughout the Bible, the concept of a day of reckoning is clearly taught. In the Old Testament, this usually involved some kind of temporal punishment meted out in this world, as when Sodom was destroyed or when Israel was defeated by its enemies. While the New Testament also includes the idea of earthly punishment, the concept of both eternal rewards and retribution is its primary focus. While some claim that a loving God would never allow anyone to go to hell, they come to this conclusion by ignoring what the Bible says on this topic, especially the teaching of the Lord Jesus Christ.

LESSON OUTLINE

I. RICH MAN, POOR MAN—
   Luke 16:19-21

II. REWARD AND RETRIBUTION—
   Luke 16:22-23

III. REQUEST DENIED—
   Luke 16:24-28

IV. REVELATION SUFFICIENT—
   Luke 16:29-31

Exposition: Verse by Verse

RICH MAN, POOR MAN

LUKE 16:19 There was a certain rich man, which was clothed in purple and fine linen, and fared sumptuously every day:

20 And there was a certain beggar named Lazarus, which was laid at his gate, full of sores,

21 And desiring to be fed with the crumbs which fell from the rich

man's table: moreover the dogs came and licked his sores.

Prosperity (Luke 16:19). {Though unnamed, the "certain rich man" in this story is often referred to as Dives. The supposed name derives from the Latin Vulgate version of the Bible, as the Latin word for "rich" is *dives.* This, however, was not a personal name.}[Q1] {In one line, the rich man is described in such a way that there is no doubt concerning his luxurious lifestyle.}[Q2] To be "clothed in purple" meant that he wore the clothing of royalty, though there is nothing to indicate that he occupied an official government post. Likewise, the "fine linen," probably imported from the Nile River valley, was another sign of wealth. In addition, the rich man "fared sumptuously every day"—he feasted on the finest food in great abundance. He would no doubt have been the envy of many people.

The context is Jesus' larger teaching concerning wealth (Luke 16:1-13) and His ongoing conflicts with the Pharisees and scribes (15:1-2). These respected opponents of Jesus loved money: "And the Pharisees also, who were covetous, heard all these things: and they derided him" (16:14). We must understand that wealth was often seen as a sign of God's special favor. That is why the Twelve were puzzled when Jesus declared, "It is easier for a camel to go through the eye of a needle, than for a rich man to enter into the kingdom of God" (Mark 10:25). The amazed disciples responded, "Who then can be saved?" (vs. 26).

One of the questions often asked concerning our lesson text concerns the nature of the story itself. Is it a parable or the recounting of actual events? Most would refer to it as a parable, but that in no way diminishes the truth it conveys. Since most parables contain one major truth or theme, some details in a parable may just add color to the story and may

not necessarily have specific meaning. "While the parable does contain a few doctrinal implications, the expositor must keep in mind that one cannot build a complete eschatology upon it" (Barker and Kohlenberger, eds., *The Expositor's Bible Commentary, Abridged,* Zondervan). Whether considering a parable or some other portion of God's Word, the best interpreter of Scripture is Scripture itself.

Poverty (Luke 16:20-21). {"Lazarus" was a rather common name in New Testament times (cf. John 11:1-44). Significantly, the name Lazarus means "he whom God has helped." This is appropriate, as Lazarus was not aided by the rich man but by God Himself.}[Q3]

Unlike today in many developed countries, there were no nonprofit organizations or government agencies to help disabled people or those who found themselves in dire straits. Even today, there are many places on earth where the ill and infirm are reduced to begging to survive.

To be placed where many people passed by, including by the gate of a wealthy man's property, was common for beggars in biblical times (cf. Mark 10:46; Acts 3:1-2). That Lazarus was "laid at his gate" (Luke 16:20) indicates a lack of mobility. Being "full of sores" reveals a condition both painful and likely infectious. The mental image we draw from this brief description certainly elicits sympathy for this man's plight.

Lazarus was not asking to be admitted to the rich man's house to be seated with him at his fine table. All he wanted was the meager leftovers from the rich man's feasts—the scraps. After one of his sumptuous meals, whatever fell to the floor would have been gathered up and tossed outside his door, presumably to be eaten by the dogs, common scavengers of the streets. Sadly, the only companions Lazarus had were the dogs that licked his sores. Whether the dogs here are to be seen in a positive or negative light is unclear, but it certainly does not paint a very pretty picture.

REWARD AND RETRIBUTION

22 And it came to pass, that the beggar died, and was carried by the angels into Abraham's bosom: the rich man also died, and was buried;

23 And in hell he lift up his eyes, being in torments, and seeth Abraham afar off, and Lazarus in his bosom.

Heaven (Luke 16:22). {As will happen to all of us, both Lazarus and the rich man died. Carried by the angels, Lazarus was escorted into the presence of Abraham to rest at his side.}[04] Being the father of the Hebrew people, Abraham was seen as the overseer of paradise, the place to which the righteous go after death (23:43). To be with Abraham meant that Lazarus was with the patriarchs of Israel (13:28). The picture is of a great banquet enjoyed by all the redeemed. Lazarus would not have to beg for food any longer. Whether paradise and heaven were seen as identical at this time is unclear. Paul seemed to use these words interchangeably (cf. II Cor. 12:1-4).

That Lazarus was taken to paradise certainly indicates that he was a righteous man, although nothing is stated about his faith or character. He was not, however, taken to paradise simply because he was poor. There are poor people who are very evil, and there are rich people who are very godly. "Lazarus was righteous not because he was poor but because he depended on God" (Walvoord and Zuck, eds., *The Bible Knowledge Commentary,* Cook). That being said, riches do present temptations never imagined by the poor. Generally speaking, Scripture depicts God as protecting the poor and opposing the oppressive rich (cf. Jas. 2:5-7; 5:1-6).

As we know, whatever we have in this world must be left behind at death

(I Tim. 6:6-10, 17-18). Since there is no mention of burial for Lazarus, we can imagine that his body met with an ignominious end. But the rich man was buried, probably in a finely carved tomb (cf. Matt. 27:57-60), including all the pomp afforded the wealthy of his day.

Hell (Luke 16:23). {In direct contrast to Lazarus, the rich man went to hell.}[04] In the King James Version, there are three Greek words rendered "hell" in the New Testament. One of these is *gehenna,* taken from the valley of Hinnom (II Kgs. 23:10), once a place of human sacrifice and later Jerusalem's garbage dump. It is used only by Jesus (Matt. 10:28; 18:9; 23:15, 33) and in James 3:6. Another word translated "hell," appearing only once in the New Testament, is *tartarus.* It was used by Greeks for the lowest place of torment (II Pet. 2:4).

{The word translated "hell" in our text is the Greek *hades,* which was understood as the world of the dead and equivalent to the Hebrew *sheol,* often found in the Old Testament.}[05] As understood by many in antiquity, hades was not necessarily a place of suffering but just the place people went after death. However, in the New Testament, hades is usually depicted as a place of torment (cf. Luke 10:15; Rev. 1:18; 6:8; 20:13-14).

As the rich man closed his eyes in death, he immediately opened them in torment. Not only could he see where he was, but he could also see where Lazarus was! Whether this means the lost can see what they have missed is an open question. If so, it will add to their mental anguish as they view the bliss of the saved.

REQUEST DENIED

24 And he cried and said, Father Abraham, have mercy on me, and send Lazarus, that he may dip the tip of his finger in water, and cool my tongue; for I am tormented in this flame.

25 But Abraham said, Son, remember that thou in thy lifetime receivedst thy good things, and likewise Lazarus evil things: but now he is comforted, and thou art tormented.

26 And beside all this, between us and you there is a great gulf fixed: so that they which would pass from hence to you cannot; neither can they pass to us, that would come from thence.

27 Then he said, I pray thee therefore, father, that thou wouldest send him to my father's house:

28 For I have five brethren; that he may testify unto them, lest they also come into this place of torment.

Great anguish (Luke 16:24). Realizing where he was caused the rich man to cry out for mercy. As a Jew, it was appropriate for him to address Abraham as "Father." But physical descent from Abraham was no guarantee of being in a correct spiritual relationship with God (cf. 3:7-9; 13:28-30).

Since the rich man was able to see Lazarus being comforted, he pleaded with the patriarch to send the former beggar to his aid. {His request was simple. He wanted Lazarus to dip the tip of his finger in some water and cool his tongue with a few drops.}[Q6]

As to references in the Bible portraying the agony of the wicked in the fires of hell (Matt. 25:41; Jude 1:7; Rev. 14:11; 20:13-15), obvious questions arise about this image. Are we to understand this literally? There is no reason not to. And as Herschel Hobbs observed, "If hell is not real fire, as some insist, then it is worse than fire; for the reality is always greater than the symbol" (*An Exposition of the Gospel of Luke,* Baker).

Great gulf (Luke 16:25-26). In reply to his plea for Lazarus to help alleviate his pain, Abraham reminded the rich man of his former life of luxury. To be sure, if we go to hell, we take our memories with us. But the memories of a life of ease would only serve to increase the mental anguish experienced by the rich man. That Lazarus by contrast received "evil things" simply means bad things—namely, poverty, privation, and pain. Now, however, the tables were turned. Lazarus was being comforted, and the rich man was being tormented.

The rich man may now have seen that he had lived foolishly, but alas, it was too late. As someone has said, "True repentance is seldom late, and late repentance is seldom true!" So it is not likely that the rich man had really changed. He was still preoccupied about his own needs and still trying to order people around!

{Even if Abraham had wanted to grant the request of the rich man, he cited a simple reason why he could not: "Between us and you there is a great gulf fixed" (vs. 26). There will be no travel between heaven and hell.}[Q7] One's eternal destiny is fixed at death. While some suggest that God might give people a second chance after death, there is no hint of this in the Bible. As was true for the rich man, if we go to hell, it will be too late to do anything about it!

Great tragedy (Luke 16:27-28). Since Lazarus could not leave paradise to aid him in his torment, the rich man made another request. {He pleaded that Lazarus might be able to return to earth for the purpose of warning the rich man's unrepentant brothers.}[Q8] While nothing else is said about these brothers, they too must have pursued selfish, ungodly lives.

Even now, there may be many such requests being made from the netherworld. Such prayers, if they could even be called that, will remain unanswered.

Christians sometimes wonder why their earnest prayers concerning their lost friends and relatives are not answered. To be sure, the Lord is "not willing that any should perish, but that all should come to repentance" (II Pet. 3:9). That people are not saved is not due to God's unwillingness or inability to redeem them but to their unwillingness to come to Him! Jesus said, "Him that cometh to me I will in no wise cast out" (John 6:37). Prayers for the lost can nevertheless open their eyes and convict them of sin, provide them additional opportunities to repent, and bring people into their lives to help lead them to Christ. It is best, perhaps, to realize that we cannot fully fathom the mysteries of God's sovereignty.

REVELATION SUFFICIENT

29 Abraham saith unto him, They have Moses and the prophets; let them hear them.

30 And he said, Nay, father Abraham: but if one went unto them from the dead, they will repent.

31 And he said unto him, If they hear not Moses and the prophets, neither will they be persuaded, though one rose from the dead.

Hear God's Word (Luke 16:29-30). {What might sound like an appropriate request to prevent others from being eternally lost was answered very succinctly by Abraham: "They have Moses and the prophets." In short, what revelation they already had from God was sufficient.}[Q9] The testimony of God's Word, whether the Old Testament for those who were under the old covenant or the completed Bible for people today, is all that is needed. We only need to listen to Scripture and believe what God says (Rom. 10:17)!

The rich man persisted, however. He argued that a miraculous demonstration—Lazarus returning from the dead—would convince his brothers and cause them to repent.

Heed God's Word (Luke 16:31). Abraham replied that if the brothers would not heed the Scriptures, they would not be persuaded by a man who returned from the dead. Indeed, even Jesus' miracles did not convince His opponents that He was the Messiah.

{"Jesus was obviously suggesting that the rich man symbolized the Pharisees. They wanted signs—signs so clear that they would compel people to believe. But since they refused to believe the Scriptures, they would not believe any sign no matter how great.}[Q10] Just a short time later Jesus did raise a man from the dead, another man named Lazarus (John 11:38-44). The result was that the religious leaders began to plot more earnestly to kill both Jesus and Lazarus (John 11:45-53; 12:10-11)" (Walvoord and Zuck).

—*John Alva Owston.*

QUESTIONS

1. What is the traditional name given the rich man? Where does it come from?
2. How is the rich man's lifestyle described?
3. Who was Lazarus, and how is he described?
4. What happened to both men once they died?
5. What is the word translated "hell" in this passage, and to what does it refer?
6. What did the rich man want Lazarus to do for him?
7. Why was it not possible for Abraham to fulfill the rich man's request?
8. What additional request did the rich man have?
9. What information did the rich man and his brothers already have?
10. How does this story relate to the Pharisees and their rejection of Christ?

—*John Alva Owston.*

Preparing to Teach the Lesson

Our lesson text today is one of those instances in the Bible where the knowledge and experience of the Lord Jesus and a factual spiritual event only He could know are linked with the present situation of many of us in this life.

This story was not given to one of the prophets, and it is not part of any other historical narrative. Yet it is told as the truth by the One who never lies. It cannot be verified or corrected by any human being. It has the ring of truth about it, although it is decidedly outside the experiential knowledge or learning of anyone living. It is not a speculation about something that could have happened. It is a clear account of something that actually did happen.

TODAY'S AIM

Facts: to learn some key details about what happens after death.

Principle: to understand that the meaning of the story will open our eyes to understanding other truths.

Application: to be alert to the fact that our lives and our beliefs have end results.

INTRODUCING THE LESSON

While not all agree, it seems the Lord Jesus is telling this story not as a parable but as a true account. It involves "a certain rich man" (Luke 16:19), not a created illustration to teach a point of truth. Although his name is tactfully not given, the Lord Jesus, by the clarity and certainty of the story as told, lets us know that He could have given his name. He was a real person.

The rich man had it made. He lived in luxury. However, he had the same problem every person does: one day he would die. Opportunities in life abounded, but they would end. Lazarus had nothing—no opportunities—and he also would die. We are captured by this story because it hits us where we live and makes us wonder about many things.

DEVELOPING THE LESSON

1. The tale of two men (Luke 16:19-23). We have no idea whether the rich man appreciated his wealth. We do not know if he was thankful for it or if he shared any of it with others. He apparently knew Lazarus was at his gate. We are told that Lazarus desired to have the table scraps from the rich man's table. Did the dogs get the table scraps? They came and licked the sores of poor Lazarus— sores that could have come from malnutrition!

We are not told about the faith of either man directly. The rich man's lack of faith would surface later. Each man had the opportunity to believe God, love Him, and obey Him. Finally, both men died. The way the Lord Jesus reported this is beautiful! Lazarus died and "was carried by the angels into Abraham's bosom" (vs. 22). We cannot take the space here to explore this further, but this is equivalent to saying Lazarus went to heaven and was comforted by Abraham, the "father of the faithful." Was his body buried? It did not matter. He, that is, the essence of what Lazarus was and is, was carried into heaven. He was ushered into peace and comfort.

When the rich man died, his body was buried, probably with all the care and attention such a person might have arranged for and might have expected. Unfortunately, he opened his eyes after dying to find himself in hell (hades). No mere mortal could have told a true story like this. We would probably say, "Well, maybe he made it to heaven. I hope he did." It is interesting that the rich man knew the status of both himself and Lazarus. And he knew who Abraham and Lazarus were.

2. The conversation between the rich man and Abraham (Luke 16:24-28). The rich man wanted relief from his pain in hell, and then he wanted Lazarus to go back to the earthly realm to warn his brothers. That was an understandable thought, but both his requests hung on the idea of Lazarus doing something for the rich man. Did he now wish he had honored God with his life and maybe helped Lazarus when he could have? As the story shows, the status of both men was now permanent. Abraham said to the rich man, "He [Lazarus] is comforted, and thou art tormented."

3. The resolution to this situation (Luke 16:29-31). The rich man's request was a logical attempt by a man who now knew better and wanted to help those he loved. His opportunities, however, were hopelessly gone. The answer given by the Lord Jesus in quoting Abraham was that the living can do no better than to live by the light God has already given them. Someone coming back from the dead would not convince them.

It may well be that at the final judgment of those who do not make it into heaven, all the opportunities they had to believe in the Lord will be revealed. Those who do not respond to the truth of God's Word will face divine judgment for their sins.

ILLUSTRATING THE LESSON

The cross is the great divider. Do you believe Christ died and rose for you? Is He your Lord and Saviour?

CONCLUDING THE LESSON

Remember, this is a story about where people will spend eternity, which is determined by the decisions we make in this life. We cannot do anything for the condition of others, other than give our testimony to the glorious gospel of Christ. Ultimately, we must leave it up to God as to what He will do to reach unbelievers. God may give extraordinary proofs of the truth of the gospel if He so chooses.

However, Scripture points out that "the just shall live by faith" (Rom. 1:17). We are asked to believe God because He is God, not because of "proof." One day all people will be convinced, but by then it will be too late, just as it was with the rich man. As much as we can, should we not explain this whole story to the unsaved? Let us not give in to the modern, liberal idea that there is no hell and eternal torment, which is clearly at odds with the teachings of the Lord Jesus.

ANTICIPATING THE NEXT LESSON

Our next lesson examines Jesus' description of the final judgment between the sheep and the goats from Matthew 25:31-46.

—*Brian D. Doud.*

PRACTICAL POINTS

1. When we have the opportunity, we should help those who are in need (Luke 16:19-21; cf. Gal. 6:10).
2. One who refuses to show kindness in this life should not expect any in the next (Luke 16:22-24).
3. One day, all people will be held accountable for their actions (vss. 25-26).
4. We should tell our loved ones about Jesus while we still can (vss. 27-28).
5. The Word of God contains everything we need to know about salvation (vss. 29-30).
6. If a person's heart is closed off to God, the greatest miracle will have no effect on him (vs. 31).

—Charity G. Carter.

RESEARCH AND DISCUSSION

1. Why did the rich man ignore Lazarus every day (Luke 16:19-20)?
2. Explain the irony of the rich man asking Abraham to send Lazarus to place a drop of water on his tongue (vs. 24).
3. What does verse 25 mean? Will some people who have more than enough on earth not be able to enter heaven?
4. What spiritual gulf in this life separates people who do not know God from those who do (vs. 26)? What can the people of God do to bridge that gap?
5. Why did the rich man believe that his brothers would listen to Lazarus when they had not listened to anyone else (vss. 27-29)?

—Charity G. Carter.

ILLUSTRATED HIGH POINTS

Carried by the angels (Luke 16:22)

Angels are called "the chariots of God" (Ps. 68:17). Angels could also have descended and broken the fall of Jesus had He chosen to jump off the cliff at Satan's urging (Matt. 4:6).

Understanding that angels are God's chariots, and suffering through more than two hundred years of bondage, slaves birthed the spiritual "Swing Low, Sweet Chariot," proclaiming with great hope, "A band of angels coming after me, coming for to carry me home." They sang that one day angels would carry them to a place of safety.

Angels are "ministering spirits" (Heb. 1:14; cf. Matt. 4:11; Mark 1:13) who can "swing low" to the depth of our troubled hearts and lift us to a place of God's comfort.

If they hear not Moses (vs. 31)

"Forever Free" was the name of an exhibition that was housed at the Massachusetts Historical Society in 2013. It featured an ordinary 150-year-old ink-stained wooden pen. But it was a mighty pen. President Abraham Lincoln used it to sign the Emancipation Proclamation of January 1, 1863, which changed the legal status of over three million people from slaves to free persons. The document, in part, reads, "I do order and declare that all persons held as slaves within said designated States, and parts of States, are, and henceforward shall be free."

There is absolutely nothing more powerful (on earth or in heaven) than God's Word. After Israel had resisted the words of every prophet sent them as well as their own God-sent emancipator, Moses, they would not even be persuaded by the resurrection of Jesus Christ.

—Therese Greenberg.

Golden Text Illuminated

"Son, remember that thou in thy lifetime receivedst thy good things, and likewise Lazarus evil things: but now he is comforted, and thou art tormented" (Luke 16:25).

In a previous lesson concerning the parables of God's kingdom, we were presented with a "macro" view of God's justice. Those parables, particularly the parable of the wheat and the tares, allowed us to see the big picture of how God's justice will be manifest at the end of time and how the saved and the lost will be separated. This current lesson, however, shows us a "micro" view of God's justice. It is not focused on the big picture but looks at two individuals' lives and final destinies.

The justice of God has very personal consequences for all people. The Lord's story of the rich man and Lazarus brings this reality to all who read it.

The rich man and Lazarus had contrasting lives and destinies, and their story has a striking twist. The rich man had all the "good" things in life, which we see from Luke 16:19 included a prosperous lifestyle, with nice clothes and whatever he wanted to eat.

On the other hand, Lazarus was a beggar who lay out in the street. He was physically unwell and did not get enough to eat. This is the classic contrast between the haves and the have nots. Some experience great prosperity in this life, and some suffer great loss and deprivation. It is the same story the world over, in every time and in every place. It is the way of a fallen world.

The interesting thing is that the Lord went on to show that how one fares materially in this life does not determine one's destiny in the next. The rich man and Lazarus had contrasting destinies, and they were not what the world would expect. Lazarus's deprived earthly condition did not prevent him from entering paradise. He was, in fact, saved and ushered to "Abraham's bosom" (vs. 22) by the angels of God. There he was comforted. The Lord was not teaching that earthly poverty is the means of salvation, but rather that having struggles and sufferings on earth will not prevent the believer from entering "comfort" in heaven.

The rich man, on the other hand, was not saved. It was a shock for him to find himself in torment after death. He learned that this end was fixed and nonnegotiable as he sought to bargain with Abraham (vss. 23-26). Earthly comforts do not necessarily mean a person is headed for heaven. We dare not trust in earthly success and riches, thinking that such things will commend us to God.

So we see great contrasts in the Lord's story of Lazarus and the rich man. The message is stark and plain. Help us, Lord, to preach this plain message for all to hear!

Abraham said that the people of the earth do not need a supernatural visitation to understand what they must do (cf. vs. 29). The truth is clear from the Scriptures. Those who repent and believe in the Lord Jesus will receive the comfort of salvation. Those who do not will be lost in eternal torment, no matter what was gained or lost in the brief years of their lives. God's justice involves everyone. The reaping comes to each individual person. Each one will be saved or lost.

—Jeff VanGoethem.

Heart of the Lesson

With the conversion of the Roman emperor Constantine, Christians went from being an often-persecuted minority to being the favored religion of the Roman Empire. In less than three hundred years after the resurrection of Christ, those who used to gather, often at risk, for worship in personal homes watched as provision was made for them with government funds. Church bishops began receiving government salaries, and churches began receiving grants directly from the Roman treasury (Eusebius, *Church History*).

Since that time, many Christians have been tempted to seek lives of wealth and comfort. Even today, some of us seem more concerned with large buildings, comfortable seating, and parking spaces than with helping those who are less fortunate. The parable of the rich man and Lazarus provides a much-needed corrective.

1. A tale of two men (Luke 16:19-23). There is a stark difference in the descriptions of the rich man and Lazarus. The rich man wore expensive clothes and ate well every day. Lazarus, on the other hand, was a poor beggar who apparently was lame and had nothing to eat. Scavenger dogs licked the sores covering his body.

Similar to others unable to work, Lazarus was laid at a gate where he could receive charity from those with the ability to help as they passed by (cf. Acts 3:1-2). But he did not receive any aid from the rich man. The rich man ignored Lazarus, all the while knowing that he was outside his gate.

While their lives on earth were different, the same fate befell both men; at some point they both died. But Lazarus was taken to the bosom of Abraham. The rich man found himself looking up from Hades in torment.

2. A word from Abraham (Luke 16:24-31). Some think that the rich man was punished for being wealthy and Lazarus was rewarded because he was poor. However, God does not judge people on outward circumstances but looks on the heart. The rich man's problem was an evil heart. Jesus had already taught that any person who had received much would be examined on the basis of what he did with it (12:48) and also that it is impossible to serve both God and money (16:13). Other passages also point to the moral responsibilities of those who have been blessed with abundance (cf. I Tim. 6:17-19).

Abraham explained to the rich man that there would be no comfort for him. The rich man then asked if Lazarus could go back and warn his brothers so that they could avoid his end. Abraham replied that what had been passed down by Moses and the prophets in the Scriptures was sufficient.

Moses had taught the people of Israel to not harden their hearts against the poor in their midst but rather to give what was needed by them (Deut. 15:7-11). Many Old Testament prophets cried out against the social injustices inflicted upon the poor by those in power. Amos preached against those who took bribes and turned away the needy at the gates (Amos 5:12). Malachi rebuked those who took advantage of hired workers concerning their wages (Mal. 3:5). Jeremiah indicted those in power who did not defend the rights of the needy (Jer. 5:27-29).

The parable of the rich man and Lazarus underscores the importance of stewardship for Christians everywhere. Those of us who have been blessed in abundance have a biblical mandate to help those in need.

—*Armondo L. Jackson.*

World Missions

Too often those who have the ability to assist others do not respond to their needs. This evil is evident in countries whose governments are laden with wealth while their impoverished and starving populations are neglected. Like the rich man in our lesson, these selfish and corrupt rulers callously disregard the suffering as they greedily pursue opulence. Christians who desire to send supplies to these countries often discover that the items rarely, if ever, get to the people. In His infinite love, however, God sends missionaries to distribute items directly to people groups whose governments cannot or will not help them. Crucial to this work is missionary aviation.

Our family recently celebrated with Ezra, the son of a family friend, upon his commissioning as a bush pilot with a missionary aviation team. His specialty is helicopters. His assignment involves flying teachers, medical teams, church planters, and construction workers into remote villages. Sensitive political circumstances will not permit Ezra to reveal the location of his assignment, but we concluded that his mission is a dangerous one.

Ezra began his journey to "fly for Jesus," as he referred to his call, as a teenager. In 2005 he observed news reports about Hurricane Katrina, which destroyed much of New Orleans, Louisiana. He watched as helicopters let down rope ladders to residents, rescuing them from their rooftops. Already fascinated by aircraft, the fourteen-year-old decided to pursue a career as a flight pilot.

Coming from a family of seven children, Ezra realized that he would have to bankroll any flight school expenses himself. During his four years of high school, he saved the proceeds from a variety of after-school and summer jobs for postgraduation flight school. His perseverance paid off as he enrolled in flight school, completed his aviation hours, and earned his helicopter pilot's license. His search then began for a missions organization he could join. He was amazed that his skills were in high demand.

After much prayer, Ezra chose a ministry with missionary aviation teams throughout the world. Our prayers and congratulations go with Ezra as he embarks on this exciting adventure with Christ.

I must admit, I had not given much thought to missionary aviation until I watched Ezra step into his calling. I asked him what we could do to help the missionaries. He gave me several suggestions. We can send financial donations to assist with providing fuel, performing maintenance, and purchasing flight equipment. Other needs include office machines and supplies for the village churches and communication, social media, and website design for a missions base at home. Also, and most important, the pilots and others affiliated with this missionary work always need our prayers and personal encouragement.

God is pleased as we extend a hand to help the "Lazaruses" of the world. Supporting a missionary aviation team is one way to assist people who have been abandoned by those who should have helped them. Find such a ministry and contribute to it, and God will richly reward you.

—*Beverly Medley Jones.*

The Jewish Aspect

A Jewish midrash (story) tells of a rabbi's visit to heaven and hell. The parable records that the rabbi visited hell first. While in hell, he saw table after table of scrumptious food. He was upset to see that although there was a great deal of delicious food, all the people there were pale and starving. Upon looking closely, he realized that every person had arms that were splinted with wooden stakes. Not one person was able to bring the delicious food to his mouth.

Next, the rabbi went to heaven. When he got there, he was surprised to find the same setting as in hell. He saw tables laden with food and people with their arms bound. However, he noticed that these people were sitting around happily content, having obviously partaken of the delicious food.

The rabbi watched as a man picked up a spoon and scooped it into the dish before him. Then he stretched forward and fed the person seated across from him. That person graciously thanked him and reciprocated. This story was intended to illustrate that people should use what they have been given to nourish others, but it also gives us some insight into the Jewish idea of heaven and hell.

This week's lesson deals with the afterlife. While many religions give a great deal of attention to the afterlife, Judaism focuses more on the here and now. Jewish tradition cherishes present-day life. Its focus, making the world better now, concerns itself with current events. As a result, Judaism contains a lesser-developed idea of the afterlife than what is found in some religions. However, it does have a few key ideas about what will happen after death.

Olam Ha-Ba means "the world to come" in Hebrew (judaism.about.com).

Many Jews believe that the present life is a corridor that leads to another world. This place, the other world, is sometimes referred to as "Sheol." Some people believe that Sheol is located in the center of the earth (reformjudaism.org).

Other people believe that the purely righteous go to the place known as Gan Eden, a place of spiritual perfection. Gan Eden is not the Garden of Eden, but it has characteristics such as perfection and peace that make it similar.

According to the most prevalent belief, most people do not go to Gan Eden. Instead, they go to a place of punishment and purification known as *Gehinnom*. Some see Gehinnom as a place of severe punishment; others see it as a place where one can review the actions of his life objectively. In either case, it is believed that the period of time in Gehinnom does not exceed twelve months; after that, the person ascends to Olam Ha-Ba (jewfaq.org).

There are different beliefs about what happens to the utterly wicked soul at the end of the twelve months. Some believe that their souls are totally destroyed. Others believe that the wicked soul exists but in a state of conscious remorse (jewfaq.org).

Many Jews believe that the Olam Ha-Ba will occur in the messianic days after the Messiah has come and judged the world. It is believed that during this period the righteous dead will be resurrected.

The doctrine of the resurrection of the dead, a fundamental concept in Judaism, was one belief that distinguished the Pharisees from the Sadducees. The Sadducees rejected the idea of the resurrection of the dead, but the Pharisees held to it vigorously.

—Robin Fitzgerald.

Guiding the Superintendent

There is a story about a man who went to an auction of a deceased artist's collection with very little money. The artist had spent his life collecting paintings, and his collection was very valuable. The man, however, only wanted something to remember the artist by, because he had cared for the artist very much while he was still alive. When the first painting was auctioned off, it was worthless in the art community, and so the man got it for a very low bid. The auctioneer announced at the closing of the bidding that the artist had stipulated that whoever purchased the seemingly worthless painting was to receive all the rest of the paintings along with it.

In this week's lesson, we learn that in our Christian walk we have no guarantee of an easy life. God's mercy in the end, however, is very great. Unlike the man in the story, we have already been told what we will inherit, and it is priceless. On the other hand, some may find that life has offered them some advantages that others lack. Without God, those riches vanish when we leave the earth. In the end, all the riches in the world mean nothing compared to faith in a God who is so generous.

DEVOTIONAL OUTLINE

1. Different stations in life (Luke 16:19-21). Here we see a picture of two men who held very different places in the community. The rich man, clothed in purple, which is the color of royalty, ate the finest food and never did without monetarily. Just outside his home, we see Lazarus, a beggar, who would gladly eat scraps from the rich man's table.

2. Death the great equalizer (Luke 16:22-23). After death, the roles of Lazarus and the rich man became switched entirely. Lazarus was imme-diately carried by angels and placed by Abraham's side. Conversely, the rich man was brought to hades, a place of torment. He received just recompense for his lack of mercy when he was alive and had been in a position to help the poor.

3. Final destinations (Luke 16:24-31). The rich man understandably cried out for mercy when he realized the consequences of his lack of faith. We see a chasm here that is impossible to cross after death. Lazarus, the beggar, could not help the rich man. It was foolish of the rich man to believe that a beggar returning from the dead would be more influential with his brothers than the laws of the Living God. Abraham told the rich man that his brothers already had the truth in front of them; they were not likely to listen to a warning message from Lazarus.

AGE-GROUP EMPHASES

Children: It is important to teach children that God is fair and just. We will reap a just reward for the things we do here on earth. Of course, we do not want children to believe that God rejects them each time they sin, for we are saved by God's grace. Teaching them to walk closely with God and to repent immediately when they displease Him is the way of wisdom.

Youths: Young people often begin to seek after a life of fame or fortune. This is a good time to teach them that the reward is far greater for a life lived for God by faith.

Adults: Many adults grumble about the unfair advantages others might have. We should remind one another that Jesus' lowering Himself and paying for our sins and sharing His kingdom with us is a wonderful, undeserved advantage.

—Paulette L. LeBlanc.

SCRIPTURE LESSON TEXT

MATT. 25:31 When the Son of man shall come in his glory, and all the holy angels with him, then shall he sit upon the throne of his glory:

32 And before him shall be gathered all nations: and he shall separate them one from another, as a shepherd divideth *his* sheep from the goats:

33 And he shall set the sheep on his right hand, but the goats on the left.

34 Then shall the King say unto them on his right hand, Come, ye blessed of my Father, inherit the kingdom prepared for you from the foundation of the world:

35 For I was an hungred, and ye gave me meat: I was thirsty, and ye gave me drink: I was a stranger, and ye took me in:

36 Naked, and ye clothed me: I was sick, and ye visited me: I was in prison, and ye came unto me.

37 Then shall the righteous answer him, saying, Lord, when saw we thee an hungred, and fed *thee?* or thirsty, and gave *thee* drink?

38 When saw we thee a stranger, and took *thee* in? or naked, and clothed *thee?*

39 Or when saw we thee sick, or in prison, and came unto thee?

40 And the King shall answer and say unto them, Verily I say unto you, Inasmuch as ye have done *it* unto one of the least of these my brethren, ye have done *it* unto me.

41 Then shall he say also unto them on the left hand, Depart from me, ye cursed, into everlasting fire, prepared for the devil and his angels:

42 For I was an hungred, and ye gave me no meat: I was thirsty, and ye gave me no drink:

43 I was a stranger, and ye took me not in: naked, and ye clothed me not: sick, and in prison, and ye visited me not.

44 Then shall they also answer him, saying, Lord, when saw we thee an hungred, or athirst, or a stranger, or naked, or sick, or in prison, and did not minister unto thee?

45 Then shall he answer them, saying, Verily I say unto you, Inasmuch as ye did *it* not to one of the least of these, ye did *it* not to me.

46 And these shall go away into everlasting punishment: but the righteous into life eternal.

NOTES

Separating the Sheep and the Goats

Lesson Text: Matthew 25:31-46

Related Scriptures: Deuteronomy 15:7-11; Daniel 7:9-14;
Matthew 16:24-28; I John 4:7-14

TIME: A.D. 30   PLACE: Jerusalem

GOLDEN TEXT—"And these shall go away into everlasting punishment: but the righteous into life eternal" (Matthew 25:46).

Introduction

The apostle Paul wrote, "For we are his workmanship, created in Christ Jesus unto good works, which God hath before ordained that we should walk in them" (Eph. 2:10). In his Pastoral Epistles, Paul repeatedly reminded Timothy and Titus of the importance of good works.

We understand that salvation is a gift from God because of His grace and is received through faith alone. We cannot earn salvation, no matter how many good works we do. Scripture does teach, however, that there will always be evidence of true salvation. James wrote, "What doth it profit, my brethren, though a man say he hath faith, and have not works?" (2:14).

Among the works that reveal the true heart of a believer is that of helping to meet the needs of others. This is so important that in the final judgment of the nations, Christ will point to what they did or did not do for others.

LESSON OUTLINE

I. JUDGING THE RIGHTEOUS—
Matt. 25:31-36

II. EVIDENCES OF
RIGHTEOUSNESS—
Matt. 25:37-40

III. JUDGING THE
UNRIGHTEOUS—Matt. 25:41-46

Exposition: Verse by Verse

JUDGING THE RIGHTEOUS

MATT. 25:31 When the Son of man shall come in his glory, and all the holy angels with him, then shall he sit upon the throne of his glory:

32 And before him shall be gathered all nations: and he shall separate them one from another, as a shepherd divideth his sheep from the goats:

33 And he shall set the sheep on his right hand, but the goats on the left.

34 Then shall the King say unto

them on his right hand, Come, ye blessed of my Father, inherit the kingdom prepared for you from the foundation of the world:

35 For I was an hungred, and ye gave me meat: I was thirsty, and ye gave me drink: I was a stranger, and ye took me in:

36 Naked, and ye clothed me: I was sick, and ye visited me: I was in prison, and ye came unto me.

A gathering (Matt. 25:31-32). Studying prophecy is not just about studying the details of the future. It is about knowing what is coming and having that knowledge affect how we live today. The text of this week's study reveals the importance of present living in the light of future events more clearly than any other passage in Matthew. This is the end of a lengthy discourse found in both chapters 24 and 25, and there is emphasis through the entire passage on the importance of how we live today in light of what is coming.

{What Jesus referred to in these verses is the last eschatological, or end-time, event prior to the establishment of the millennial kingdom.}[Q1] First will come the rapture, when all living believers will be taken directly into heaven (I Thess. 4:13-17). This will be followed by a time of tribulation on the earth. Many will suffer during that time, but many also will turn to Christ for salvation. At the conclusion of the tribulation, Christ will return to earth. Then will follow the time of judgment described in Matthew 25:31-46, which will determine whether the survivors of the tribulation will enter Christ's earthly kingdom. The two parables preceding this passage (vss. 1-30) seem to explain the judgment that will come upon Israel when they are unprepared for the return of the Lord. Verses 31 through 46 describe the judgment that will come upon the Gentile nations at Christ's return.

The coming of the Son of man is described in Daniel 7:13-14. There He was seen appearing before the "Ancient of days" and receiving dominion and a kingdom so that all the world will serve Him. Jesus said the holy angels will come too, and He will be given a throne of glory. All the nations will come before Him, and He will separate believers from unbelievers, similar to the way a shepherd separates his sheep and goats.

A dividing (Matt. 25:33-34). The context indicates that this will not be a judgment of entire nations but rather a judgment of individuals from within each nation. If entire nations were judged as entities, some unbelievers would be allowed into the kingdom of Christ along with the believers; that will not happen. {Jesus referred to those on His right hand as sheep and to those on His left as goats.}[Q2] The sheep represent believers, while the goats represent unbelievers. It will not be possible for anyone to fool the Lord at this time.

{It is the group on Christ's right hand that will be invited to enter into the kingdom with Him.}[Q3] {Throughout the Bible the place at the right hand is viewed as the place of honor and authority (Pss. 45:9; 110:1).}[Q4] The terms "sheep" and "goats" actually refer to people, of course, and notice that from Matthew 25:34 on they are no longer referred to in that way. They are spoken of as those on the right and those on the left. The people coming from the nations of the world will be divided into believers and unbelievers.

All believers at that time will be invited to enter the kingdom that has been prepared for them. This is the millennial kingdom, in which Christ will reign on the earth for one thousand years (Rev. 20:6). This group will enter the kingdom without dying, so they will be in their fleshly bodies. These are the saints who survive the horrors of the tribulation.

A pronouncement (Matt. 25:35-36). {At this point Jesus explains why this group is being invited to enter the kingdom. He specifies six different actions that they took at one time or another that benefited Him. When He was hungry, they gave Him food. When He was thirsty, they gave Him drink. When He was a stranger, they took Him in and cared for Him. When He was naked, they gave Him clothing. When He was sick, they visited Him and nursed Him. When He was in prison, they came to Him, revealing their caring hearts.}^Q5

These are six needy conditions that represent the kinds of needs people experience at one time or another. This is not intended to be an exhaustive list. Each need has something to do with survival or quality of life and is important to every one of us. We could think of many additional needs that arise in our lives in which others can minister to us, helping and encouraging us. Jesus speaks as if these actions were done directly for Him, meeting needs He faced personally.

EVIDENCES OF RIGHTEOUSNESS

37 Then shall the righteous answer him, saying, Lord, when saw we thee an hungred, and fed thee? or thirsty, and gave thee drink?

38 When saw we thee a stranger, and took thee in? or naked, and clothed thee?

39 Or when saw we thee sick, or in prison, and came unto thee?

40 And the King shall answer and say unto them, Verily I say unto you, Inasmuch as ye have done it unto one of the least of these my brethren, ye have done it unto me.

A sense of confusion (Matt. 25:37-39). {The group at the right hand of Jesus, previously called sheep, is now referred to as "the righteous." They are portrayed as being confused and surprised at the descriptions they had just heard. They reiterate each need in the same order Jesus gave them and ask when they met these needs. They do not remember even seeing Him, let alone doing these things for His personal benefit.}^Q6

Remember that this is a group of people who will have survived the tribulation; so they will not have seen Jesus until His return to earth just prior to this event (vs. 31). In their minds, therefore, they will have trouble understanding what He means. No doubt they would have been more than glad to do any and all of these things for their Saviour, but He will not have been physically present on earth. They will not know He had such needs or be aware of ways they met them. They will interpret His pronouncement literally.

We are about to see how God views the importance of meeting the needs of our fellow believers. While we might enjoy studying prophecy and be enamored of the many details that are given about future events, what is really important to us now is the way we live in the present. {As we anticipate Christ's coming, we must remain aware of the circumstances around us. These circumstances include needs people face daily, and we cannot allow ourselves to become so engrossed in the study of the future that we forget these present needs.}^Q7

A reassurance (Matt. 25:40). Did you notice that in verse 34 Jesus referred to Himself as the King? The Son of man will come accompanied by His holy angels. He will sit on the throne of His glory, and He will set up His reign as King over all the earth at this time. In verse 40 He again referred to Himself as the King. This King will reassure the righteous that whenever they did acts of kindness in order to help His people, they were in essence doing those acts for Him.

The phrase "unto one of the least of these my brethren" has been understood in several different ways. Since those gathered are divided into two categories designated as sheep and goats, these "brethren" appear to be another, separate group. Since the Jews will have already been dealt with, according to the two parables (vss. 1-30), this must be a different and special group. It is possible the reference is to the 144,000 Jewish evangelists who will spread the gospel of Christ during the tribulation (Rev. 7).

This group will have suffered by refusing to take the mark of the beast (Rev. 13:16-17). They will be under a death threat and not be allowed to buy or sell in order to meet their needs. Of course, all believers will have faced the same discrimination, so it is possible Jesus was simply referring to those who had needs to whom others reached out, ministering unselfishly. The point is obvious: we are not saved just to care for ourselves; we are saved to be concerned and to reach out to meet the needs of God's people.

JUDGING THE UNRIGHTEOUS

41 Then shall he say also unto them on the left hand, Depart from me, ye cursed, into everlasting fire, prepared for the devil and his angels:

42 For I was an hungred, and ye gave me no meat: I was thirsty, and ye gave me no drink:

43 I was a stranger, and ye took me not in: naked, and ye clothed me not: sick, and in prison, and ye visited me not.

44 Then shall they also answer him, saying, Lord, when saw we thee an hungred, or athirst, or a stranger, or naked, or sick, or in prison, and did not minister unto thee?

45 Then shall he answer them, saying, Verily I say unto you, Inasmuch as ye did it not to one of the least of these, ye did it not to me.

46 And these shall go away into everlasting punishment: but the righteous into life eternal.

Damnation (Matt. 25:41). {Jesus then explains what will happen to those at His left side. They will be commanded to depart, being referred to as "ye cursed." Their destination is "everlasting fire," a description of hell, which has been prepared for Satan and his angels.}[Q8] Among the ones addressed there probably will be many pretenders, those who profess to be believers in Christ but in reality are deceivers. No pretender will ever be able to deceive the Lord at the time of judgment.

Hell was not originally prepared for people. Paul wrote, "For this is good and acceptable in the sight of God our Saviour; who will have all men to be saved, and to come unto the knowledge of the truth" (I Tim. 2:3-4). God wants people to be saved. Hell was prepared for Satan and the demons, but those people who refuse to trust Jesus as Saviour will be sent there too.

Condemnation (Matt. 25:42-43). {The King now lists the same six physical needs He mentioned to the righteous: hunger, thirst, being a stranger, being naked, being sick, and being in prison. This time, however, He declares that this group did not meet any of those needs.}[Q9] We see the contrast between these two groups becoming clearer. They are characterized by entirely different sets of attitudes that lead to entirely different actions. One group is totally self-centered, while the other group reaches out to those around them.

Is this not often the case in the world today? Believers have a special bond that draws them together. When other believers are hurting, they are pulled toward them with a desire to encourage and help—at least, that is the way it should be. It is possible to be a coldhearted believer and not be moved by the needs of others, but it certainly should not be that way. God's people ought to have tender hearts toward those who are suffering and in need. This is one of the evidences of the presence of Christ within a person.

Affirmation (Matt. 25:44-45). The people in this group also seem confused and surprised. They have not seen Jesus either and wonder when they could possibly have missed doing these things for Him. Perhaps some will cry out, "This is not fair. You were not there telling us what You wanted us to do for You." There will be no good excuses however, for there has always been opportunity to know His will. God has given the world His Word, in which His will is clearly revealed.

Jesus explains that when they refused to reach out and help "one of the least of these" (vs. 45), they in essence refused to help Him. Life is not meant to be for the benefit of ourselves only. There are needy people all around us, and every one of us can help them in some way. We are not equally equipped to help, but we all have something we can do to assist and encourage. Believers should have a special burden for fellow believers simply because we are all part of the same family, with God as our Father.

The "goats" evidence the fact that they are unbelievers through the uncaring attitudes that caused them to turn deaf ears to those in need. They cannot blame God for the sentence pronounced against them, for they made their own decision to turn away from Him in unbelief. This truth cannot be ignored.

Separation (Matt. 25:46). The long discourse of Jesus (chaps. 24—25) and the final judgment scene He described are now summarized in a single sentence. {There are two categories of people and two eternal destinies. People are either believers in Jesus Christ or unbelievers who refuse to accept Him. There is no middle ground, and there will be no second chance for those who come to the end of life on earth without having trusted in Him. What we do about Jesus now has eternal implications.}Q10

There are also two destinies, heaven and hell. Heaven is where God dwells and where believers will live for all eternity. It is described in the Bible as a beautiful place of joy, peace, and contentment. A detailed description is included in the final two chapters of Revelation, where we are assured that God will wipe away all tears, death, and sorrow (21:4). Every-thing will be new (vs. 5), and we will be with the Lord forever.

Hell is described as a place of eternal torment. Mark 9:42-48 warns that it is a place where the fire is never quenched. In that passage Jesus said it would be better to be disfigured on earth, if that is what it took to stay away from sin, than to enter hell and be punished forever. It is this place where Jesus said unbelievers will go, in contrast to heaven, where those who trust in Christ will enjoy eternal life.

The greatest human need is that of receiving Jesus as Saviour. Once we have done that, we should be so grateful for our salvation that we gladly reach out to those around us with the message of eternal life and we should be ready to come to the aid of fellow believers.

—Keith E. Eggert.

QUESTIONS

1. When will the event that Jesus speaks of in Matthew 25:31 take place?
2. How did Jesus refer to the two groups of people?
3. Which group will be invited to enter the kingdom?
4. What is the significance of the right-hand side in Scripture?
5. What does Jesus say they did to qualify them for this invitation?
6. Why are they surprised and confused by Jesus' statement?
7. What practical lesson should we learn from this?
8. What is Jesus' message for the ones at His left side?
9. How does Jesus explain this decision?
10. What are the two eternal destinies, and what determines one's destiny?

—Keith E. Eggert.

Preparing to Teach the Lesson

Our lesson this week shows us our obligation as Christians to help fellow believers in need, and they are all around us. If we believe in Jesus, we will give our lives in service to Him. That will involve helping those in need.

TODAY'S AIM

Facts: to show that our spiritual condition is revealed by how we treat needy fellow believers we meet.

Principle: to show that as Christians we are accountable to God for the way in which we treat the needy among us.

Application: to urge believers to seek opportunities to help the needy.

INTRODUCING THE LESSON

In many churches there is a great emphasis on salvation without the corresponding emphasis on Christian living and growth in Christian discipleship. Part of discipleship involves helping fellow believers who are needy.

James reminds us in his letter that our faith is no good if we do not show it through our works. Beliefs have to be translated into action. The church must seek to actively help those in their number who need help.

DEVELOPING THE LESSON

1. Jesus speaks to the righteous (Matt. 25:31-36). One reason we Christians have been given life and salvation is so that we can serve our Lord and others around us.

Jesus told His disciples that when He comes again at the end of the age in all His glory, along with His angels, He will sit on His throne as Judge. Sitting on a throne indicates that He is King, and it is a king's task to pass judgment.

When Jesus returns to earth, all the nations will be gathered before Him (vs. 32). The word "nations" here refers to all the living peoples of the world, who will stand before Him to be judged. Jesus will then separate them as one would separate sheep from goats. His disciples knew that analogy well because they came from an agricultural society. The "sheep" will be put on His right hand and the "goats" on His left.

Jesus will then speak to those on His right hand. He will commend them for taking care of His people who were needy and they will be invited to enter the messianic kingdom prepared for them.

The King's words will be those of welcome and affirmation. Jesus will describe these people as blessed by the Father. Ultimately, after all we have done on this earth, it is important that we receive the blessing of God the Father. Everything else will mean nothing when we stand before Him.

Jesus also emphasized that the righteous were called to inherit the kingdom prepared for them before the foundation of the world. It is amazing that God would think of those who are His children long before we were born and prepare the very best for us.

The King then will give the reasons He accepts those on His right. When they saw Him hungry, they fed Him. When He was thirsty, they gave Him drink. When He was a stranger, they invited Him to share their homes with them. When He was without clothing, they clothed Him. When He was in prison, they visited Him. In other words, their genuine faith was evidenced by their helping fellow believers around them, and their faith in

Christ was the basis for their inheritance of the kingdom.

True Christianity is not isolated from everyday life. Stress to the students the importance of living out our faith by ministering to those who need our help. Ask them to identify specific ways in which they can actively help others.

2. The question of the righteous (Matt. 25:37-40). Here we see the righteous asking Jesus when they saw Him hungry or thirsty or a stranger in need of hospitality or naked or sick or in prison and in need of comfort and companionship. Jesus replied that when they did it to the Lord's needy brethren, they did it to Him. In other words, Jesus identifies with His needy people; so helping those people is like serving Jesus.

3. Jesus speaks to the wicked (Matt. 25:41-43). The words that Jesus spoke to the wicked on His left were very strong. They were cursed to eternal fire, which was prepared for the devil and his angels. Notice here that just as heaven and all its glory is the inheritance of the righteous, so hell is the inheritance of the wicked. This tells us that a day of judgment is coming and that all will be held accountable to our Maker for their deeds.

These wicked people demonstrate their unsaved condition by failing to help the needy believers around them. They ignored the poor and did not visit them in prison or feed or clothe them or give them drink or provide them hospitality when they needed it.

Encourage your students to think about sins of omission. Are we failing to help those in need because we are so caught up in the practice of our religion that we forget the legitimate demands of our faith? We are saved to serve, and that means we must seek to meet real human needs.

4. The question of the wicked (Matt. 25:44-46). Here Jesus responds to the unrighteous. They will ask Him where they had seen Him hungry and thirsty and naked or sick or in prison or in need of hospitality. Jesus will tell them that in refusing to help the needy believers around them, they were neglecting to help Him.

The wicked will be revealed for what they are, and they will be consigned to eternal punishment. The righteous, however, will enjoy life eternal. It is a characteristic mark of these and all true Christians that they care for those in need.

ILLUSTRATING THE LESSON

Our faith life cannot be isolated from our life in the world. The church must be active in helping the needy and thus serve Christ.

CHRISTIANS MEET HUMAN NEEDS

CONCLUDING THE LESSON

As Christians it is important that we express our faith through our works, serving Christ by helping others who are in need. In so doing the church will make its mark on the world.

ANTICIPATING THE NEXT LESSON

In our lesson next week we will see how Jesus used parables to communicate truths about God's kingdom.

—A. Koshy Muthalaly.

PRACTICAL POINTS

1. We need to be conscious of the fact that everyone we know and meet will one day stand before the Lord (Matt. 25:31-33).
2. It is comforting to know that we have been in God's plan from the beginning (vs. 34).
3. The best way to serve the Lord is to meet the real needs of other people (vss. 35-40).
4. The fate of all who reject Christ should motivate us to proclaim the gospel (vs. 41).
5. A lack of compassion for hurting people shows a lack of love for the Lord (vss. 42-45).
6. How we live today reveals where we will be in eternity (vs. 46).

—Jarl K. Waggoner.

RESEARCH AND DISCUSSION

1. How does the description in Matthew 25:31-46 differ from the one given in Revelation 20:11-15?
2. Why is the compassionate treatment of other people, rather than what one believes, set forth as the measure of one's salvation (Matt. 25:34-38)?
3. What role should the church have in helping the poor and hurting? Would it be proper to seek government assistance in doing so?
4. Does the reaction of both the "sheep" (vss. 37-39) and the "goats" (vs. 44) suggest that a person can never know for sure in this life whether he is truly saved? Explain.
5. What principles for ministry does Jesus' parable give us?

—Jarl K. Waggoner.

ILLUSTRATED HIGH POINTS

Ye took me in (Matt. 25:35)

Due to the moral situation in North America, many babies are conceived out of wedlock. That often leaves young, pregnant women with no idea of what to do. Hundreds of women's pregnancy centers now exist across our land, and they offer tender, loving support to many young women. These Christian establishments are antiabortion in their stance and thus encourage the young women to carry their babies to term and give birth to them. They share the gospel and distribute the Scriptures. A number of the young women trust in Christ or rededicate their lives to God.

These pregnancy centers give pregnancy tests and, if needed, provide clothing, food, and furniture, as the Lord supplies. Most operate strictly on the basis of faith as they support women in need.

Ye have done it unto me (vs. 40)

Bill Bright, founder of Campus Crusade for Christ, passed into the Lord's presence in July 2003. He was one of the twentieth century's greatest examples of meeting human needs.

Bright also was a prolific writer and penned much literature for evangelistic and revivalistic causes in our day. Under Bright's leadership, 26,000 full-time workers served people in 191 countries. In addition, 225,000 trained volunteers have followed his example in various aspects of the ministry.

Bill Bright was fueled by his passion to present the love and claims of Jesus to as many people on earth as possible. To him, no human need could surpass the need to hear and receive the gospel of Christ. His "secret" was giving priority to serving Christ and doing His will.

—P. Fredrick Fogle.

Golden Text Illuminated

"And these shall go away into everlasting punishment: but the righteous into life eternal" (Matthew 25:46).

Life can seem very complicated at times. When approaching many issues, there are numerous nuances and points of view to consider. But as our golden text for this week illustrates, on some questions the situation is not at all ambiguous.

The concluding words of what is called Jesus' Olivet Discourse make very clear that there are only two possible eternal destinations for mankind. People will either suffer "everlasting punishment," or they will enjoy joyous eternal life.

Needless to say, this stark reality is not popular in the unsaved world. Christians will find when they maintain this truth that they may be called simple-minded, extremists, or even bigots. People may say something like, *How conceited of you to think that you are among the fortunate ones to go to heaven and that those who disagree with you will be in hell.*

Another approach the world might take is to center their fire on the character of God Himself. *What kind of a God would send people to eternal punishment?* they might ask.

How should we respond to these various attacks? First of all, we must clearly declare what our presuppositions are. Scripture teaches that since the Fall, man in his natural state is in a hopeless, spiritually dead, condition. The world rejects this truth, and so we must pray that the Holy Spirit will be at work convicting them of the undeniable reality of it.

Recognizing man's fallen condition, it becomes a matter of sheer grace on God's part that He provided a way of deliverance and renewed fellowship with Him through Christ. As has often been said, the real wonder is that God chose to save anyone at all in the face of man's continual rebellion. Indeed,

the "righteous" of the golden text are only called such because they have been clothed in Christ's righteousness and been transformed by God's Spirit. When people reject the way of salvation, they are rejecting the very Son of God, the One who sacrificed His life on the cross to pay for humanity's sins.

Another presupposition that underlies our faith is that God is the Creator. He breathes life into every creature on the earth, including man. He is the very source of life. When man rejects God, he is rejecting life itself. As C.S. Lewis declared in his book *Mere Christianity,* "God cannot give us a happiness and peace apart from Himself, because it is not there. There is no such thing."

So those whose lives demonstrate that they have rejected the eternal Son of God will experience everlasting punishment (cf. Dan. 12:2), and many Scriptures give vivid pictures of the severity of that judgment. That it is *eternal* punishment is clear in the golden text from the fact that in the Greek the same adjective is used to describe the duration of the punishment as well as the duration of the life.

The best way to answer the gainsayers who would attack God or His people about the truths of this verse is to give them glimpses of what eternal life is like by the joy and love evident in our lives. Eternal life does mean living forever in heaven, but the term also involves a quality of life, a reflection of what it means to live in fellowship with the eternally good and perfect God.

Life is more than just drawing breath. As Christ Himself declared, "And this is life eternal, that they might know thee the only true God, and Jesus Christ, whom thou hast sent" (John 17:3).

—*Stephen H. Barnhart.*

Heart of the Lesson

Many years ago in *Peanuts,* Linus told his sister Lucy, "I love mankind. It's people I can't stand." That was humorous and cynical, but it was thought-provoking too. There are days when many of us feel that way.

Conversely, when some people talk about all the people of the world—of every color and nation—they get a warm, fuzzy feeling. A soft drink had an advertising campaign many years ago that highlighted this idea of the world singing together in perfect harmony. How wonderful it is to imagine everyone living in peace and harmony!

When it comes to actually interacting with someone who is different culturally, though, many of us are hesitant at best. We may even be afraid of or hostile to the idea. People who are different from us in skin color or culture may be hard for us to understand, and we do not take the time or make the effort to get to know them.

When Jesus was here on earth, He went about doing good to people. He had time for people, even when He was tired. Jesus loved people and had compassion for them.

This lesson tells us about something Jesus taught His disciples just days before His suffering and death.

1. Reward for loving action (Matt. 25:31-36). Jesus described a time in the future when He will sit on His throne and reign as King and Judge. He will be like a shepherd, dividing those who follow Him from those who refuse Him. The "sheep" will be placed on the right, the place of power and honor, while the "goats" will be relegated to the left, the place of dishonor.

Jesus will call those on His right "blessed of my Father" (vs. 34). He will invite them to enter His kingdom because of the love and compassion they have shown toward Him.

2. Loving action explained (Matt. 25:37-40). Jesus explained that those He invited to enter His kingdom had demonstrated love and compassion for Him by aiding His needy and hurting brethren. Their loving actions in meeting basic human needs were proof of their faith in Christ.

When we serve the needy, we actually serve Jesus too. We show that we are true children of the Father. Our reward will be blessing from God the Father and inheritance of the kingdom He has prepared for us.

3. Punishment for unloving action (Matt. 25:41-46). Those who fail to live as children of the King will be banished from His presence. They will be cursed and driven from Him. There will be no place in His kingdom for them.

Those who are concerned only about themselves live as the devil does. They shut their eyes to the human misery around them. Because they have not put their trust in Christ and received God's gracious salvation themselves, they do not show loving-kindness to others.

Jesus knows our hearts. He sees our motives and knows why we do good for others. Jesus is interested in a righteousness of the heart.

Christians need to be spiritually aware and alert for opportunities to show God's love in physical, tangible ways. With all the needy people around us, we need God's guidance in knowing whom we can help and how.

Good works do not save us. Our salvation comes from God's grace when we accept His gift of Jesus Christ as our personal Saviour. However, salvation should lead to good works. Just as Jesus went about doing good, so should we.

—Judy Carlsen.

World Missions

Our text for this week's lesson treats the judgment of the nations at the close of the future seven-year tribulation period. In the prophetic Scriptures, it is easy to overlook the fact that gospel ministry will go on in that troubled time.

The Word of God will still have its transforming power. Many will dare to read the Bible, and many will be saved through its message of hope.

Some years ago, the late Dr. David L. Cooper, a scholar and a missionary to the Jews, had large caches of New Testaments buried in Israel. Bank trustees were instructed to await worldwide rumors of great numbers of people vanishing from homes, offices, and public life. In that event, the trustees were to release the New Testaments to the Israeli citizens without charge. Dr. Cooper expected that great numbers will be saved through reading the Scriptures. The Word of God will offer an escape at a time of unprecedented catastrophes, natural and man-made.

The total missionary force throughout the world today is around 200,000. In Revelation 7 we learn that 144,000 sealed Jewish witnesses for the Lord will be raised up during the future tribulation (Rev. 7:1-8).

This represents more than half the size of the current missionary force in the world before the church is raptured (cf. I Thess. 4:13-18). The fruit of the labors of the 144,000 is a great number out of all the nations of earth (Rev. 7:9-10). It seems likely that the "sheep" in this week's lesson text (Matt. 25:33-40) will include those reached through the end-time missionary activity of these chosen witnesses.

What soul-winning lessons can we learn from this week's study? It is thrilling to learn that great numbers will be saved during the most serious trials ever suffered by mankind, but that truth should move our hearts to reach out right where we are, right now. The ones who will experience the bitter trials of the Great Tribulation could even include some who are alive today. Reaching them now could preclude great suffering—not just for the short period looming ahead but, more important, for all eternity. That is where Jesus' concern lay, and it is where He focused all of His warnings. If we share His heart, we will want to proclaim the truth to everyone we possibly can.

I grieve over those who give nodding assent to the truth of the gospel but put off the most important decision of life. A relative of mine, now well up in years, has heard the gospel again and again for years. "It is not the right time for me," she pleads, but as I have told her, the Bible says, "Behold, now is the day of salvation" (II Cor. 6:2).

I also grieve over those who flatly reject the testimony of the Word of God and thus the only way of salvation. I met with Jim for three years. He patiently listened to the gospel message. He said that salvation was good for me but that he had his religion. I was convinced I had not made the gospel sufficiently clear, so I wrote it out carefully and mailed it to him.

I called at Jim's residence, and he angrily refused to talk with me. He became one more person to weep over; yet I still pray he will come to the truth.

Whatever the response, we should diligently give out the gospel to as many as we can, and we should make sure that our words are backed up by consistent deeds of compassion and love.

—Lyle P. Murphy.

The Jewish Aspect

Jesus referred to three groups of people as He taught about the future judgment. Two groups he identified figuratively with animals—sheep and goats. He referred to the third group as the King's brethren.

The identity of the King's brethren is crucial, especially since the sheep and the goats will be judged according to the way they treat these brethren. Context and subject matter indicate that the brethren are the believing Jewish remnant who will survive the Great Tribulation period.

Jeremiah spoke of the Great Tribulation as the time of Jacob's trouble (Jer. 30:7). While the tribulation period will be a time of judgment for the entire world, it will especially be a time of testing for the Jews.

Satan himself, by means of his empowered antichrist, will attempt to annihilate the Jewish people (Rev. 12:13-17). This danger to the Jews will be the most serious in history, shrinking even the horrors of the Holocaust by comparison.

During the Holocaust there were many Gentiles who came to the aid of the endangered Jews, often at great risk to themselves. Many suffered and died. The people who help the Jews during the tribulation will be the ones who will choose to follow Christ no matter what the cost. In so doing they will also choose to assist the Jewish people. Their good works will be an evidence of their saving relationship with Christ.

Jesus called these compassionate tribulation Christians "sheep" (Matt. 25:32). Along with the "goats," they are individuals from within the greater groups of nations. The Greek word for "nations" can, and in this case should, be translated as "Gentiles" in contrast to the Jewish brethren.

The Bible consistently makes mention of the two groups Jews and Gentiles. While God will use the tribulation to purify and redeem Israel, He also will use this time to judge the world and redeem millions. The end of the tribulation will mark the beginning of the judgment of the nations to determine who will enter the millennial kingdom of the Messiah.

Part of the long-standing Jewish expectation for the future was that God will one day judge the nations. This is found in Isaiah 2:4 and Micah 4:3. It was also expected, as Daniel foretold (Dan. 7:13-14), that the Messiah will reign on the earth. The separation of the sheep from the goats is pictured in Ezekiel (Ezek. 34:17).

The separation of sheep from goats was a common practice in the Middle East. Because of their different needs and sleeping habits, although they grazed together during the day, they slept separately at night. Sheep preferred open air, while goats huddled together to keep warm. From a shepherd's standpoint, goats were considered comparatively less valuable than sheep.

Ancient texts speak of the right side as the preferred side and the side of power. The left side consequently is the side of dishonor.

As Jesus used the sheep imagery, it is clear and in keeping with tradition that the sheep represent those people with whom He is pleased. These are His people. The goats represent those with whom He is displeased and with whom He has no relationship.

—Carter Corbrey.

Guiding the Superintendent

The body of Christ continues to experience a long-standing tension over the subject of ministry priorities. A portion of the church believes that preaching the gospel must be its priority mission. Another portion believes that meeting the basic needs of human beings should be the priority ministry. Sadly, for many, these two ministry priorities will never find common ground.

When one investigates the Scriptures on this subject, a wonderful balance between the two seems to be present. Yes, the preaching of the gospel must remain a focal point of the church. But meeting the basic human needs of people also has a prominent position.

In this week's lesson text Matthew recorded the words of Jesus in relation to an indispensable element of Christian ministry.

DEVOTIONAL OUTLINE

1. A separation of individuals (Matt. 25:31-33). When Jesus Christ returns to earth as King and Judge, all nations will be gathered in His presence. He will then place one segment of individuals on His right hand—the place of prominence—and the other segment on His left hand—the place of condemnation.

2. The individuals on Christ's right (Matt. 25:34-40). The individuals on Jesus' right will receive their inheritance—"the kingdom prepared for you from the foundation of the world." This blessing is theirs because of their willingness to demonstrate their faith by giving themselves in compassionate service for the sake of fellow believers.

3. The individuals on His left (Matt. 25:41-46). To the individuals on His left, Jesus will proclaim a message of eternal rejection. Their eternal state is "everlasting fire, prepared for the devil and his angels." The basis of their eternal separation from God is the fact that although they had the same opportunities to show compassion and love that the first group had, they consistently turned their backs on the needs. Their self-serving, selfish lifestyle betrayed an absence of saving faith.

The individuals on Jesus' left refused to perform compassionate acts to meet basic human needs. As a result, their eternity is one of everlasting punishment.

AGE-GROUP EMPHASES

Children: As children learn more about God's great love for them in Jesus Christ, it is important that they learn that God wants them to share His love with fellow believers.

Your teachers can use this week's lesson text to teach their students that performing acts of kindness toward others pleases God's heart.

Youths: Adolescence is a time of life when young people are especially prone to to self-centeredness. Living life for the moment and giving very little thought to others, many young people pursue their selfish dreams with a reckless delusion of their own immortality.

Have your teachers use this week's lesson text to counter this selfish view of life. Challenge your young people to obey God's desire for them to selflessly give themselves to His service.

Adults: Adults need to avoid getting into arguments over priorities and simply get down to business serving the Lord. They need to be sharing the gospel with others. They also need to be reminded that Jesus considers compassionate acts toward fellow believers as having been done for Him.

—*Thomas R. Chmura.*

Scripture Lesson Text

MATT. 13:9 Who hath ears to hear, let him hear.

10 And the disciples came, and said unto him, Why speakest thou unto them in parables?

11 He answered and said unto them, Because it is given unto you to know the mysteries of the kingdom of heaven, but to them it is not given.

12 For whosoever hath, to him shall be given, and he shall have more abundance: but whosoever hath not, from him shall be taken away even that he hath.

13 Therefore speak I to them in parables: because they seeing see not; and hearing they hear not, neither do they understand.

14 And in them is fulfilled the prophecy of Esaias, which saith,

By hearing ye shall hear, and shall not understand; and seeing ye shall see, and shall not perceive:

15 For this people's heart is waxed gross, and *their* ears are dull of hearing, and their eyes they have closed; lest at any time they should see with *their* eyes, and hear with *their* ears, and should understand with *their* heart, and should be converted, and I should heal them.

16 But blessed *are* your eyes, for they see: and your ears, for they hear.

17 For verily I say unto you, That many prophets and righteous *men* have desired to see *those things* which ye see, and have not seen *them;* and to hear *those things* which ye hear, and have not heard *them.*

NOTES

Ears to Hear

Lesson Text: Matthew 13:9-17

Related Scriptures: Matthew 13:18-23; I Corinthians 2:6-16

TIME: A.D. 28 PLACE: Sea of Galilee

GOLDEN TEXT—"Who hath ears to hear, let him hear" (Matthew 13:9).

Introduction

Oday ouyay ememberray enwhay ouyay okespay inay Igpay Atinlay osay atthay ouryay ildrenchay ouldway otnay owknay atwhay ouyay ereway ayingsay? You did this with your spouse in order to communicate a message that he or she would understand but that the children would miss.

Do you know that parables were something like that? Jesus taught His followers in parables so that they could gain spiritual understanding while others listening in could not. Without spiritual insight, people were incapable of grasping the truths being taught. In I Corinthians 2:1 through 3:4, Paul wrote of different types of people: spiritually mature, spiritually immature, and natural (unsaved). Each group responds differently to the truth.

When a person preaches or teaches the Word of God, his listeners hear him through preconceived ideas that determine what they understand from the message. Unsaved people cannot grasp spiritual truth. They hear the message one way. Spiritually immature, people cannot grasp much spiritual truth, so they hear in a different way. Spiritually mature people hear in a distinctive way as well. They are able to grasp truth the others cannot.

LESSON OUTLINE

I. THE IMPORTANCE OF LISTENING—Matt. 13:9-13

II. THE DISCREPANCIES IN LISTENING—Matt. 13:14-17

Exposition: Verse by Verse

THE IMPORTANCE OF LISTENING

MATT. 13:9 Who hath ears to hear, let him hear.

10 And the disciples came, and said unto him, Why speakest thou unto them in parables?

11 He answered and said unto them, Because it is given unto you to know the mysteries of the kingdom of heaven, but to them it is not given.

12 For whosoever hath, to him shall be given, and he shall have more abundance: but whosoever hath not, from him shall be taken away even that he hath.

13 Therefore speak I to them in parables: because they seeing see not; and hearing they hear not, neither do they understand.

Hearing parables (Matt. 13:9-10). In the Sermon on the Mount Jesus said, "Give not that which is holy unto the dogs, neither cast ye your pearls before swine, lest they trample them under their feet, and turn again and rend you" (Matt. 7:6). There are spiritual truths that ungodly people cannot possibly comprehend. In their ignorance they often take what they think they understand and twist it into something with a completely different meaning. This is repeatedly demonstrated by many Hollywood stars in their references to God and holy matters.

{In New Testament days, there were ungodly people who apparently had a curious interest in spiritual matters but were not interested in embracing the gospel of Jesus Christ. From them spiritual truth was withheld. They could neither grasp it nor apply it to their lives in meaningful ways.}[Q1] When Jesus taught His disciples the "mysteries of the kingdom" (Matt. 13:11), He used a method of teaching that kept ungodly listeners from comprehending what He was saying. When He said, "Who hath ears to hear, let him hear" (vs. 9), He was referring to the godly, who could understand.

Jesus had just finished telling the parable of the sower (vss. 3-8). {As we find out later in the chapter, even the disciples could not initially understand the meaning of this parable (vss. 18-23). But when it was explained to them, they would have the capability of comprehending the message Jesus conveyed. They were puzzled, however, as to why Jesus was teaching in parables. It did not seem difficult to them to understand the spiritual truths He was communicating, but why did He do it in this somewhat roundabout way?}[Q2]

The disciples probably did not realize how deaf ungodly ears are to spiritual teaching. Perhaps many of us never realized previously how differently biblical teaching is perceived by unbelievers. It is a curious matter to us that some people hear the same message we do and get something entirely different from it.

Hearing and understanding (Matt. 13:11-12a). {Jesus had offered Himself to Israel as her Messiah, but she had rejected Him. The epitome of the rejection can be seen in the statement in Matthew 12:24. The religious leaders had concluded, "This fellow doth not cast out devils, but by Beelzebub the prince of the devils." In saying this they attributed His power and authority to Satan. It appears that it was after this rejection that Jesus began teaching in parables much more extensively.}[Q3] The disciples noticed the different emphasis and asked Jesus the reason for it.

{In response to their question about teaching in parables, Jesus gave three reasons. The first is given in these verses. Jesus wanted to pass on to His followers the mysteries of the kingdom of heaven. These truths were not meant for unbelievers.}[Q4] The word "mysteries" refers to truth that had not previously been revealed to anyone. There are truths in the New Testament that were never given in the Old. The apostle Paul referred to this, for example, in I Corinthians 4:1.

Those who believed in the Lord were enjoying the privilege of learning more about Him, His Father, and the eternal plan coming from them. Those who rejected the Lord were being denied any further comprehension because of their refusal to believe. This still occurs today. Those who receive the Saviour are given insight into the Word of God, while those who reject Him cannot understand it. Likewise, those endeavoring to grow in their knowledge of the Lord learn more and more of His will and ways than Christians who are stuck in spiritual immaturity

This should become a challenge to every believer. Spiritual growth does not come from perfunctory Christian activities. While it is good to attend church regularly, it is possible to listen passively and leave the services without having received a message in the heart. For example, how many times do we sing thought-provoking words in hymns and gospel songs without even thinking of those words while we sing? How often do the soloist and preacher present meaningful messages and we remain unmoved in our hearts?

It is widely known that many believers do not engage in daily devotions, let alone in-depth Bible study on their own. God has filled His Word with wisdom beyond our imagination, but as Proverbs 2 teaches, we must search diligently for that wisdom. When we do, we are promised wisdom and insight far beyond what is granted to those who have little interest in God's Word. God graciously adds to what we already have when we search diligently for more.

Hearing and not understanding (Matt. 13:12b-13). {The second reason Jesus gave for teaching in parables was His desire to hide spiritual insight from those who were rejecting Him.}[Q4] We saw this fact as part of His first reason, but He especially emphasized it in these verses. {Verse 11 includes the phrase "to them it is not given," indicating that those outside the circle of believers were not being given the same spiritual instruction as the believers. While they could hear what Jesus was saying, they could not understand it.}[Q5]

Note the statement "whosoever hath not, from him shall be taken away even that he hath" (vs. 12). Prior to His rejection by the Pharisees (12:24), Jesus had presented Himself to Israel as their Messiah. Everyone had been given enough information to be able to respond positively to Him. Those who did so were now learning more; those who did not were now having what little they did understand taken from them.

It has already been established that rejection of the truth stops any learning of further truth. Jesus now seemed to be saying that it also causes a person to forget the truth that brought him to consider God's message. {We see the reality of this in people we know who once were under conviction of their need for salvation but turned away from it. They then apparently forgot what they heard. This is probably best illustrated in the example of the first person described in the parable of the sower. He received the truth but did not understand it and so rejected it. As a result the truth was snatched away from his heart by the enemy (13:18-19).}[Q6]

{Jesus described such a person as one who saw but did not see and heard but did not hear. Those who rejected Him saw Him teaching the people and listened to His words, but they could not understand His messages. They had physical hearing without an ability to hear spiritually. They had physical sight without an ability to comprehend spiritual reality. A mental comprehension of what is going on in a church service is not the same thing as spiritual comprehension. It is possible to be physically present and miss the meaning.}[Q7]

First Corinthians 2:14 explains it this way: "But the natural man receiveth not the things of the Spirit of God: for they are foolishness unto him: neither can he know them, because they are spiritually discerned." Is it possible that someone in your Sunday school class has never received Jesus as personal Saviour and so is without the ability to discern spiritual truth? When we trust in Him, God sends His Holy Spirit to dwell in us and enable us to understand things we have never been able to grasp before (I Cor. 2:9-12, 14).

THE DISCREPANCIES IN LISTENING

14 And in them is fulfilled the prophecy of Esaias, which saith, By hearing ye shall hear, and shall not understand; and seeing ye shall see, and shall not perceive:

15 For this people's heart is waxed gross, and their ears are dull of hearing, and their eyes they have closed; lest at any time they should see with their eyes, and hear with their ears, and should understand with their heart, and should be converted, and I should heal them.

16 But blessed are your eyes, for they see: and your ears, for they hear.

17 For verily I say unto you, That many prophets and righteous men have desired to see those things which ye see, and have not seen them; and to hear those things which ye hear, and have not heard them.

Isaiah's prophecy (Matt. 13:14-15). {These words are quoted from Isaiah 6:9-10. Isaiah 6 records the call of Isaiah to his prophetic ministry.}[08] He described how he saw the Lord sitting on a throne high and exalted, with seraphim around Him proclaiming His holiness. Upon seeing this, Isaiah felt completely unworthy and cried out, "Woe is me! for I am undone; because I am a man of unclean lips, and I dwell in the midst of a people of unclean lips: for mine eyes have seen the King, the Lord of hosts" (vs. 5).

One of the seraphim then took a live coal from the altar and touched Isaiah's mouth with it, proclaiming that his iniquity was taken away and his sin purged (vs. 7). After this, Isaiah heard God asking whom He could send with His message. Isaiah responded that he would go. God then commissioned him as a prophet to His people Israel. It was at that point that God spoke the words that are quoted in Matthew 13. As it turned out, this became a call to a very long and discouraging ministry for Isaiah.

Isaiah was to tell the people to keep listening without understanding and to keep looking without perceiving. His ministry began around 739 B.C., prior to the captivity of the northern nation of Israel (which occurred in 722 B.C.). By then Israel was so corrupt that God would not turn from His determination to punish her with captivity. Sadly, Judah, the southern kingdom, was also filled with corruption. The people's worship was largely empty ritualism (Isa. 1:10-15), and idolatry was rampant (40:18-20; 46:5-7).

Since the hearts of the people in Isaiah's day were already hardened against God, the more he preached, the more hardened they would become. As he ministered, their hearts would become increasingly dull (the meaning of "make the heart of this people fat" [6:10]), their ears would become less receptive to this message, and their eyes would remain blinded to the truth. They had reached the point in their rejection of God where He refused to enable them to turn back and be healed. Judgment was already on its way.

{The same thing that happened to the people in Isaiah's day was now happening in Jesus' day. People had rejected God and the Messiah He had sent. To fulfill Isaiah's prophecy was the third reason Jesus spoke in parables. Just as in Isaiah's time, there would be a remnant of believers, but on the whole, the people were rejecting Him and would suffer the consequences.}[09]

The disciples' blessing (Matt. 13:16-17). {The disciples were a great contrast to those who rejected Jesus, and as a result they were unusually blessed. They had believed that Jesus was indeed the Messiah sent from God; therefore, they were able to comprehend further spiritual truths.}[Q10] Using the same terminology, Jesus said their eyes could see and their ears could hear. That is completely the opposite of those who had no spiritual comprehension at all. This contrast still applies between believers and nonbelievers.

Perhaps the greatest privilege of all was the fact that these disciples lived in the actual days of Messiah's appearance and ministry. This is brought out by Jesus' saying that many prophets and righteous men from the past had a great desire to see the fulfillment of the things they spoke. Isaiah is an example, for his words included many prophecies about the coming, ministry, and death of the Messiah. When he came to the end of his life, however, Isaiah had not seen any of those things actually come to pass.

Read what Peter wrote about this subject: "Though now ye see him not, yet believing, ye rejoice with joy unspeakable and full of glory: receiving the end of your faith, even the salvation of your souls. Of which salvation the prophets have enquired and searched diligently, who prophesied of the grace that should come unto you: searching what, or what manner of time the Spirit of Christ which was in them did signify, when it testified beforehand the sufferings of Christ, and the glory that should follow.

"Unto whom it was revealed, that not unto themselves, but unto us they did minister the things, which are now reported unto you by them that have preached the gospel unto you with the Holy Ghost sent down from heaven; which things the angels desire to look into" (I Pet. 1:8-12). Today we rejoice in the full revelation of the salvation available through Jesus Christ!

It is a serious thing to hear spiritual truth and then reject it. The ministries of all the Old Testament prophets emphasized this. They repeatedly warned Israel that God's judgment would come upon them if they continued to ignore His Word. The history of the Old Testament verifies that God's warnings came to pass. Both Israel and Judah went into captivity. Once spiritual truth has been heard, the listeners become accountable for what they do with it.

Let no one ignore the truth that salvation is only through Jesus Christ. To ignore this is to face eternal separation from God.

—*Keith E. Eggert.*

QUESTIONS

1. What type of people among those listening to Jesus could not comprehend what He was saying?

2. What question did the disciples ask Jesus, and why?

3. At what point in His ministry did Jesus begin to use parables more extensively?

4. What were the first two reasons Jesus gave for using parables?

5. What does the phrase "to them it is not given" mean (Matt. 13:11)?

6. What happens in the hearts of people today when they reject the truth after they hear it?

7. How can people see but not see?

8. Who did Jesus quote, and what was the context of that quote?

9. How did that Old Testament passage apply in Jesus' day?

10. How were the disciples blessed in a particularly wonderful way?

—*Keith E. Eggert.*

Preparing to Teach the Lesson

Sometimes it is said that we hear but do not listen. Listening involves the whole person and by its very nature demands a response. In our lesson text Jesus teaches about truly listening to Him.

TODAY'S AIM

Facts: to teach the nature of true listening.

Principle: to show that truly listening to God involves a willing heart.

Application: to encourage students to listen to God with their hearts as well as their ears.

INTRODUCING THE LESSON

As adults and as parents, we all have the experience of talking to children. We tell them to do something, and sometimes they seem to listen but do not obey. As adults, we tend to do the same thing with God. He knows we are not listening.

DEVELOPING THE LESSON

1. Listening is a prerequisite to understanding (Matt. 13:9). After telling a parable, Jesus said that those who truly listen will understand the seemingly difficult things of God. It must be remembered that Jesus often astounded His hearers with the things He said, and those hearers did not easily grasp the things of God. When they found it hard to comprehend matters about the kingdom of God, Jesus indicated that they would understand if they took the time to listen carefully. This applies to us today as well.

Ask the class members whether they think that God deliberately makes matters of the spiritual life hard for us to understand. You will have further opportunity to discuss this point when you come to verse 13.

Most preachers and teachers use stories to make the things of God simpler to their congregations. Jesus did this too.

2. Why Jesus spoke in parables (Matt. 13:10-13). The disciples now crowded around Jesus and questioned Him about His use of parables for teaching. Jesus often used real-life illustrations and anecdotes to explain the things of God so that they would understand.

Jesus said that the disciples were privileged to understand the things of God, while others were not. God opened up the mysteries of His kingdom to them.

Sometimes we wonder why we have the opportunity to go to church and hear the gospel while people in other cultures worship idols and follow other religions. Should we not have an attitude of gratitude for this and listen to God more because of it? Allow the students time to discuss this.

Jesus went on to explain that those who understood and received what they had been taught would be taught greater things. In other words, if you cannot pass spiritual kindergarten, you are not qualified to learn what is taught in first grade. On another occasion, Jesus told His disciples that He had much to teach them but that they were not ready to receive it yet (John 16:12). This implies that there are stages of growth in learning and that we are accountable to God for what He teaches us. We are shown the things of God for a purpose.

Those who reject the Lord's message, however, will be deprived even of what they have already been taught. God's truth will be hidden from them. This is why Jesus said He taught in parables. Parables are earthly stories with heavenly meanings, and they have the unique quality of being able to hide the truth from some while revealing the truth to others. Those who have rejected Christ and have closed their eyes and ears to the truth will not understand the truth taught in His parables. Those truths, however, become clear to those who have seeking hearts.

3. The prophecy fulfilled (Matt. 13:14-15). Jesus knew the writings of the prophets. When His disciples asked Him about His use of parables, He was reminded of the prophecy of Isaiah that said the people of Isaiah's day would hear but not understand. They did not understand because they had hearts that were hardened to the things of God. Jesus implied that His own teaching could be understood only by those who had open and pliable hearts.

Jesus also was indicating that the people of His day, like those in Isaiah's day, did not understand the things He said because they had shut God out of their lives. As such, God would not break through and heal and restore their lives. This situation highlights the need for God's grace. He heals lives as He draws people to willingly turn to Him.

Here is a lesson for us. As we turn to the Lord, acknowledging our need for Him and our own powerlessness to help ourselves, He begins His work of transformation and healing in our lives. Isaiah was right on target with his prophetic words.

4. Blessing for those who listen (Matt. 13:16-17). Jesus then pronounced a blessing on His disciples, who listened and saw with their hearts. They perceived the things of God with their hearts. Jesus said that because they were able to understand the things of God from the heart, they were given a privilege greater than the prophets of old, who had not heard or seen many of these truths Jesus taught. As His children today, we have free access to the things of God, but it begins with a listening heart.

In the New Testament era, people were privileged to experience the promises of God more personally because Jesus, the incarnate God, was walking with them. We are blessed too because we also can see and understand the things of God with our hearts because God the Holy Spirit indwells us.

ILLUSTRATING THE LESSON

Listening to God is not just a matter of hearing with our physical ears but also of listening with the heart.

CONCLUDING THE LESSON

Our lesson this week has shown us that we truly listen to God when we listen with our hearts and not just our ears. We are then truly blessed by Him.

ANTICIPATING THE NEXT LESSON

Our lesson next week shows us how to forgive others in the same manner in which we have been forgiven our sins by our loving God.

—*A. Koshy Muthalaly.*

PRACTICAL POINTS

1. We should take advantage of every opportunity to hear God's Word (Matt. 13:9).
2. We cannot know God's plans apart from His gracious revelation of them (vss. 10-11).
3. Spiritual truth can be grasped only by those who are indwelt by God's Spirit (vss. 12-13).
4. Hearing God's truth is of no value unless the hearing is accompanied by faith (vss. 14-15).
5. We should never take for granted the divine blessing of spiritual understanding (vs. 16).
6. The privilege of having God's full revelation obligates us to learn it and live it (vs. 17).

—Jarl K. Waggoner.

RESEARCH AND DISCUSSION

1. Is there ever any reason for us to withhold God's truth from particular individuals (Matt. 13:10-11)? Why or why not?
2. What is required for us to fully understand God's revelation (vss. 12-13)?
3. Have you encountered people who have heard God's Word repeatedly but never understood it (vss. 14-15)? What accounts for this? Is it fruitless to try to reach them with the gospel? Why or why not?
4. What are some of the blessings we enjoy that the Old Testament saints did not (vss. 16-17)?
5. What does Jesus' teaching in parables tell us about the character of God and how He deals with mankind?

—Jarl K. Waggoner.

ILLUSTRATED HIGH POINTS

Let him hear (Matt. 13:9)

God has given each of us two ears, well-positioned so that we will benefit from stereo sound. He has also given each of us a spirit, made in His image, so that He can communicate with us.

What do we often do with that tremendous privilege? Do we avoid communicating with God and miss some essential messages that He tries to send us to help us in our Christian lives and to make us more fruitful?

Jesus used the expression, "Who hath ears to hear, let him hear" (Matt. 13:9). He was pointing out our need to open our minds and hearts to let the message penetrate our being.

When God speaks to us through His Spirit and His Word, what is our reaction? Do we sometimes suppress His voice as if we had not heard a thing, or are we constantly on the alert to catch what He has to say to us?

Dull of hearing (vs. 15)

An important area of life where we need to learn to listen is the family. It has become a popular joke (although it is not really funny) that a husband turns off his wife like a hearing aid, and she may do the same to him.

That practice has spread to parents and children as well, leading to misunderstanding, misconceptions, and misconstrued messages. The end result can be hurt feelings or lost opportunities to be of service to each other. The damaged feelings can be overcome or forgiven, but lost opportunities to help those we love may never be regained.

By reexamining our love for the people with whom we share a residence and by strengthening our concern for their wants and needs, defective communication can be corrected.

—P. Fredrick Fogle.

Golden Text Illuminated

"Who hath ears to hear, let him hear" (Matthew 13:9).

One of the challenges Jesus faced in His few years of public ministry was to get the attention of the people. The very thing that held the Jewish people together was the Bible (Old Testament). From childhood on it was part of their everyday lives, and such things as their days off and holidays were dictated by it. Jesus spoke, therefore, to a biblically literate people who had heard the Scriptures over and over again.

When Jesus came, He had much to say to the Jews about many things, but how does one get and hold the attention of those who have heard it all many times? Jesus used contrast (Matt. 5:21-22), hyperbole (vs. 30), reversal of order (placing the "amen," or "verily," at the beginning of statements rather than at the end [cf. John 1:51]), and other methods such as parables.

Our golden text appears at the end of a parable. The word "parable" literally refers to something set alongside; thus, it is a story set alongside some spiritual truth and meant to teach or illustrate it. A parable was a story that might need interpretation, and those who wanted to learn the meaning of it would ask (cf. Matt. 13:36). Jesus was a master of every teaching method He used, and this was certainly true of His use of parables. He used them to separate the spiritually hungry from those with no interest at all.

Our golden text, coming as it does at the end of a parable, was in itself a mini-parable. Everyone has physical ears. Obviously, some with ears may in fact be deaf, but the point Jesus was making was that some people also have spiritual ears. The person who had an interest in spiritual matters would either understand the intent of the story or would seek it by asking that it be explained to him. Those who had only physical ears and thus no interest in learning spiritual truths would go on their way, content to have heard a nice little story.

People today are little different from people back then, though in general they are more biblically illiterate. Jesus' challenge, however, is valid for everyone today. Upon hearing the Word of God, whether it is a parable or some other portion of Scripture, those with an interest in spiritual things should pay close attention and learn the lesson because of the importance it has to their lives.

Pastors and Sunday school teachers today must deal with the biblically illiterate as well as those who grew up in church and know the Bible quite well. One thing they must keep in mind, however, is the ministry of the Spirit.

Those with spiritual ears are those who usually come to the Bible lesson with the desire to learn. They are intent on hearing anew what the Holy Spirit will say to them. These same people are usually the ones who ask for clarification if they do not understand the point being made. To have such people in one's class or congregation is one of the more encouraging things for those who present the Word.

We also must personally apply the challenge of the golden text to ourselves. Do we come to Bible studies or church services with ears to hear, or do we inwardly tune out familiar texts? "Who hath ears to hear, let him hear" is spoken to us as much as it is to our neighbors in the pew.

—*Darrell W. McKay.*

Heart of the Lesson

"It is time to come in for supper!" Mother calls to her child, who is busy at play in the yard. There is no response. Did the child hear his mother's voice? "Time for supper!" Mother repeats. There is still no response. Mother walks over to her child, taps him on the shoulder, and says once again, "Come in for supper." "Oh, did you call me, Mother?" he asks.

Sometimes we wonder whether our children hear what we say. Does it go in one ear and right out the other? Do they choose not to hear what they wish to avoid?

Of course, it is not only children who are apparently deaf to words they would rather not hear. Adults can be just as bad.

In our lesson text Jesus used the parable of the sower to talk about the importance of having listening ears.

1. Mysteries (Matt. 13:9-12). Jesus told His disciples, "Who hath ears to hear, let him hear." The men found Jesus' parables hard to understand. They wanted Him to explain the stories to them in private.

Jesus used parables to help explain the mysteries of the kingdom of heaven. Before, they had been hidden from people. Now, Jesus was ready to tell people about God's kingdom—if they were ready to receive the truths.

Their spiritual eyes needed to be open. They needed to be like the soil in Jesus' parable that was ready to receive the seed of the gospel and respond to its message (Matt. 13:8).

2. Closed ears (Matt. 13:13-15). People who did not believe in Jesus had ears closed to the truth. They refused to truly listen and were deaf to Jesus' claims. Isaiah prophesied that there would be such obstinate unbelief.

With hardened hearts, dull ears, and closed eyes, there could be no conversion or healing. In Jesus' parable, this compared to the rocky soil that prohibited any growth of the seed.

3. Open ears (Matt. 13:16-17). Jesus talked further about people's response to hearing the gospel. Those who listened and received the truths were blessed, or happy. Their eyes and ears were actually functioning as they were meant to.

Jesus' first coming to earth did not fulfill all the Old Testament prophecies. Prophets such as Isaiah and Daniel looked forward with longing to that coming when He would rule and reign on earth. It will not be until Jesus' second coming that His kingdom will be completely in place so that He will rule the earth.

Jesus' parable of the sower pointed out some important differences among people who hear the claims of the gospel. Some apparently hear the message but immediately reject it because their hearts are hardened. Their spiritual ears are completely closed.

Some seem to accept the good news when they hear it, but nothing comes of their initial positive reaction because no root takes hold. They will not truly listen to God.

Others also seem to readily accept the seed of the gospel for a while, but when troubles come, they reject its power in their lives. Their hearing ears close.

Finally, those who learn to listen to Jesus' truth have ears that are open to whatever He is trying to teach them. Learning to listen is a skill that Jesus has honed in them. They have listened to Him and taken small steps of faith, resulting in spiritual growth, which produces fruit in their lives.

—*Judy Carlsen.*

World Missions

As the Lord said, prophets and righteous men of the Old Testament era had no opportunity to hear the words and teachings of Jesus (Matt. 13:17). Peter explained to his readers that even though they had eyewitness accounts of the Lord's ministry, they had "a more sure word of prophecy" (II Pet. 1:19). The "more sure word" is the inerrant, infallible Bible. It is of central importance in soul-winning and missions.

"Perspicuity," an important term, is related to the word "perspicuous." This is an adjective meaning "clear and legible, easily understood." That perfectly defines the Bible. The doctrine of perspicuity holds that anyone who can read the Scriptures in his own language or dialect can be saved.

No doubt many missionaries have never heard the word "perspicuity," but every missionary believes in it and acts on it. The Gideons, Wycliffe Bible Translators, the Pocket Testament League, and Ethnos360 (New Tribes Mission) confidently believe in the perspicuity of Scripture. These societies have thousands of testimonies of people who were saved through reading the Word of God without a believer's assistance.

Barry was a traveling salesman. He checked into the last motel in town with a vacancy just before a heavy snowstorm. He was disgusted that he had no reading matter. Then he found a Gideon New Testament in the nightstand. He read large portions of the book until he concluded that it called him a sinner. He then hurled it against the motel room door.

The storm worsened, and Barry was marooned for another day. The New Testament lay on the floor where it had landed. With nothing else to read, Barry gave in and picked up the rejected book. In his reading he found the answer to the indictment for sin. He opened the cover and followed the instructions on how to be saved. The perspicuity of Scripture had worked again! Today, Barry heads up an important missionary society.

The Bible's perspicuity means every Christian can be a missionary in one way or another. Carrying gospel tracts in pocket or purse and passing them to clerks and waiters can return eternal rewards in the saving of souls without a word of personal testimony. Enclosing a tract in letters and bill payments is also a great way to make the gospel known.

Adherents of cults and rigid religious groups may be difficult to reach with a personal testimony, but a tract or Scripture portion lovingly given may turn the lost one to the light. In the city of New York, for example, there was a unique witnessing approach. For many years, faithful believers set up tables filled with tracts and New Testaments for Jews. The goal was to attract businessmen waiting for public transportation to Manhattan offices. Time alone will tell what was achieved without a word from the Christians.

We live in a world that emphasizes the visual, and millions of people in all parts of the world have seen the Jesus film or video. The film uses the Word of God to give the salvation message. Many churches and missionaries have placed the film on neighborhood doors without comment. The perspicuity of Scripture thus is at work through a splendid, full-color presentation. It will be exciting one day to meet those saved through this outreach.

—*Lyle P. Murphy.*

The Jewish Aspect

The word "parable" comes from the Greek word *parabolē*. It literally means "a placing of one thing beside another." A parable is a comparison or illustration and is often in story form. The Hebrew term for a proverb or parable is *mashal.*

The *mashal* refers to proverbial sayings, similitudes, or sentences of ethical wisdom. The Old Testament contains several parables, or *mashals.*

The word *mashal* was used of Balaam's prophecies when he was called upon to curse Israel (Num. 23:7, 18; 24:3). When David committed his sins of adultery and murder, Nathan confronted him with a *mashal,* or parable, about a poor man and his pet ewe lamb (II Sam. 12:1-15).

When the Shechemites selected Abimelech as their king, Jotham presented them with a parable in which trees went on a desperate and indiscriminate search for a king to reign over them (Judg. 9:7-21). The point of his parable was that the Shechemites were accountable to God for choosing a murderer as their king.

Ezekiel used parables while in exile in Babylon. One parable was about an eagle and a vine, representing Nebuchadnezzar's invasion of Jerusalem and the removal of its people and king (Ezek. 17:3-10).

Another parable was about a lion and her whelps. This referred to the fate of Judah's last kings (Ezek. 19:2-9). A third parable told of a boiling pot, a reference to the wickedness and destruction of Jerusalem (24:3-14).

The *mashal,* or parable, is a part of Jewish folk culture that has continued to the present. It is still found in traditional circles but especially in schools.

"You want to know why it's so hard to be a Jew? Let me tell you a moshl," Lewis Glinert wrote in *The Joys of Hebrew* (Oxford), illustrating the ease with which a parable would slip appropriately and naturally into a conversation.

Jesus spoke of the people of Israel in His day as fulfilling Isaiah's prophecy of people who hear but do not understand. They heard Jesus' parables but did not understand their meaning.

At first glance at Isaiah's message, it almost appears that God did not want Israel to understand; however, Israel's history of insensitivity to God and His prophets resulted in the lack of perception and understanding.

Isaiah directly told the people how they were going to react to Isaiah's message, and they responded exactly that way. They heard the words but did not want to accept the message, so they closed their ears to it.

This was consistent with other instances in which the truth was declared, but because the people did not like that truth, it was rejected, thus deepening their plight.

Isaiah's audience did not have soft hearts. They did not listen to God. Isaiah's message simply brought the hardness that already existed in varying degrees to the surface. Isaiah's message did not make the people unresponsive. It simply exposed their existing unresponsiveness. Just as Pharaoh's heart was hardened because he continued to reject God's instructions, so Israel's people hardened themselves against repentance, both in Isaiah's day and in Jesus'.

—Carter Corbrey.

Guiding the Superintendent

In my current ministry I devote most of my time to working with volunteers, who, out of the goodness of their hearts, give of themselves so that others can benefit. In order to prepare them for the task of dealing with people who have urgent needs, we ask our volunteers to attend training sessions. One of the most popular training sessions deals with learning the art of active listening.

Active listening is the ability not only to hear what an individual is saying but also to concentrate on the individual's body language, voiced intonations, and other significant nonverbal cues in order to better understand what the person is trying to communicate.

In this week's lesson text, Matthew recorded one of the times that Jesus taught in parables and how He used that occasion to impress on His disciples their accountability not only to listen to His teaching but also to receive it with spiritual understanding.

DEVOTIONAL OUTLINE

1. A parable (Matt. 13:9). Jesus assumed the role of a teacher and taught the multitudes from a boat, using a parable about a farmer who sowed his seed in various types of soils (vss. 1-8). Jesus then stated that His teaching must be carefully listened to.

2. Questions (Matt. 13:10-17). Jesus' disciples approached Him and asked why He spoke to the multitudes in parables. His answer cannot be minimized. Jesus taught the multitudes in parables "in such a way as to harden and reject those who [were] hard of heart and to enlighten—often with further explanation—his disciples" (Gaebelein, ed., *The Expositor's Bible Commentary,* Zondervan).

Jesus told His disciples that His parable was about the spread of the gospel message concerning the kingdom of God and how various people responded to it (cf. vss. 18-23). Impenetrable hearts, thoughtless, shallow lives, and noncommittal attitudes keep the message from having any fruitful sort of effect in the lives of many hearers.

Some, however, embrace the gospel message of God's kingdom with spiritual understanding. Soon thereafter, the appearance of spiritual fruitfulness in their lives reveals the gospel was genuinely received in true faith.

AGE-GROUP EMPHASES

Children: As your teachers continue to tell their students about God's amazing love for them, encourage them to use this week's lesson text to help their students understand that God loves them enough to give them His magnificent story called the gospel. The Lord wants the children not only to listen to it but also to believe it with joy.

Youths: Young people often look for the easiest way to accomplish a task. However, when it comes to sharing the gospel with their peers, a more serious dedication is warranted. Even though only a minority who hear the gospel embrace it by faith, encourage your teachers to challenge their students to faithfully share the gospel and trust the Lord for the results.

Adults: Challenge your adult students to take a personal inventory of how much spiritual fruit their lives are producing. Remind them that God still takes delight in His children when they share the gospel message. The Holy Spirit may lead some of their listeners into God's kingdom.

—*Thomas R. Chmura.*

SCRIPTURE LESSON TEXT

MATT. 18:21 Then came Peter to him, and said, Lord, how oft shall my brother sin against me, and I forgive him? till seven times?

22 Jesus saith unto him, I say not unto thee, Until seven times: but, Until seventy times seven.

23 Therefore is the kingdom of heaven likened unto a certain king, which would take account of his servants.

24 And when he had begun to reckon, one was brought unto him, which owed him ten thousand talents.

25 But forasmuch as he had not to pay, his lord commanded him to be sold, and his wife, and children, and all that he had, and payment to be made.

26 The servant therefore fell down, and worshipped him, saying, Lord, have patience with me, and I will pay thee all.

27 Then the lord of that servant was moved with compassion, and loosed him, and forgave him the debt.

28 But the same servant went out, and found one of his fellowservants, which owed him an hundred pence: and he laid hands on him, and took *him* by the throat, saying, Pay me that thou owest.

29 And his fellowservant fell down at his feet, and besought him, saying, Have patience with me, and I will pay thee all.

30 And he would not: but went and cast him into prison, till he should pay the debt.

31 So when his fellowservants saw what was done, they were very sorry, and came and told unto their lord all that was done.

32 Then his lord, after that he had called him, said unto him, O thou wicked servant, I forgave thee all that debt, because thou desiredst me:

33 Shouldest not thou also have had compassion on thy fellowservant, even as I had pity on thee?

34 And his lord was wroth, and delivered him to the tormentors, till he should pay all that was due unto him.

35 So likewise shall my heavenly Father do also unto you, if ye from your hearts forgive not every one his brother their trespasses.

NOTES

Forgiving One Another

Lesson Text: Matthew 18:21-35

Related Scriptures: Luke 6:27-38; 17:1-

TIME: A.D. 29   PLACE: Capernaum

GOLDEN TEXT—"Then his lord, after that he had called him, said unto him, O thou wicked servant, I forgave thee all that debt, because thou desiredst me: shouldest not thou also have had compassion on thy fellowservant, even as I had pity on thee?" (Matthew 18:32-33).

Introduction

While all the principles for living included in God's Word are important, the principle of forgiveness is one of the most rewarding. It is also one of the most difficult for many people to put into practice, maybe because of the have-it-your-way philosophy of the culture we live in. We are repeatedly told that we have the right to experience all the pleasure we can get and that no one has the right to reach into our area of enjoyment and diminish it in any way whatsoever. We live in an extremely self-centered society.

Abraham Lincoln was once asked how he was going to treat the rebellious Southerners after they were finally defeated and returned to the Union. Although the questioner expected an indication of revenge, Lincoln is said to have answered, "I will treat them as if they had never been away." Archibald Hart is quoted as defining forgiveness as "surrendering my right to hurt you for hurting me." These two quotes capture the essence of true forgiveness. It is a willingness not to get even with someone who has hurt us.

LESSON OUTLINE

I. THE SERVANT FORGIVEN—
   Matt. 18:21-27

II. THE SERVANT UNFORGIVING—
    Matt. 18:28-35

Exposition: Verse by Verse

THE SERVANT FORGIVEN

MATT. 18:21 Then came Peter to him, and said, Lord, how oft shall my brother sin against me, and I forgive him? till seven times?

22 Jesus saith unto him, I say not unto thee, Until seven times: but, Until seventy times seven.

23 Therefore is the kingdom of heaven likened unto a certain king, which would take account of his servants.

24 And when he had begun to reckon, one was brought unto him, which owed him ten thousand talents.

25 But forasmuch as he had not to pay, his lord commanded him to

be sold, and his wife, and children, and all that he had, and payment to be made.

26 The servant therefore fell down, and worshipped him, saying, Lord, have patience with me, and I will pay thee all.

27 Then the lord of that servant was moved with compassion, and loosed him, and forgave him the debt.

Seeking guidance (Matt. 18:21-22). {Jesus had just finished telling the disciples how believers are to handle someone who has sinned against them. Peter had a logical follow-up question: How often are we required to forgive a person who repeatedly sins against us?}Q1 In suggesting seven times, Peter was actually being generous, for the rabbis taught that a person should forgive someone who has sinned against him up to three times. They apparently based this on the repeated phrase about three transgressions found in Amos 1 and 2.

{It is important to note that Peter was asking about a relationship between believers. This is evident from the term "my brother" (Matt. 18:21).}Q2 In the family of God, it is extremely important that we get along and not allow offenses to separate us from one another. Grudges should not be part of our lifestyle, even though they are quite prominent in the social, political, and business world, where most people are determined to look out for themselves.

"Forgiving our sinning brothers and sisters is a part of our duty toward God's children, just as it is our duty to pursue them for restoration to righteousness. To fail to forgive fellow believers is to abuse God's children, and so incur the Father's wrath. Forgiveness is a foundational characteristic of the family of God" (Weber, *Matthew,* Broadman and Holman). {It is not surprising, then, that Jesus responded to Peter as He did.

Jesus' answer did not mean we should count up to 490 offenses! He was teaching that forgiveness should go on endlessly, no matter how many times we are offended.}Q3 A child of God should never carry a grudge against another child of God or, for that matter, against anyone else. This can be more difficult when unsaved friends or family members hurt us badly.

Settling accounts (Matt. 18:23-24). Jesus then told a parable to illustrate how those in His kingdom should handle forgiveness. He told of a king who wanted to settle accounts with his servants, perhaps provincial governors who owed the king money from taxation. The man brought before him owed ten thousand talents, which in our economy would amount to millions of dollars. A denarius was a day's pay, and a talent equaled six thousand denarii. This was an impossible amount to repay.

This man found himself in a hopeless position. Whether this was the result of poor administration or dishonesty does not really make any difference at this point. The fact is he faced a debt he had no way to pay, and yet his master was demanding to have the account settled right then. {The concept of debt can be applied to offenses because when we find ourselves offended by someone, we feel the person owes us something to make up for it.}Q4 In our minds he owes us a debt of some sort, if only an apology.

It is this feeling that another person owes us something that we must deal with. The concept of forgiveness includes willingly canceling anything owed to us. When someone has offended us or hurt us deeply, our part in the matter is to not withhold a willingness to forgive and a loving, forgiving spirit. If the other person asks forgiveness, we should immediately grant it; but it is also true that if that person never does ask for our forgiveness, we should forgive him in our hearts for what he has done.

There are times when we feel the debt is enormous. How does a daughter, for example, forgive her father's sexual abuse? How does one forgive a spouse's marital infidelity?

Releasing debts (Matt. 18:25-27). When it was realized that the king's servant would not be able to pay his debt, the king ordered that he, his wife, his children, and all his property be sold and the money used to settle part of the debt. It does not take much calculation to realize that even with all this, it would be impossible to come anywhere near settling such a huge debt. The servant fell down before his master, begging for an extension of time and promising to pay it all off, but it was a totally unrealistic request.

As the king listened to his servant's pleas, he was moved with compassion. In the most amazing move he could possibly make, the king forgave his servant the entire debt and released him from the obligation of paying any of it back. {No doubt Jesus purposely used such a huge amount of debt in His parable to clearly demonstrate the greatness of God's forgiveness of our sins. There is no humanly possible means of paying the Father what we owe because of our sins.}^Q5 He is holy, while we are unholy and sinful.

In ourselves we have no way of bridging the enormous gap of unholiness that separates us from God. If He were to leave everything (or anything) up to us, we would be hopelessly lost for all eternity, with no hope of salvation and heaven. God, in His mercy and grace, provided a means for us that does not depend on our own ability. In the death of His Son, Jesus, He provided the payment for our sins. Our trust in Christ as personal Saviour is all God requires. When we receive Him, we are forgiven and released from the entire debt.

The release that the king gave his servant was astonishing, but even more so is the salvation we receive in Jesus Christ. We are saved simply because of His great grace.

THE SERVANT UNFORGIVING

28 But the same servant went out, and found one of his fellowservants, which owed him an hundred pence: and he laid hands on him, and took him by the throat, saying, Pay me that thou owest.

29 And his fellowservant fell down at his feet, and besought him, saying, Have patience with me, and I will pay thee all.

30 And he would not: but went and cast him into prison, till he should pay the debt.

31 So when his fellowservants saw what was done, they were very sorry, and came and told unto their lord all that was done.

32 Then his lord, after that he had called him, said unto him, O thou wicked servant, I forgave thee all that debt, because thou desiredst me:

33 Shouldest not thou also have had compassion on thy fellowservant, even as I had pity on thee?

34 And his lord was wroth, and delivered him to the tormentors, till he should pay all that was due unto him.

35 So likewise shall my heavenly Father do also unto you, if ye from your hearts forgive not every one his brother their trespasses.

Demanding payment (Matt. 18:28-29). The opening word "but" lets us know there is a contrast coming with what has gone before. The situation here is similar to the previous one in that it involves a creditor and a debtor; however, the man who had been forgiven his debt by the king responded very differently to a man who owed him money. One of his fellow servants owed him one hundred denarii. This would amount to a little over three months' wages, which was no small sum. It was minuscule, however, compared to what he had been forgiven.

Proverbs 22:7 says, "The rich ruleth over the poor, and the borrower is servant to the lender." It is never good to be in debt, because to a degree indebtedness puts us under the control of the one we owe. Sadly, our society has made it very easy to get caught in indebtedness through the use of credit cards. As a result, many are so deeply in debt that they will need years to get free of it. This is not the primary teaching of this parable, but it does serve as an indirect warning to us about these dangers.

{The first servant treated his fellow servant roughly and thoughtlessly. He took him by the throat, apparently choking him, and demanding payment of what was owed him. Just as this man had done before the king, his fellow servant fell down before him, pleading for time and promising to repay everything. Everything the first servant did indicated a completely merciless attitude—difficult to understand in light of the mercy he had just received.}Q6

{We must keep in mind that this is a parable, not an actual incident. The Lord purposely set up an immense contrast in order to make His point. We must also keep in mind that in a parable, not every detail demands an application. Rather, we should look for the central message being communicated by the Lord.}Q7

Reporting injustice (Matt. 18:30-31). The merciless attitude of the first servant caused him to ignore the pleading of his fellow servant. He had him thrown into prison until he could repay everything. It is difficult to see any purpose in this action beyond cruelty, for as long as the man was in prison, it would be difficult if not impossible to earn the money to repay his debt! It is clear that the attitude of the first servant is paramount to the lesson Jesus was teaching. Even though he had been forgiven, he would not forgive.

Although the man had a legal right to have his fellow servant put in prison, his action infuriated and grieved the other servants. They went to the master and reported everything that had happened.

Remember that we do not need to make application of every detail of a parable and here is an example. Jesus was not teaching that we should tattle to God every time we see another believer doing something wrong. God already knows all about it, and our place in His family is not to resemble that of a police officer. We can, however, talk with God about injustices that grieve us.

Jesus clearly was emphasizing the unforgiving attitude of the man who had himself been forgiven. The contrast is so vast that it would seem unlikely that such a thing could ever really happen. That might be exactly what Jesus was teaching: surely no believer who has been forgiven for all his sins would ever dare to be so unforgiving of others.

Confronting inequity (Matt. 18:32-33). {Once again the first servant was called into the presence of his master, the king, who was very angry about what he had heard. While he had shown great mercy toward this servant, the servant had responded by being angry, bitter, unforgiving, and compassionless toward a fellow servant.}Q8 Since the master in Jesus' parable was being portrayed in the role of God, surely this teaches us that our Master is deeply affected when our attitude toward other believers resembles this attitude.

One of the greatest blemishes on Christianity today is church fights. What a devastating testimony we give to the world when we cannot get along as fellow believers in the Lord Jesus! There will often be differences of opinions among church members, but it is possible to defer to others instead of demanding our own way, and it is possible to spend time in discussion and prayer that lead to resolutions that protect the unity of the body of Christ. How the church must grieve the Father when we, as His children, portray a fractured body in the eyes of those who are not part of His family!

The master confronted his servant by calling him wicked and reminding him of the great debt he had been forgiven. He then asked this pointed question: "Shouldest not thou also have had compassion on thy fellow-servant, even as I had pity on thee?" (vs. 33). {It is clear that Jesus expects His followers, who have been forgiven, to be forgiving. The basis of our forgiving others is the forgiveness we have already received ourselves.}Q9

"We tend to forget our king's grace, often refusing to forgive even the most trifling of offenses against us. Such behavior among God's family is infantile. It is time for us to grow up! When we refuse to forgive our brothers, we hold punishment over their heads, and they are affected by our decision. But the person who is truly imprisoned is the one who refuses to forgive. Long-term bitterness is a grinding burden" (Weber).

Teaching forgiveness (Matt. 18:34-35). The master immediately had the first servant thrown into prison. Jesus summarized by saying, "So likewise shall my heavenly Father do also unto you, if ye from your hearts forgive not every one his brother their trespasses." What Jesus seems to be saying here is that someone who truly knows what it means to have his enormous debt of sin forgiven will manifest a spirit of forgiveness himself. There is cause for self-examination here.

Jesus said there would be consequences for having an unforgiving spirit. We should take this to heart. Envision Him looking into the faces of His hearers and pressing upon them the importance of individual responsibility in this matter. He had answered Peter's question clearly: a child of God has been completely forgiven of all his sin and should be willing, in turn, to forgive repeatedly those who offend or hurt him.

{Ephesians 4:32 states the principle by which each of God's children should live: "Be ye kind one to another, tenderhearted, forgiving one another, even as God for Christ's sake hath forgiven you." This would be a good time for each of us to examine our heart and be certain that there is no spirit of bitterness or unwillingness to forgive. This is especially important if there has been a long-standing hurt or grudge from which we need emotional and spiritual healing.}Q10

—Keith E. Eggert.

QUESTIONS

1. What had caused Peter to wonder about how often to forgive?
2. How do we know his concern was about fellow believers?
3. How did Jesus respond to Peter's seemingly generous offer to forgive seven times? What did He mean?
4. How does the concept of debt relate to our need to forgive?
5. What was Jesus portraying in the first servant's huge debt?
6. What did the servant do after being forgiven, and what did this reveal about him?
7. What must we keep in mind about interpreting a parable?
8. How did the master respond to what he heard about the servant?
9. What does this parable teach?
10. What is a practical way in which we can apply this parable?

—Keith E. Eggert.

Preparing to Teach the Lesson

Our lesson this week brings another test of our faith. It is the test of being able to forgive others. Jesus set us a good example by forgiving His enemies even as He died on the cross. We are called to follow His example.

TODAY'S AIM

Facts: to show the merciless nature of the forgiven debtor who refused to forgive his own debtor.

Principle: to understand that we are called to forgive others even as we have been forgiven by God.

Application: to urge Christians to put no limits on their willingness to forgive others.

INTRODUCING THE LESSON

Sometimes we come across well-meaning Christians who have a great deal of righteous indignation. They are very angry about the injustices they face every day, and they probably have very good reason to be. Our lesson this week, however, helps us see that we are called to forgive others of their wrongs against us, just as we have been forgiven by our loving God. We get a proper perspective when we see how much God has done for us and the obligations that come with it.

DEVELOPING THE LESSON

1. Boundaries for forgiveness (Matt. 18:21-22). Are there any boundaries for forgiveness? Peter, the disciple of Jesus, wondered that too and openly asked Jesus about it. His question was a legitimate one from a social perspective.

Peter asked Jesus how often he should forgive someone who deliberately sinned against him. He then suggested an answer. He asked whether seven times would be sufficient. The number seven was considered the number of completion or wholeness, and, in fact, Peter was being very generous in light of the common teaching of that time that forgiveness was to be given three times. Peter had a good attitude and was earnest in his desire to do what was right and to follow God.

Jesus' reply to Peter was succinct and just as straightforward. It went beyond the demands of tradition and entered the realm of grace. Jesus replied that it was not enough to forgive seven times. Rather, one should forgive seventy times seven. In other words, Jesus was saying that Peter ought to put no limits on forgiveness! He was to grant unending forgiveness from his heart.

2. The debtor forgiven (Matt. 18:23-27). Jesus then went on to elaborate by telling a story to illustrate the values of the kingdom of heaven. A certain king was settling accounts with his servants when he found a man who owed him an enormous sum of money. When the man could not pay, the king ordered that he and everything that he had, including his wife and children, be sold to pay the debt. The debtor fell on his knees and pleaded with the king to give him time to repay him. The king felt sorry for him and forgave him all his debt.

Here we have a beautiful picture of God's grace. We were all in the depths of sin and could never clear that debt of sin by ourselves. Then Jesus came on the scene and died for us and paid the debt. Through faith in Him we are free. Our debt is completely paid. What we could not do, God did for us in His mercy and His grace.

Discuss the things people do to try to clear themselves of the debt of sin. Help your students acknowledge what Christ has done for us on the cross.

3. The debtor's failure to forgive (Matt. 18:28-30). The man who was set free from his huge debt left the king's presence and found another man who owed him a small amount of money. Forgetting the huge debt that he had just been forgiven, he grabbed that man by the throat and insisted that he pay him immediately. He put that man in jail until he could pay him all of what he owed.

How quickly we forget how much we have been forgiven ourselves! Ask the class members what makes this man's actions so detestable. Then ask them to ponder their own attitudes toward those who have sinned against them. Consider the fact that although we did not deserve forgiveness, it was given to us freely. We ought to respond in similar fashion to others who need our forgiveness. Discuss why it is so hard for us to extend forgiveness to others. What is it that keeps us from reaching out in love and acceptance?

4. Unforgiveness punished (Matt. 18:31-34). The man learned a lesson the hard way. When the other servants of the king saw what he had done to a fellow servant, they were disturbed and reported it to the king. The angry king called in the man who had been forgiven his debt and scolded him for not demonstrating to others the same mercy that he had been shown. Notice that the king implied that this was expected of him. It is the same for us. As Christians we are obligated to forgive others as we have been forgiven.

As a result of his unforgiveness, the man was severely punished. He was turned over to torturers to be punished until he was able to pay the whole amount, something he could never do. The point of Jesus' story is very clear. It is unthinkable that those whom God has freely and completely forgiven would not willingly and continually forgive others. When we are forgiven by God, we are called to show mercy to others.

5. A warning about forgiveness (Matt. 18:35). Jesus ended His teaching here with a warning. Serious consequences await those who refuse to forgive others. We have to take this warning seriously. We do not want to stand before God knowing that there are people we have not forgiven. In fact, an unforgiving spirit may well indicate that we have not truly experienced God's forgiveness. Christians are to be known by the grace they show to others daily.

ILLUSTRATING THE LESSON

When God forgives us, we must turn around and forgive others in the same manner.

FORGIVEN TO FORGIVE

GOD

CONCLUDING THE LESSON

It is truly amazing how much our Lord has forgiven us. We are sinners by nature, and yet He showed us His mercy by forgiving and accepting us. Let us encourage each other to forgive someone this week.

ANTICIPATING THE NEXT LESSON

Our lesson next week deals with the story of the prodigal son from Luke 15:11-24.

—A. Koshy Muthalaly.

PRACTICAL POINTS

1. Followers of Christ do not have the option of withholding forgiveness (Matt. 18:21-22).

2. Forgiveness is not something that is earned; it is something that is given (vss. 23-27).

3. If we do not forgive, we demonstrate ingratitude for God's forgiveness of us (vss. 28-30).

4. Hypocrisy and a lack of mercy are sins that cannot be hidden (vss. 31-33).

5. An unforgiving spirit brings God's displeasure, as well as His discipline (vs. 34).

6. Forgiveness that is not heartfelt is no forgiveness at all (vs. 35).

—Jarl K. Waggoner.

RESEARCH AND DISCUSSION

1. What attitude do you think prompted Peter's question (Matt. 18:21)? What did he not understand about forgiveness?

2. Are there no limits at all on forgiveness (vs. 22)? Do we do others harm by routinely forgiving them for repeated offenses?

3. Why do you think Jesus used a story to illustrate the answer He had given Peter (vss. 23-34)?

4. What does an unwillingness to forgive others reveal about us?

5. Should we forgive even those who do not ask for forgiveness?

6. How can we be sure that we are truly forgiving others from the heart and not simply going through the motions (vs. 35)?

—Jarl K. Waggoner.

ILLUSTRATED HIGH POINTS

How oft shall . . . I forgive him? (Matt. 18:21)

Why is forgiveness necessary and desirable in this world? It is because it is a principle devised by God Himself, who applied it to Adam and Eve in the Garden of Eden.

Following Adam and Eve's devilish sin of outright disobedience (Gen. 3), God's justice called for punishment.

Though the Lord cast them out of the garden, however, He also provided for their forgiveness by applying a sacrificial remedy (Gen. 4). This provision indicated that God was eager to forgive. It also pointed to the ultimate sacrifice of Christ at Calvary, where Jesus would take away the sin of the world (John 1:29).

Shouldest not thou also have had compassion? (vs. 33)

Even though forgiveness is essential to harmonious relationships, mankind finds it very hard to forgive. For the Lord, it is natural. For people, it is unnatural and annoying and at times even seems inappropriate.

In our hearts, there is often a desire for vengeance. Children at play hit each other. Teenagers may warn an offender of payback. Adults lash out at one another.

The illustration Jesus used shows how difficult it is for members of fallen humanity to forgive each other. Sadly, a similar situation can occur in Christian families and churches. Some might say, "I will forgive you if you forgive me," thus offering a conditional forgiveness. In other cases, some might state, "I will forgive you, but one thing is sure—I will never forget." The lesson from Jesus' words is that if we do not forgive, we cannot expect to be forgiven by God.

—P. Fredrick Fogle.

Golden Text Illuminated

"Then his lord, after that he had called him, said unto him, O thou wicked servant, I forgave thee all that debt, because thou desiredst me: shouldest not thou also have had compassion on thy fellowservant, even as I had pity on thee?" (Matthew 18:32-33).

Our world is full of fractured relationships. In the Parable of the Unmerciful Servant, Jesus masterfully illustrates one reason for that. Sinful man desperately needs and seeks mercy for himself, but he has the tendency to demand strict justice for everyone else, particularly when it comes to what he believes is his due.

This week's golden text expresses the moral of Jesus' parable as the king exposes the hypocrisy of his wicked servant. *How could a person act so badly?* we may wonder. He had been forgiven so much ("all that debt"), but then he had turned around and had not shown any patience with the man who owed him much less.

In this case, mercy over a financial matter is the example used. But the truth urged here also applies to all areas that call for mercy or forgiveness. Scripture is very clear that extending forgiveness is not an optional matter for the believer.

In the Lord's Prayer, which is to serve as a model for our interaction with God, we are told to ask the Lord to "forgive us our debts, as we forgive our debtors" (Matt. 6:12). Just after giving this model prayer, Jesus chose to stress this point by saying, "If ye forgive men their trespasses, your heavenly father will also forgive you: But if ye forgive not . . . neither will your Father forgive your trespasses" (vss. 14-15). Pretty strong language!

Does this mean that we have to earn our salvation by doing certain things? No, what it means is that our actions reveal whether we have a genuine relationship with God.

If we are unable or unwilling to extend mercy or forgiveness to others, do we really have a true understanding of what God has done for us? Do we, in fact, have a heart knowledge of God's character that is born out of a genuine relationship with Him?

These are serious questions. We must remember that we are saved by faith, a genuine transforming belief in Christ. But this faith produces godly fruit. The wicked cruelty of the servant in this week's parable indicated a heart not acquainted with the grace of His master, even though he had just experienced an example of it.

God pours out His mercies on the world every day. He "maketh his sun to rise on the evil and on the good, and sendeth rain on the just and on the unjust" (Matt. 5:45). The theological term for this is common grace. The world generally does not acknowledge God's kindnesses. And just as gratitude to God is rare in this fallen world, so is mercy and forgiveness.

As believers in Christ, we are to demonstrate the love of God in our lives by extending mercy and forgiveness to others. Lives characterized by these qualities will make an impact in this cruel world.

We will not, of course, live life perfectly while we struggle with our sinful natures this side of heaven. The fact that we are actively fighting against sin indicates the Holy Spirit's work in our hearts. One of our chief aims should be to cultivate a spirit of humility and gratitude to God. Then we will not find ourselves acting like the unmerciful servant in this week's parable.

—*Stephen H. Barnhart.*

Heart of the Lesson

"I will never forgive him for doing that to me!" Sometimes even Christians make these kinds of rash vows. Never is an extremely long time. Even more important, though, we should have an attitude of forgiveness rather than look for a reason not to forgive a wrong done to us.

What is the worst thing a person could do to you? He certainly could injure you in such a way that you would be permanently disabled, either physically or emotionally. Or someone could damage your reputation by spreading lies about you.

Perhaps a person could damage someone you truly love in one of these ways. Those who do not know Christ in a personal way would say that a circumstance such as that would be ample grounds for not forgiving the wrongdoer.

In our text, Jesus addressed the whole idea of forgiveness by telling a parable. He told this story in responding to Peter's question about how many times it should be necessary to forgive a wrong done to us.

1. Forgiving much (Matt. 18:21-27). Jesus' story centered on a man who owed an impossible amount of money to his king. The king had every right to sell the man and his family into slavery to pay off the debt. But when the man begged for more time to somehow begin to pay off his debt, the king was moved with compassion. He graciously forgave the servant the entire debt.

Can you imagine the relief this man must have felt? It was as if a million-pound rock had been lifted from his shoulders! He surely went away rejoicing at his good fortune.

2. Unforgiving (Matt. 18:28-35). Jesus' story did not end there, though. It took an unexpected turn. The recently forgiven man went on his way until he ran into a man who owed *him* money. This man who had just experienced unbelievable grace turned around and demanded full payment from his fellow servant.

The debtor pleaded for more time, just as the forgiven man had pleaded with the king. Would the forgiven man show grace and allow his debtor more time to come up with the money? No. Rather than show mercy as he had been shown, the forgiven man ordered the debtor to be thrown into prison.

Other servants, watching this drama unfolding, saw how wrong this was. They told the king what had happened with the man whose debt he had graciously forgiven. Furious, the king withdrew his forgiveness of the first man and had him punished.

Jesus told this story to explain an important truth. Those who have experienced God's forgiveness—that is, Christians—are accountable to God to display forgiveness to others who have wronged them. God expects His children to forgive from the heart, not grudgingly.

Even the worst sin a person could do against us can still be forgiven by God. We have all sinned. God forgave us our sins, so we need to forgive others too.

God continually shows mercy. We need to do the same.

Forgiving one who has wronged us does not make that sin right by any means. God will rightly judge people for the wrongs they have done to us. It is not up to us to somehow bring judgment on another person. After all, God can do a much fairer job of punishing a person for doing wrong than we ever could!

An unforgiving heart brings bondage. When we forgive, we are free of the hatred and bitterness that unforgiveness causes.

—*Judy Carlsen.*

World Missions

It was a rude awakening each morning for the girls in Ruth dormitory. Just after dawn, Barbara and her roommate, a girl from Arkansas, greeted the day with a lusty rendition of the "Hallelujah Chorus." Dormitory neighbors protested the intrusion into their dreams with a barrage of shoes that rained on the singers' door.

The singers were members of the Calvary Bible College musical gospel team. The impromptu concert was their own alarm clock.

The girl from Arkansas was Gracia Jones, a preacher's daughter. Gracia's father had been a Calvary professor but now was back in the pastorate.

Gracia remained at the college after completing her education, holding down four administrative jobs. Mr. Right came along for Gracia in the person of Martin Burnham, a Calvary student. Martin was Kansas born and bred, but his parents were missionaries to the Philippines. As a licensed pilot, he taught part-time in the Bible college aviation program.

For both it was love at first sight. The courtship was proper, involved both families, and held promise of the blessing of God.

The newly married couple applied to New Tribes Mission for foreign service and were accepted. Raising support for the field was not comfortable for Gracia, but Martin, blessed with a sunny disposition and the experience of deputation with his parents as a child, fared better. In time the funds were raised, and there was a second Burnham family on the field in the Philippines (Burnham, *In the Presence of My Enemies,* Tyndale).

Martin provided valuable service to mission stations and to missionaries by air. Gracia, who believed she was called to be Martin's wife rather than a missionary, monitored radio traffic between her flier husband and his scheduled stops. Three beautiful children were born on the field.

Their wedding anniversary was coming up. Gracia urged that they treat themselves to an island getaway in a pricey, offshore resort. During the first night of their vacation, they were rudely awakened by terrorists bent on taking hostages for ransom.

For more than a year, the Burnhams were captives on the run in the dense jungles of the southern Philippines. A worldwide prayer campaign was waged for their release. For long months, political and military pressures failed to bring them to safety.

Finally, a shoot-out left Martin dead and Gracia wounded but freed. For Gracia it was the beginning of a new and very different life. She now had three children to raise alone at home in America.

Recovering from the ordeal required certain steps—most particularly, the act of forgiveness. Gracia admitted that for a long time she was angry with God. Confession of that sin provided release and allowed healing to begin (Burnham).

Gracia then had to forgive the world, which she was sure had forgotten them. Government officials had to be forgiven for their failure to act responsibly and decisively in dealing with rampant terrorism.

Finally, the Philippine army had to be forgiven for recklessly firing on the hostages, which resulted in Martin's death and Gracia's wounds. The grace of God enabled her to be free to forgive.

—Lyle P. Murphy.

The Jewish Aspect

In the King James Version of the Bible, the word "forgive" is found only twenty-eight times in the Old Testament. There are three different Hebrew words that are translated "forgive."

The word *salach* is used nineteen times in its various forms. It means to "pardon" or "forgive." *Salach* is used only of God forgiving sin.

The word *nasa'* is used eight times. Its root form means to "lift," "carry," or "take." It is translated in a wide variety of ways besides "forgive." With respect to forgiveness, it seems to carry the nuance of the lifting away of sin or guilt. When one person forgives another, he lifts away the influence of the offending person's guilt from the relationship. This does not suggest approval of the sin but refers to how one deals with sin that has led to repentance. *Nasa'* can refer to either human or divine forgiveness.

A third word translated "forgive" is *kaphar,* meaning to "cover" or "cancel." This is the word translated "atonement" in Leviticus 16. On the Day of Atonement, the sins of the people were covered by the blood of the sacrifice. This word is used only of God's forgiveness of people.

When God forgives sin, it involves the actual removal of the sin and guilt of the sinner. When man forgives sin, it is merely the momentary overlooking of an offense. A person who forgives another person for sinning against him is only able to overlook in a limited way the personal offense and restore a personal relationship that may have been broken by that offense.

Forgiveness is an implied standard in many Old Testament passages. According to the law, when an enemy's ox or donkey needed assistance, one was to offer help (Ex. 23:4-5). There is an underlying, implied element of forgiveness of the animal's owner.

Proverbs instructs a person to be slow to anger and in so doing to overlook another person's sin against him (19:11). The Israelite was also instructed not to revel in an enemy's misfortune (24:17). Again, an attitude of forgiveness and compassion underlies such an action.

An element of self-awareness also aids the ability to forgive, as Solomon advised (Eccl. 7:21-22).

One of the most powerful examples of forgiveness in the Old Testament involves Joseph and his brothers (Gen. 45:5-15). Joseph forgave them for selling him into slavery. Essential to that forgiveness was his understanding of God's sovereignty.

The traditional rabbinic interpretation as to how many times a person was to forgive another was three times. The Old Testament did not prescribe any limit. In fact, when Jesus advised Peter to forgive seventy times seven, He may have been deliberately making a contrast with Lamech's threat in Genesis 4:24.

According to Jewish teaching, it is important for the sinner to seek out and ask forgiveness from those against whom he has sinned. Sins against other people are regarded as double sins, for they include sins against God and sins against another human. It was Jewish practice that until a sinner had been forgiven by the offended person, he is unable to seek God's pardon on the holiest of days, Yom Kippur, the Day of Atonement.

Such Jewish beliefs show the importance of forgiving others when they have been offended.

—*Carter Corbrey.*

Guiding the Superintendent

I must confess that I always had a difficult time interpreting and applying Matthew 18:21-22 in the context of Christian forgiveness. While I was listening to the radio one day, a pastor communicated his understanding of this verse. Suddenly, my difficulty was removed.

This godly man stated that the emphasis of Matthew 18:21-22 should not be on any specific amount of forgiveness but on control. His definition of forgiveness, which I have since adopted, is this: No sinful act in the past will control me by dominating my thought life. If I have truly forgiven the offending party, no matter how often I remember the past act, I will forgive and live my life for Christ in godly freedom.

In this week's lesson text Matthew recorded Jesus' parable that helped His disciples understand the significance of Christian forgiveness.

DEVOTIONAL OUTLINE

1. Peter's question about forgiveness (Matt. 18:21-22). Peter questioned the Lord concerning the concept of forgiveness. Peter knew the Jewish standard of forgiving someone a minimum of three times; so in his mind, his stated standard of "till seven times" must have seemed exceptionally generous.

Jesus' response to Peter's query gives the true measure of grace. He wanted Peter to know that true forgiveness is limitless in scope. To drive home His point, He followed His response with a parable.

2. Jesus' parable (Matt. 18:23-35). Jesus taught about a king who had discovered that one of his servants owed him a vast sum of money. Rather than exercise deserved discipline, the compassionate king forgave the debt.

When the forgiven servant responded to a coworker who owed him a relatively small sum by having the man thrown into prison, other coworkers told the king about the harsh treatment. The king then called the forgiven servant into his presence and angrily confronted him over his hypocrisy. The king then delivered the servant to be tortured until the immense debt was paid.

Jesus' conclusion to His parable was a dynamic statement of truth. He wanted His disciples to clearly understand that people who have been forgiven by their heavenly Father must also extend forgiveness to others. Their failure to do so will demonstrate that they have not truly embraced the Father's forgiveness.

AGE-GROUP EMPHASES

Children: Children need to be continually taught that God's love for them includes His wonderful forgiveness of their sin. Your teachers can use this spiritual truth to help their young students know that God has given them the ability to treat others the same way.

Youths: Young people are masters at holding grudges. They strenuously cling to past offenses, imprisoning themselves in a cage of unhappiness.

This week's lesson text allows your teachers to show their students an alternative to living in bitterness. God's awesome forgiveness frees them to forgive others and experience a life of abounding joy.

Adults: Adults often think about the past and wonder whether they could have done things differently. Many times, this contemplation leads to guilt, shame, and self-pity.

Have your teachers use this week's lesson text to help free their adults from emotional bondage. Embracing Christ's forgiveness—and forgiving others—will free them to delight in the Lord as never before!

—*Thomas R. Chmura.*

SCRIPTURE LESSON TEXT

LUKE 15:11 And he said, A certain man had two sons:

12 And the younger of them said to *his* **father, Father, give me the portion of goods that falleth** *to me.* **And he divided unto them** *his* **living.**

13 And not many days after the younger son gathered all together, and took his journey into a far country, and there wasted his substance with riotous living.

14 And when he had spent all, there arose a mighty famine in that land; and he began to be in want.

15 And he went and joined himself to a citizen of that country; and he sent him into his fields to feed swine.

16 And he would fain have filled his belly with the husks that the swine did eat: and no man gave unto him.

17 And when he came to himself, he said, How many hired servants of my father's have bread enough and to spare, and I perish with hunger!

18 I will arise and go to my father, and will say unto him, Father, I have sinned against heaven, and before thee,

19 And am no more worthy to be called thy son: make me as one of thy hired servants.

20 And he arose, and came to his father. But when he was yet a great way off, his father saw him, and had compassion, and ran, and fell on his neck, and kissed him.

21 And the son said unto him, Father, I have sinned against heaven, and in thy sight, and am no more worthy to be called thy son.

22 But the father said to his servants, Bring forth the best robe, and put *it* **on him; and put a ring on his hand, and shoes on** *his* **feet:**

23 And bring hither the fatted calf, and kill *it;* and let us eat, and be merry:

24 For this my son was dead, and is alive again; he was lost, and is found. And they began to be merry.

NOTES

-Country or citizen of that country - Gentile pig farma

-Parable of the Prodigal Son

-Sinned against heaven - sinned against God

A Story of Forgiveness

Lesson Text: Luke 15:11-24

Related Scriptures: Luke 15:25-32; Romans 12:9-21; II Corinthians 5:17-21

TIME: A.D. 30   PLACE: probably Perea

GOLDEN TEXT—"This my son was dead, and is alive again; he was lost, and is found" (Luke 15:24).

Introduction

On this particular day, Jesus was speaking to a mixed audience. Two distinct groups are mentioned (Luke 15:1-2). Tax collectors and others considered to be sinners by the religious elite were there for the specific purpose of hearing Jesus teach.

Since tax collectors worked for the Roman government, they were viewed as traitors and outcasts. The problem for the religious leaders was that Jesus sat and ate with these less-than-desirable people! Such action indicated identification and welcome, something they avoided at all costs. In their minds, Jesus was also guilty because of His association with such bad people of low reputation.

Because of their condescending attitudes, Jesus decided to instruct them in His special style of teaching—namely, parables. On this particular occasion, He used a series of three parables with a lost object being found in each one. What we learn is that such reconciling causes joy in heaven.

LESSON OUTLINE

I. A BROKEN RELATIONSHIP—Luke 15:11-16

II. A RESTORED RELATIONSHIP—Luke 15:17-24

Exposition: Verse by Verse

A BROKEN RELATIONSHIP

LUKE 15:11 And he said, A certain man had two sons:

12 And the younger of them said to his father, Father, give me the portion of goods that falleth to me. And he divided unto them his living.

13 And not many days after the younger son gathered all together, and took his journey into a far country, and there wasted his substance with riotous living.

14 And when he had spent all, there arose a mighty famine in that land; and he began to be in want.

15 And he went and joined himself to a citizen of that country; and he sent him into his fields to feed swine.

16 And he would fain have filled

his belly with the husks that the swine did eat: and no man gave unto him.

The son's request (Luke 15:11-12). This is the third of the three parables. It is about a man and his two sons. For some unknown reason, the younger son asked for his portion of the inheritance early. We are not told why he did this or why his father agreed to it, but they did. Normally, such division of an inheritance did not occur until after the death of the father; at that time, the older brother would receive a double portion. In this case, the older would get two-thirds and the younger one-third.

Jesus did not explain the details of the division because that was not important to the illustration and the point He was making. The only thing we can know for certain is that after this, the son would have no more claim to further inheritance. The request seems to be one of arrogant disregard for the authority of his father. Constable wrote that "to request it prematurely was tantamount to expressing a wish that the father would die" (*Thomas Constable's Notes on the Bible,* Tyndale). No wonder the older brother later became upset.

{The father's response was a very gracious and generous act on his part.}Q1 He did not force his son to stay with him but instead granted his request by giving him his portion of the inheritance early. We are not told whether the older son received his portion at the same time, though in such circumstances he likely would. Since the younger son was unmarried, it is also likely that he was an older teenager. It is quite obvious that his intention was to sever the relationship and leave.

{In order to understand the parable, we need to recognize that the father represents God, the older brother represents the religious leaders, and the younger brother represents sinners.}Q2 Just as this father did not force his son to stay with him, so God does not deal with us in that way. Every created person owes his or her very existence to God. He has revealed His love for us by sending His Son to die for our sins, but we often respond to His grace with rebellion.

The son's wastefulness (Luke 15:13-14). {As planned, the younger son took his new fortune and left home, traveling to another country a good distance from home. He must have become something of a party animal, making himself popular with everybody because of his willingness to spend money on them.}Q3 The Greek word translated "wasted" here is *diaskorpizō,* meaning "to dissipate" or "to squander." An English dictionary definition of "squander" is "to spend extravagantly or foolishly" (*Merriam-Webster's Collegiate Dictionary,* Eleventh Edition).

The *Life Application Bible Commentary* notes, "The young man apparently had wanted to live his own way, be his own master, get out from under the rules of his home and his father. Money was his ticket, so he took it and ran" (Osborne, ed., Tyndale). He is described as participating in riotous, or wild, living. He fell into a lifestyle marked by indulgence in the baser vices, uninhibited by parental or societal restraints. He had cast off all moral standards and lived for pleasure and popularity.

This is the kind of thing some young people seem to desire, what is sometimes called sowing their wild oats. While some adults smile and simply say, "Kids will be kids," it can be a very dangerous pathway for young people to take. This is especially true in today's culture, where drugs have become so prominent. These, as well as addiction to alcohol, can produce serious mental and emotional disturbances from which it might be impossible to ever recover.

The root problem in all of this is the focus on the temporal instead of on the permanent and eternal. Parental example and teaching can do much to steer children away from such perils, although, as this parable implies, some will stray even from the godliest of upbringings. When that happens, there is still hope for redemption and reconciliation.

In the eyes of this wayward young man, everything was going just as he had hoped. We know there can be no genuine joy in such living, but sometimes God has to use drastic means to get a person's attention. That is what He did in this case. A severe famine occurred, and the young man was left in desperate need.

The son's desperation (Luke 15:15-16). The prodigal son soon learned what happens when one lives recklessly and self-indulgently. He ran out off money and friends and his situation became quite desperate. He would have to be brought low before he came to his senses. The young man took the most menial job possible in order to survive. Necessity caused him to forgo personal desires in order to meet his critical needs.

He hired himself out to a Gentile pig farmer, thereby working for a foreigner and caring for animals that were unclean to Jews. To add to his destitution, he became so hungry that he wanted to eat their food. He wanted to eat "the husks, or the hulls of the leguminous plant, which in the East is the food of cattle and swine. It is known that the poor in time of distress also relied upon these pods for nourishment. No one cared enough for the young man to give him anything better" (Douglas, ed., *New Commentary on the Whole Bible*, Tyndale).

{To feed pigs was great humiliation for a Jewish young man, and to eat their food was complete degradation.}Q4 Did he actually eat this food? We cannot tell for sure. "He was fortunate. He found a job, but what a job for a Jew! He fed pigs in a pigpen. Destitute of other resources, he longed to eat what he fed the pigs. How repulsive for a law-abiding Jew. But he had no authority to eat pig food. So he fattened pigs and starved himself" (Anders, ed., *Holman New Testament Commentary*, Broadman & Holman).

Remembering the analogy to this parable, we recognize that sometimes God allows people to reach rock bottom in order to get them to look to Him. That is where this man was at this time. A life that was supposed to be wonderful had turned out to be one huge disappointment.

A RESTORED RELATIONSHIP

17 And when he came to himself, he said, How many hired servants of my father's have bread enough and to spare, and I perish with hunger!

18 I will arise and go to my father, and will say unto him, Father, I have sinned against heaven, and before thee,

19 And am no more worthy to be called thy son: make me as one of thy hired servants.

20 And he arose, and came to his father. But when he was yet a great way off, his father saw him, and had compassion, and ran, and fell on his neck, and kissed him.

21 And the son said unto him, Father, I have sinned against heaven, and in thy sight, and am no more worthy to be called thy son.

22 But the father said to his ser-

vants, Bring forth the best robe, and put it on him; and put a ring on his hand, and shoes on his feet:

23 And bring hither the fatted calf, and kill it; and let us eat, and be merry:

24 For this my son was dead, and is alive again; he was lost, and is found. And they began to be merry.

The son's decision (Luke 15:17-19). {It was while sitting among the pigs that were better fed than he was that he finally came to his senses and thought about home. He realized that what he had run from was far better than anything he had found since.}Q5 This is a good testimony to the quality of homelife he had once enjoyed with his family. How many parents wait and long for their child to come to a realization like this? Jesus' story can be a means of encouragement and hope for such parents.

The young man's greatest realization was that his father's servants had it a whole lot better than he did right then. He no longer had any money, he no longer had any dignity, he no longer had friends, and he no longer had a familial relationship he could enjoy. He had severed all of that. Could he get any of it back? His only recourse was to try. His experiences had taken away his pride and replaced it with genuine brokenness. He would make his appeal by acknowledging that he no longer had any rights as a son.

If his father would allow it, he would return to his home, confess his sin, and ask to be allowed to live there as a servant. That way he could at least have food regularly. He had reached the point where all he could hope for was mercy. Note that he planned to admit his sin not only against his father, but also against God ("I have sinned against heaven" [vs. 18]). This is a statement of his repentance, because he would go to the father with nothing but an expression of his need.

Why is it that for so many it takes a tragedy before they realize their need for God? Why do they go to God only when they have "foxhole" prayers, in times of desperation? Perhaps what is even more crucial to ask, Why do so many offer those prayers of desperation and then forget about them after God provides the deliverance? How much better it is to know the love and mercy of God without having to experience such deep trials!

The son's return (Luke 15:20-21). "Finally, his mind went to work again. Humans have the capacity to change. We do not have to remain in the pigpen. We do not have to continue to live as sinners. We can become responsible for our lives. We can quit our riotous living. We can come home" (Anders). {When the young man returned, the father's response was priceless! He had been watching every day for his son. When he saw him, his fatherly compassion rose to the fore, and he ran to meet him.

The son was still a long way off when his father spotted him. His longing for his son's return is fully evident in his actions.}Q6 Imagine if he had not been watching in this manner and if the son had arrived at his door before he knew he was anywhere around. {We cannot help noticing that the focus of attention has now changed from the son to the father. Jesus made this shift on purpose in order to portray His Father as the loving God waiting for the return of those He loves so dearly.}Q7

The son began his rehearsed speech, but we soon see that it was ignored. The father heard it but chose to act according to his own wishes.

There are two perspectives about the parables in Luke 15. Some think they teach the restoration of a sinning believer to fellowship with God. Others

What was lost now is found
↳ Parables of Luke 15

believe they teach the salvation of one who is lost. We should note the key words here: the father said his son had been "dead" and was now "alive," "lost" and now "found" (vs. 24).

Jesus was speaking to those who were rejecting His message and objecting to His association with sinners. Such sinners needed more than restoration. The primary emphasis, therefore, seems to be salvation. The sheep, coin, and son were all lost and sought by their owners (picturing God, the Creator). At the same time, we know that God rejoices over every wandering child of His who returns to Him as much as He does over those who are redeemed from their sinful conditions.

The father's welcome (Luke 15:22-24). {Contrary to the son's intent to be a hired servant, the father made him a full member of the family again. He gave him a standing like that which he had previously, one that was full of privileges.}Q8 He had the best robe brought out and put on him, along with a ring, and sandals for his feet. Since hired servants probably went barefoot, this was a clear indication that the father was receiving him back as his son and not as a hired servant.

The fatted calf was reserved for a banquet of celebration, usually during one of the national feasts. The boy's return was cause enough for the father to celebrate. Did you notice that he was so eager for his son's return that he ran to meet him (vs. 20), something that no dignified man in that culture would do? {Since this father's joy is a reflection of God's when someone comes back to Him, we need to reflect on these details.}Q9

"Everything the younger son had hoped to find in the far country, he discovered back home: clothes, jewelry, friends, joyful celebration, love, and assurance for the future. . . . The father did not ask him to 'earn' his for-giveness, because no amount of good works can save us from our sins (Eph 2:8-10; Titus 3:3-7). In the far country, the prodigal learned the meaning of misery; but back home, he discovered the meaning of mercy" (Wiersbe, *The Bible Exposition Commentary,* Cook).

{This father portrays our Heavenly Father in His love, kindness, grace, and mercy. If any one of us needs to be reconciled to Him, we can be certain that He is waiting and watching and will never turn away someone coming to Him.}Q10 For this young man, the return was just the beginning. From then on, his relationship with his father would no doubt be full of blessings. So it is for every person who comes to our Father.

—Keith E. Eggert.

QUESTIONS

1. How did the father respond to his son's arrogant request?
2. What persons or groups are portrayed by the parable?
3. What did the son do after receiving what he asked for?
4. What was especially degrading about the son's circumstances and employment?
5. What brought him to his senses, and what did he decide to do?
6. How do we know the father never stopped longing for his son?
7. Why did Jesus shift the attention of His parable from the son to the father?
8. What did the father do to restore and rejoice over his son?
9. Why is it important that we focus on the father?
10. What does this reconciliation show us about God our Father?

—Keith E. Eggert.

Preparing to Teach the Lesson

This first lesson on "Entering God's Kingdom" looks at a familiar passage from a fresh perspective. Usually the account of the prodigal son focuses on the son himself. This study focuses on the father. The father showed love and faith by reconciling with his wayward son. The older brother did not exercise faith to reconcile with his younger brother.

Use this lesson to emphasize the truth that faith in Christ will lead us to reconcile with others, including family members.

TODAY'S AIM

Facts: to understand the spiritual element in reconciling with others.

Principle: to have the spiritual courage to reconcile with someone who may not deserve it.

Application: to reconcile with a person with whom there may be a broken relationship.

INTRODUCING THE LESSON

(Present the following case study, and ask your learners the questions that follow.)

A mother and her adult daughter had a small disagreement. At first the relationship was only a little awkward, but neither woman took any steps to reconcile. As the years wore on, the mother and her daughter drifted further apart. Now they do not speak to each other, and both seem entrenched in their ways.

1. What is the real cause of this problem?

2. What are the potential consequences of their actions?

3. What steps should one or the other take now?

In Luke 15 we find instructions on how to handle this type of situation.

DEVELOPING THE LESSON

1. The younger son's request (Luke 15:11-19). This parable features three men: a wealthy father, a bitter older son, and a wayward younger son. The relationship between this father and his sons highlights the important issue of reconciliation.

The younger son decided he did not want to wait for his portion of the family's inheritance. So one day he approached his father with the request, "Father, give me the portion of goods that falleth to me" (vs. 12). His father, showing remarkable self-control and restraint, complied and divided his wealth between his two sons.

The younger son "took his journey into a far country, and there wasted his substance with riotous living" (vs. 13). After some time of want and hunger, he came to his senses. He realized that his father's servants had a better life than he had. So he determined to return to his father and ask to be treated as one of the servants.

2. The father's reconciliation (Luke 15:20-24). As the wayward son neared home, his father saw him. What reaction would he display toward his son? Would he reject his son and say, "Son, you have disgraced me and my family. You have no place here anymore"? Would the father accept his son on his son's own terms and say, "Son, you are welcome to return, but we will not have the same relationship. You will live and eat with my servants"?

The father did not display either one of those attitudes. Rather, when he first saw his son, he "had compassion, and ran, and fell on his neck, and kissed him" (vs. 20). Then he told his servants to bring his son a robe, a ring, and sandals. He further instructed his servants to prepare a great feast, saying, "This my son was dead, and is alive again; he was lost, and is found" (vs. 24).

The father could have rejected his son; instead, he made the choice to reconcile with him, even though, humanly speaking, the son did not deserve such favor.

When the older son discovered what had happened, he became angry (vss. 25-28). His father pleaded with him to show the same spirit of reconciliation, but he refused to do so. "These many years do I serve thee, neither transgressed I at any time thy commandment: and yet thou never gavest me a kid, that I might make merry with my friends" (vs. 29). He was scandalized by his father's mercy and felt it was unfair to him.

The older son's recalcitrance appears to be directed more toward his father than his younger brother. He could have agreed with his father and joined the festivities, happy that his brother had returned. Instead, he made the choice to resist reconciliation, creating a barrier that would have a negative impact on all three of them.

ILLUSTRATING THE LESSON

We should act in faith and seek reconciliation and restoration when necessary.

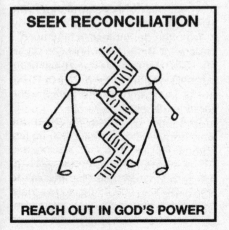

CONCLUDING THE LESSON

In our fallen world, we often live with broken relationships. We face choices just like the father and the older brother. We can choose to continue a broken relationship or seek reconciliation. Our faith in Christ should lead us to take the lead in seeking reconciliation, even if the problem is not our fault.

Who is someone with whom you need to reconcile? (Allow your learners to reflect on this question.) Perhaps the problem between you and this person has only recently surfaced. Or maybe it has festered for years. Either way, let us determine to act in faith to seek reconciliation.

The Scripture gives an important principle in Matthew 5:23-24. "Therefore if thou bring thy gift to the altar, and there rememberest that thy brother hath ought against thee; leave there thy gift . . . first be reconciled to thy brother, and then come and offer thy gift."

We cannot wait for the person to come to us. We must take the first step, or we may never experience restoration. Before we approach the person, we must make sure we have forgiven him or her unconditionally. Will the person always respond positively? No, but we are still obligated to seek reconciliation. (Allow your learners to spend a couple of minutes in prayer forgiving the person and asking for strength to seek reconciliation.)

ANTICIPATING THE NEXT LESSON

Next week's lesson examines Jesus' parable of the vineyard owner from Matthew 20:1-16. God is generous to all who faithfully serve Him in His kingdom. His rewards are based on His own grace and generosity, and not on what we have earned. We should receive whatever rewards our heavenly Father bestows on us with gratitude and thanksgiving

—*Don Anderson.*

PRACTICAL POINTS

1. Affluence absent spiritual discernment often leads to a squandering of it all (Luke 15:11-13).
2. The world is a cruel place to those who have foolishly lost everything (vss. 14-16).
3. Sometimes we have to hit bottom before we wise up (vs. 17).
4. We try to bargain with God; He wants to show us His grace (vss. 18-20).
5. We really are not worthy to be called God's children; thankfully, it does not depend on that (vss. 21-22).
6. We should join heaven in celebrating every time a lost sinner is found (vss. 23-24).

—Kenneth A. Sponsler.

RESEARCH AND DISCUSSION

1. Why did the father agree to such an offensive and unprecedented request (Luke 15:12)? What does this tell us about God and His dealings with us?
2. Why is the allure of a far country and wild living so strong for many young people (vs. 13)? Could the father have done anything to allay it?
3. Everyone suffers in a famine. Why was it especially hard on the wayward son (vss. 14-16)?
4. Do you think the son was sincere in his plan to confess sinning against his father and heaven (vss. 18-19)? Why or why not?
5. Why was such an extravagant celebration appropriate for the wayward son's empty-handed return after wasting his father's money (vss. 22-24)? How does this apply to us?

—Kenneth A. Sponsler.

ILLUSTRATED HIGH POINTS

A certain man had two sons (Luke 15:11)

I once worked as a Bible salesperson. Striving to master the role, I studied the features of many Bibles. When a customer came to my counter, I would ply him with the amazing features of the seven or eight Bibles that lay before him. To my dismay, most customers walked away dumbfounded. The problem? Too many choices! I soon learned to show customers only two Bibles, limiting their choices.

In philosophy, there is a principle called Hobson's choice. It takes its name from Charles Hobson, an English liveryman who told his customers that they could either ride the horse nearest the stable door or not ride at all—it was their choice.

Unlike Mr. Hobson, God is gracious in His limitation of choice. We should choose the Lord over spiritual death (cf. Deut. 30:19).

Filled his belly with the husks (vs. 16)

The younger son took his father's hard-earned inheritance for granted. He wasted it, and in Luke 15:14, he found himself "in want." This was the beginning of his salvation (cf. Ps. 107:9; Matt. 5:6).

We often do not realize how hungry we are for the true Bread from Heaven—God Himself. We have been filling our bellies with pig food. These carob husks (indicated by the Greek word *keration,* "husks") were cheap and in abundance. Once the carob seeds were removed, the husks became a fibrous pig slop.

The world around us is brimming with advice and diversions, but it is all pig slop compared to the Father's bread (cf. Isa. 55:2; Luke 1:53; John 6:27).

—Therese Greenberg.

Golden Text Illuminated

"This my son was dead, and is alive again; he was lost, and is found" (Luke 15:24).

In 1961, the world was stunned when the Berlin Wall was erected. After World War II, Germany had been split into four sections, each controlled by a different country. While the West offered freedom, the Soviet Union tightened its grip. Germany was divided into East and West. The city of Berlin was divided by a barrier that could not be crossed. Many who tried to cross were killed.

For decades, this remained the status quo. During that time, families were torn apart. Relatives on one side were not permitted to see their loved ones on the other side. Children grew up with the reality of this barricade that closed them off from precious relatives known only through stories told by their elders.

When the Berlin Wall was torn down, those who had been forcibly divided were reunited. Grandchildren were able to meet grandparents for the first time, and parents were able to meet their children's spouses. People cheered as the last remnants fell. For Germans, this did not merely represent the ousting of an oppressive system. It enabled the process of reconciliation as people were brought back together.

In the same way, sin creates a barrier between God and us. When sin initially creeps into our lives, we may not think much about it. Often we rationalize it: "It is only just this one time." That sin seems small and insignificant.

However, sin grows swiftly. Just as the Berlin Wall was initially erected section by section, so a wall is built up in our souls. In a short time, we discover that our prayer lives are lacking and our walk has grown stale. We are trapped by the barrier. No matter how we attempt to get around it, sin becomes an impenetrable wall that blocks our path to Him. All access has been cut off. Our sin has separated us from Him (Isa. 59:2).

As the families separated by the Berlin Wall longed to be reunited, so our Father yearns for us. When the sin wall went up, His family was torn apart. We are the relatives on the other side whom He misses. His desire to be with us never wanes. And, like the father from this week's passage, He eagerly awaits our return (Luke 15:20).

However, His righteousness is such that there can be no sin in His presence. Thus, we are unable to break down the sin wall by our own volition. No matter how we try, we cannot breach that barrier.

That is where Jesus comes into the story. His death changed that. The sin wall was not just broken but abolished. No trace of it remains (Eph. 2:14). The barrier that separated us from God is no longer standing, enabling Him to call us His people again (Hos. 2:23).

When we turn to God and become reconciled to Him, there is nothing that can separate us from His love through Christ (Rom. 8:38-39). His Word tells us that there is great joy in being reconciled to God (5:10-11). Even the angels rejoice (Luke 15:7).

We have a Heavenly Father who wants to shower us with His love. Sadly for us, sin gets in our way. The great news is that He does not condemn us when we come to Him, because Jesus tore down the wall (Rom. 8:1). We can look with joy to a glorious reunion with our Father, knowing that the barrier no longer stands. How wonderful it is that Christ reconciled us!

—*Jennifer Lautermilch.*

Heart of the Lesson

Most of us can tell a lost-and-found story. No matter what it was that was lost—whether a prized possession, a well-loved pet, or even a roaming child—there is great joy when the lost is found. Today's lesson is a magnificent lost-and-found story. Jesus told a parable that, among other things, illustrates the joy that fills heaven when a lost person repents and is found.

1. An ungrateful son and a gracious father (Luke 15:11-12). How shocking that a son would ask his father for his inheritance! In effect, he was saying, "I wish you were dead." Here was a young man who had been fed, clothed, and housed by his loving father; yet the young man was not satisfied. He wanted to be independent of the father and be his own boss, so he asked for his share early. And the father gave it to him—not because he had to or because the son deserved it—but because he understood (like all wise fathers) that some people must learn the lessons of life the hard way. Our Heavenly Father is all-wise. He always acts in ways that are for the ultimate good of His people. He could force us to obey Him, but He does not. In His wisdom He often allows us to "go our own way."

2. A sinful son and a watching father (Luke 15:13-20). Taking his newly inherited wealth, the young man headed for a far country, where he was free to do what he wanted when he wanted without any interference from his father, family, or friends. He spent all that he had on riotous living, so when famine came he was reduced to feeding pigs and wishing he could eat with them. He found the often-quoted adage very true: "Sin will take you farther than you want to go, keep you longer than you want to stay, and cost you more than you want to pay."

Then he remembered his father. He remembered his father's previous provision, protection, grace, and mercy. Although he was far from home, the lessons learned at home were not far from him. This is a reminder to parents that children may stray from what we teach them, but they will never be able to forget what we taught them (cf. Deut. 6:1-7; Prov. 22:6).

Having come to himself, the young man recognized his foolishness and his sin. He decided that it would be better to be a servant in his father's household than to continue in the life he had chosen. So he prepared his speech and headed for home. While he was still "a great way off" (Luke 15:20), his father, who had been watching and waiting since his departure, saw him and in compassion ran to greet his sinful son.

3. A repentant son and a forgiving father (Luke 15:21-24). The repentant son humbly began his prepared speech, expressing his willingness to suffer the consequences of his sin. But the father would not have that. Instead, he interrupted him in the middle of his speech and called the servants to bring the best that he had and to plan a party for his son who had been dead but was now alive again.

How ready our Heavenly Father is to reconcile with those who will humbly repent! He knows our hearts. He perceives the true intent of our actions and is eager to give us His best. Be reconciled to God and rejoice (cf. II Cor. 5:17-21)!

—Don Kakavecos.

World Missions

In some cultures, the group is valued over the individual, and the characteristics that make up the American dream are considered selfish and undesired. It is selfish to leave your family and neighborhood situation wanting more, for that is condemning or judging those you would leave behind. To strive for better is to criticize your family line or to reach outside a thousand-year-old caste system; who would be arrogant enough to do that? To work harder only brings criticism and possibly demotion, for hard workers make the others look bad.

The Jewish culture of Jesus' time was more like those group cultures than our Western culture. Those hearing the story of the prodigal son were surely horrified at the idea of a son asking for his inheritance before the father died, especially the younger son. To do so was to reject the father and his legacy and remove himself from his place in the family. Jesus' listeners that day likely empathized with the older brother's feelings.

That is important to note when reading this story or using it in other cultures. The prodigal son dishonored his family and harmed their place in the fabric of society. For the father to run and embrace him and accept him home was extremely unusual. This likely would have been an unexpected twist in the story not contemplated by those in attendance.

Although this story tells about two sons, it is really about the father. The father wanted his family to be whole and to rejoice. To accomplish that, he welcomed home the son who had wandered and spent all. Then he also went to find the older brother, whose heart had wandered even though he had never physically walked away.

The father wanted them both to rejoice—both the one who felt grief and regret and the one who felt anger and bitterness. Each needed to take the focus off himself, turn from the direction he was going, and come to the father. It is interesting how each son, when talking with the father, was primarily worried about himself. Had they focused on the father, they would have found his goodness and grace, ready and available for each of them.

When we read this story, we likely think of each person individually within the story. Others may see the story as a whole and the family as one entity, with each person's actions affecting the whole. God wants to restore whole families. Each individual within the whole must make the choice himself; and if he does, the entire group can choose to come to Christ as a unit. This happens in many cultures today and happened several times in the New Testament (see passages in which a person and his house were saved).

We should think of the family of God as a whole as well. The family of God as a unit should be a more important priority to us than the individual. If we look at God's desire for the world's salvation from that perspective, it may change our outreach strategy. We, like the servants in the story, will not only gladly get the robe and ring for the redeemed prodigal but also go into the field to call the others in to celebrate. We will want to keep the whole family of God a priority and help individuals find their place in it as they enjoy the goodness of the loving and kind Father.

—Kimberly Rae.

The Jewish Aspect

When the prodigal son obtained a job that required him to "feed swine" (Luke 15:15), he had sunk about as low as a Jewish person could go. Ancient Jews abhorred the pig and everything connected with it. That same attitude continues among contemporary Jews who observe kosher standards.

The Mosaic Law twice specified the pig as being unclean and prohibited from the Jewish diet (Lev. 11:7; Deut. 14:8). Exactly why God chose some animals to be clean and others unclean has been debated among both Jews and Christians.

Some suggest that the unclean animals were forbidden because of health reasons. No evidence exists, however, that all forbidden foods were unhealthy. Others have thought that the prohibitions came because of utilitarian reasons. The camel, for example, is better fit as a beast of burden rather than for food. No evidence exists, however, that Jews ever thought such reasons existed. Another suggests that the "basic reason for kosher rules is for a person to cultivate the value that 'you can't eat everything'" ("Kosher Laws and Health"). The reality is that this is always the case, no matter what a person's diet is.

"The only hint or clue that the Biblical text itself provides as to the reason for all these regulations is that in almost every instance where the food laws are referred to in the Torah, we find a call to holiness" (Donin, *To Be A Jew,* Basic Books). God wanted His people to be distinct from all others. The "short answer to why Jews observe these laws is: because the Torah says so. The Torah does not specify any reason for these laws, and for a Torah-observant, traditional Jew, there is no need for any other reason" ("Kashrut: Jewish Dietary Laws").

In biblical times Jews clearly regarded pigs as unclean. They did not touch them and also avoided contact with Gentiles who raised them. Jewish teachers forbade raising pigs anywhere (*Mishneh Torah,* Laws of Property Damages 5:9).

The Talmud states that Jews refused to call pigs by name, referring to them by the term "another thing" (*Shabbat* 129a). They also had strong feelings concerning what they perceived as detrimental effects of pigs. In explaining the origin and extent of many items in the world, it also asserts that "[forty pints] of sores descended to the world: nine were taken by swine" (*Kiddushin* 49b). Jews regarded the curse of sores in the world to be centered in pigs. Coming in contact with a pig, therefore, exposed a Jew to contamination and illness.

Since pigs wallow in the muck, ancient Jews considered them filthy animals. The Talmud declares that "the snout of a pig is like manure" (*Berachoth* 25a). The Jewish scholar Maimonedes (A.D. 1135–1204) said that if Jews ate "swine's flesh, the streets and houses would be more dirty than any cesspool" (*Guide for the Perplexed* 3.48).

Modern Jews do not usually hold such extreme thoughts, but observant Jews continue to practice kosher regulations. Diet is critical because rabbinic teaching through the years has emphasized that the dinner table has replaced the temple altar. As a result, observant Jews diligently abide by a strict diet. While their efforts are well intentioned, they miss the deeper issues of heart cleanness leading to spiritual life, which comes only through the Messiah, Jesus Christ.

—R. Larry Overstreet.

Guiding the Superintendent

"When the now-famous poet Elizabeth Barrett became the wife of Robert Browning, her parents disowned her because they disapproved of the marriage. Their daughter Elizabeth, however, wrote almost every week, telling them that she loved them and longed for a reconciliation.

"After 10 years, she received a huge box in the mail that contained all the notes she had sent. Not one had been opened! Although these 'love letters' have now become a precious part of classical English literature, it's really sad to think that they were never read by Elizabeth Barrett's own parents. Had they looked at just one, the broken relationship with their daughter might have been healed" ("When The Now-famous Poet Elizabeth Barrett Became . . .").

In this week's lesson, we learn of a happy ending to a broken relationship.

DEVOTIONAL OUTLINE

1. A son's selfish departure (Luke 15:11-13). A father had two sons. The younger son asked his father to allow him to receive his inheritance early. The father agreed with the younger son's request and gave him his portion of the inheritance. Several days later, the son left his father's house and traveled to a region that was far removed from any family interference. There the younger son expended all of his material resources on an extravagant and sensual lifestyle.

2. A son's sensible decision (Luke 15:14-19). In the midst of his excessive and sensual living, the younger son experienced a devastating turn of events. A severe famine shrouded the land, and the young man sought employment to meet his needs. He was hired as a swineherd, the vilest and most degrading employment that a Jewish person could engage in.

Alone and with no one to pity him, the younger son survived by eating the only food he could find—the same food he was feeding to the swine. While doing so, he resolved to return to his father's house and confess that he had made a selfish decision to leave.

3. A son's sorrowful declaration (Luke 15:20-24). The son's father compassionately embraced him, showered him with loving affection, and listened to his confession. The father then clothed his son with the best raiment, expressed his favor and affection to him, and honored his son's return with a joyous celebration.

AGE-GROUP EMPHASES

Children: Children thoroughly enjoy attending parties. Their youthful innocence revels in these times of celebration and energetic joy. You may consider holding a celebration in Sunday school and using it as an example of the joy and love that Jesus has for His children.

Youths: Young people often believe they are invincible. As a result, they often engage in impulsive behavior that can have miserable consequences. Remind your young people that as followers of Jesus Christ, they have committed to live righteous lives that will result in celebration and joy.

Adults: Some of your adults may be experiencing the emotional pain of their children's hasty and irresponsible decision making. Whether their children remain at home or have left to "find their own way," parents know the strength and faith it takes to commit the welfare of their children to the Lord. Encourage your adults by reminding them that their hearts can be filled with hope, believing that Jesus Christ will never abandon His loving pursuit of His children.

—*Thomas R. Chmura.*

SCRIPTURE LESSON TEXT

MATT. 20:1 For the kingdom of heaven is like unto a man *that is* an householder, which went out early in the morning to hire labourers into his vineyard.

2 And when he had agreed with the labourers for a penny a day, he sent them into his vineyard.

3 And he went out about the third hour, and saw others standing idle in the marketplace,

4 And said unto them; Go ye also into the vineyard, and whatsoever is right I will give you. And they went their way.

5 Again he went out about the sixth and ninth hour, and did likewise.

6 And about the eleventh hour he went out, and found others standing idle, and saith unto them, Why stand ye here all the day idle?

7 They say unto him, Because no man hath hired us. He saith unto them, Go ye also into the vineyard; and whatsoever is right, *that* shall ye receive.

8 So when even was come, the lord of the vineyard saith unto his steward, Call the labourers, and give them *their* hire, beginning from the last unto the first.

9 And when they came that *were hired* about the eleventh hour, they received every man a penny.

10 But when the first came, they supposed that they should have received more; and they likewise received every man a penny.

11 And when they had received *it,* they murmured against the goodman of the house,

12 Saying, These last have wrought *but* one hour, and thou hast made them equal unto us, which have borne the burden and heat of the day.

13 But he answered one of them, and said, Friend, I do thee no wrong: didst not thou agree with me for a penny?

14 Take *that* thine *is,* and go thy way: I will give unto this last, even as unto thee.

15 Is it not lawful for me to do what I will with mine own? Is thine eye evil, because I am good?

16 So the last shall be first, and the first last: for many be called, but few chosen.

NOTES

God's Gracious Rewards

Lesson Text: Matthew 20:1-16

Related Scriptures: Matthew 19:16-30; 20:20-28; Luke 13:22-30

TIME: A.D. 30   PLACE: Perea

GOLDEN TEXT—"[The man] said unto them; Go ye also into the vineyard, and whatsoever is right I will give you. And they went their way" (Matthew 20:4).

Introduction

Jesus took pictures from everyday life to help His hearers understand how God works with people. By using familiar things in life, Jesus enabled a wide range of people to comprehend the truth that He wanted them to learn.

The parable of the laborers in the vineyard teaches that what we receive from God is due solely to His grace. The teaching of the Pharisees was that people could earn God's favor by their righteous deeds. Jesus' story demonstrated that God compensates people according to His own goodness.

When the laborers who had toiled the full day complained that they should receive more than those who had worked for only a short time, the owner answered them. They had received what they were promised. As the owner, he could treat others graciously if he so chose.

LESSON OUTLINE

I. **CALL TO THE LABORERS—Matt. 20:1-7**

II. **COMPENSATION FOR THE LABORERS—Matt. 20:8-10**

III. **COMPLAINT BY THE LABORERS—Matt. 20:11-16**

Exposition: Verse by Verse

CALL TO THE LABORERS

MATT. 20:1 For the kingdom of heaven is like unto a man that is an householder, which went out early in the morning to hire labourers into his vineyard.

2 And when he had agreed with the labourers for a penny a day, he sent them into his vineyard.

3 And he went out about the third hour, and saw others standing idle in the marketplace,

4 And said unto them; Go ye also into the vineyard, and whatsoever is right I will give you. And they went their way.

5 Again he went out about the sixth and ninth hour, and did likewise.

6 And about the eleventh hour he went out, and found others standing

idle, and saith unto them, Why stand ye here all the day idle?

7 They say unto him, Because no man hath hired us. He saith unto them, Go ye also into the vineyard; and whatsoever is right, that shall ye receive.

First shift of laborers (Matt. 20:1-2). The Gospel of Matthew contains numerous parables that Jesus used in His teaching ministry. {Just as a preacher will use stories to illustrate spiritual principles, so Jesus used parables to clarify what He was teaching.}Q1 Many of the parables began, "For the kingdom of heaven is like. . . ." These stories describe what is involved in living under God's rule. God orders His kingdom by different priorities and values than those of human governments.

Parables employ familiar imagery, but they are not typically real-life examples of what actually happened. Instead, they are stories that were especially composed to teach lessons. In an allegory most of the details have specific meanings, but a parable usually illustrates one principle or truth. To interpret a parable properly, we need to determine the main idea that Jesus was endeavoring to communicate.

The parable in this passage tells of a man who owned a large vineyard. At harvesttime he needed a number of laborers to pick the grapes. In Israel there were always people who did not have permanent, full-time employment. These people would hire themselves out as day laborers. If an employer needed day laborers, he would go to the marketplace, where potential workers would gather, hoping to gain work.

{The man went out early in the morning to get the workers he needed to harvest his grapes. The standard wage for work like this was a "penny" (vs. 2), or a denarius, per day. The man and the laborers agreed to these terms, and he sent them into the vineyard at the beginning of the workday, which was about six o'clock in the morning.}Q2

Second shift of laborers (Matt. 20:3-4). After a few hours, the man realized that he needed more laborers to get the harvest completed. Ripe grapes do not stay good for long, especially in a hot climate like that in Israel; so the work had to be done quickly. The landowner thus went back to the marketplace to hire some more workers around the third hour, or nine o'clock. {He found some men there who were willing to work. Instead of agreeing on a set wage for them, the man promised to give them whatever was right.}Q3 Probably laborers assumed that they would get a fraction of a denarius relative to how much of the day they worked. With only this vague promise from the owner, they went to the vineyard and began their work.

Third and fourth shifts of laborers (Matt. 20:5). As the workday went on, the owner became more and more intent on getting the harvest completed. {At noon and then again at three o'clock in the afternoon, he went back to the marketplace to get more workers.}Q4 Each time, he found more available laborers to join those already in the vineyard.

With these later shifts of laborers, the owner made the same vague agreement that he had made with the second shift. He simply promised to do what was right for them. Apparently satisfied with these terms and trusting the judgment of the owner, the workers proceeded to join those who had been toiling in the vineyard since the early morning.

Final shift of laborers (Matt. 20:6-7). The workday in ancient Israel ended around six o'clock in the evening. Just one hour before the end of the day, the owner recruited a final shift of workers. We do not know what these people had been doing, but no one had hired them. They too joined the rest of the laborers.

Once again, the owner did not set a specific wage for them. No doubt they supposed that they would get only a small compensation for one hour's work; nevertheless, they trusted him to give them whatever was right.

During the last hour of the day, then, some workers were just beginning their labor. Others had worked for a few hours or since early morning. All of the laborers were involved in getting the owner's grapes harvested. All expected that he would pay them what they had agreed on—either a denarius or what the owner determined was right.

COMPENSATION FOR THE LABORERS

8 So when even was come, the lord of the vineyard saith unto his steward, Call the labourers, and give them their hire, beginning from the last unto the first.

9 And when they came that were hired about the eleventh hour, they received every man a penny.

10 But when the first came, they supposed that they should have received more; and they likewise received every man a penny.

Procedure for wages (Matt. 20:8). The Old Testament law was careful to protect both the employer and the employee. The owner could expect to receive the full amount of labor agreed upon. The laborer was entitled to receive the full wage for which he had contracted. In addition, the law required that the wage be paid on the evening of the day that the laborer had worked (Lev. 19:13; Deut. 24:14-15).

Because typical day laborers were poor, they had no savings to fall back on. If the owner waited until the next day to pay them, he could be depriving them and their families of their evening meal. God's law prohibited the employer from exploiting his workers in this way.

{When evening came, the owner gave his steward specific instructions about paying the laborers. The fact that they were to be paid was expected. The manner in which they were paid, beginning with those hired last, was almost certainly different from the norm.}[Q5] The amount they would be paid would be totally unprecedented. This was a payday that was certain to be remembered by all the workers.

Payment to the final shift (Matt. 20:9). The first group to be paid were those who had begun last. Their work had started at the eleventh hour; so they had labored in the vineyard for only about an hour.

When the owner had hired them, he had not quoted them a particular wage. He had told them only that they would receive whatever was right. No doubt they were prepared to receive about one-twelfth of a denarius, because that would be the proportional rate for their labor. That small amount would be better than nothing at all, but it would hardly provide an adequate meal for an individual and would certainly not be sufficient for an entire family.

{When the last shift of workers came to the steward, they were amazed at the wage that they received. The owner had authorized them to get a full day's wage, a denarius.}[Q6] This was the same amount that those who worked all day had contracted to receive. The full denarius was twelve times what they expected—or deserved.

The owner had compensated them according to his goodness, not according to what they had earned. The ample payment to the later shifts demonstrated his generosity. It was a measure of his grace and kindness to those who were undeserving.

Payment to the first shift (Matt. 20:10). The parable turns from the payment of the last shift to the payment of the first shift of workers. They knew what the group that had worked for only one hour had received. As they came before the steward, they reasoned that they would certainly receive more than one denarius. After all, it was only just that those who had labored all day should be paid more than those who had worked for just one hour.

{If the last shift had been surprised to get a full denarius, the first shift was stunned by receiving the same amount. The steward gave to them exactly what they had agreed to as a wage, no less and no more. Although in their own minds they supposed that they would receive more than the wages they had agreed to, that was not in fact the case. Their wage was the same as that of all the other workers, the one denarius for which they had contracted.}[Q7]

COMPLAINT BY THE LABORERS

11 And when they had received it, they murmured against the goodman of the house,

12 Saying, These last have wrought but one hour, and thou hast made them equal unto us, which have borne the burden and heat of the day.

13 But he answered one of them, and said, Friend, I do thee no wrong: didst not thou agree with me for a penny?

14 Take that thine is, and go thy way: I will give unto this last, even as unto thee.

15 Is it not lawful for me to do what I will with mine own? Is thine eye evil, because I am good?

16 So the last shall be first, and the first last: for many be called, but few chosen.

Charge of unfairness (Matt. 20:11-12). Even though the first shift of laborers had received exactly what they had agreed to for their wage, they began to grumble. They knew that the workers who had started later in the day had

received much more per hour than they had. To their way of thinking, it seemed only right that they should be paid a bonus beyond what their contract called for. If the last workers received one denarius for one hour's work, certainly they deserved to receive more than a denarius for twelve hours of labor.

Their complaint was that the owner was being unjust to them. By paying those who had worked just one hour the same wage as those who had labored all day, the owner had made the two groups equal. To compound the supposed injustice, the first shift had toiled throughout the heat of the day, but the last shift had begun and ended their work in the cooler evening breeze. The first shift's work had been much longer and much more arduous than what the last shift had endured.

{The earlier workers were offended that the latecomers were treated as well as they. Instead of rejoicing for the others, they insisted that those who had worked just one hour had no right to be compensated as the owner had determined. Consequently, those who had labored all day began to criticize the owner, accusing him of being unjust and unfair in his dealings.}[Q8]

Choice of grace (Matt. 20:13-14). The owner was not intimidated by the murmuring of the laborers. On the other hand, he was not angry with them either. His answer to them centered upon some basic facts and principles that they needed to digest.

{Apparently the owner took one of the first-shift workers aside to talk with him. He addressed him as a friend, a term that implied a kind response rather than an angry retort. The charge that the workers had made against the owner was of injustice; so he began at that point as he talked with the laborer. He stated firmly, "I do thee no wrong" (vs. 13). The first workers had agreed to work in the vineyard for a penny, or a denarius. That was precisely what they had been paid. This was not a case of an unjust owner failing to pay the contracted wage.}[Q9]

Because they had received the complete wage to which they had agreed, their charge of injustice could not be sustained. The owner had not defrauded them at all. He urged the worker to take his denarius and go his way rather than complain about it.

The owner then reaffirmed what he had done for the last workers. He had indeed determined to give to them the same wage he had given to the first workers he had hired. That was his instruction to the steward, and that decision would stand despite the murmuring and grumbling by the first workers.

Challenge to gratitude (Matt. 20:15-16). The first workers spoke in terms of justice, but the owner gave in terms of grace. His resources belonged to him, and he had the right to dispense them as he pleased. If the owner, in his goodness, chose to give to some workers more than what they deserved, that was his choice to make.

By their grumbling, the first workers were in effect saying that the owner was wrong for showing grace to others. In reality, they themselves were at fault. The fact that the last shift received the full denarius, just as the first shift did, caused the first-shift workers to become jealous. They had received all that they had agreed to, but they felt that others who came later did not deserve to get the same payment. By begrudging the grace shown to others, the laborers demonstrated a selfish, evil attitude that contrasted with the heart of the owner.

Jesus concluded the parable with the important lesson the story illustrated: "So the last shall be first, and the first last" (vs. 16). Peter had just asked what the disciples could expect to receive as compensation for forsaking all and following Jesus (19:27). This parable may have been intended to reinforce Jesus' assurances that we can trust Him to be abundant in blessings, providing for us far more even than we could possibly deserve (cf. vss. 28-30).

{The parable reminded the disciples that while there is reward for faithful service to God, they must not think about it in strictly human terms. Rather, God gives freely according to His grace. In His kingdom the Lord blesses according to His pleasure, not necessarily according to what we humans think we deserve.}[Q10]

—Daniel J. Estes.

QUESTIONS

1. Why did Jesus use parables as He described what the kingdom of heaven is like?

2. What agreement did the owner make with the first shift of workers?

3. How did the agreement with the later shifts differ from that with the first shift?

4. At what times of the day did the owner recruit workers?

5. How did the owner instruct the steward to pay the workers?

6. Why was the final shift of workers surprised at their wages?

7. Why were the first workers disappointed when they received their wages?

8. Why did the first workers murmur against the owner?

9. How did the owner show that their charge of injustice was not justified?

10. How does the parable illustrate God's grace to people?

—Daniel J. Estes.

Preparing to Teach the Lesson

Jesus taught many great lessons with parables. In the parable of the laborers in the vineyard, we learn of God's sovereign grace in giving rewards.

TODAY'S AIM

Facts: to investigate and interpret Jesus' parable of the laborers in the vineyard.

Principle: to teach that God sovereignly rewards according to His grace, not according to human standards.

Application: to help students appreciate and accept the actions of their sovereign God.

INTRODUCING THE LESSON

Bill was hired in 1969. His benefit package was generous and comprehensive. Medical and dental insurance was included, along with a pension plan that was entirely paid for by the company.

Steve was hired by the same company in 1994. The John Doe Company was still a good employer. The hourly wage offered was competitive in the industry, but Steve was not offered the same generous benefit package that earlier workers had received. Competition had grown stronger. Downsizing had occurred. The union had been forced to make concessions. New workers had to pick up a portion of their health insurance premium. Vacations were shorter, and the pension plan was dropped altogether.

Some of the newer workers envied their older colleagues, but there was nothing they could do. They knew what they would receive when they were hired. What other workers had received in the past had nothing to do with the newer workers' terms of employment. The parable in this week's lesson presents an interesting twist on this believable scenario.

DEVELOPING THE LESSON

1. Workers hired (Matt. 20:1-2). Read 19:16-30 to gain a sense of context for the lesson. After the incident with the rich young man, Jesus had been discussing rewards with His disciples. This led Him to offer the parable. Matthew was true to his purpose in reminding us that Jesus' words related to the kingdom of heaven.

Ripe fruit must be harvested immediately. The householder in Jesus' parable suddenly had an abundance of ripe fruit that needed to be taken care of. Nowadays there are temporary job services available to employers who need short-term help. In Jesus' day a man in need of workers would go to the marketplace.

The word translated "penny" in the Authorized Version is *denarius*. A denarius was the normal pay for a day's work in Palestine at that time. No worker objected to the rate of pay at the time of hiring.

2. More workers hired (Matt. 20:3-7). The crop of grapes must have been very good, for the householder went back to recruit more workers at 9:00 A.M., noon, 3:00 P.M., and 5:00 P.M. The workers hired at 5:00 P.M. had to work only one hour. The landowner had not agreed to pay these later workers a denarius. He had simply said that he would pay them "whatsoever is right."

3. The workers paid (Matt. 20:8-9). The householder had promised the later workers fair payment. Imagine how pleasantly surprised the later workers were when they received a full day's wage for just a few hours work. This generous action illustrates God's grace. The workers who started at 5:00 P.M. did not deserve to be paid for a full day, but they were paid a day's wage anyway. Notice that nobody complained about being paid too much!

4. Some workers complain (Matt. 20:10-12). The first workers expected more when they saw how generous the employer had been with the latecomers. Class members will be able to identify with the disappointment of those people. Perhaps someone in the class can share a similar experience. On the surface, the original workers had a point. They had worked harder and longer than the men hired later and had been paid the same.

5. The householder's response (Matt. 20:13-16). Explain that verse 13 is a key to understanding the parable. The original workers had agreed to a certain amount and were satisfied to work for that amount when they were hired. The householder had lived up to his agreement with them. The later workers had not agreed to any set amount. They had simply trusted the householder to give them what was right. Their faith in the man had been generously rewarded.

God's grace and sovereignty are illustrated by the statement made in Matthew 20:14. God is not accountable to men. Men are accountable to God. God has a right to extend His grace to whomsoever He will. The later workers did not deserve to be so well paid, but the householder was certainly within his rights to pay them anything he wanted. Discuss the implications of this.

In verse 15, the householder asked, "Is thine eye evil, because I am good?" In what sense were the complaining workers in the wrong? They were envious of others. They were suggesting that the householder was being unfair when he was not. God is not unjust because He exercises His sovereignty in the affairs of people. He is God!

One writer summed up his comments on these verses with these words: "God is the One before whom all accounts will be settled. Many who have prominent places will someday find themselves demoted. And many who often find themselves at the end of the line will find themselves promoted to the head of the line" (Walvoord and Zuck, eds., *The Bible Knowledge Commentary,* Victor).

ILLUSTRATING THE LESSON

The visual aid depicts the main idea conveyed by Jesus' parable—that God's rewards are based solely on His grace and sovereignty, not on human standards.

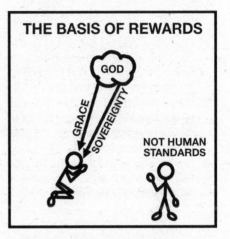

THE BASIS OF REWARDS

GOD

GRACE SOVEREIGNTY

NOT HUMAN STANDARDS

CONCLUDING THE LESSON

God's ways are not our ways. There are many things that God does that we do not understand. We should remember that God is sovereign and gracious. He is just and faithful in keeping His promises. He also is a gracious rewarder of those who put their trust in Him.

As Christians, it is not our place to murmur at God's judgments or to be envious of those who seem to be more blessed than ourselves. We should worship our sovereign God and trust Him to always do what is right.

ANTICIPATING THE NEXT LESSON

Next week is our final lesson for this quarter. It deals with Jesus' parable of the Pharisee and the tax collector from Luke 18:9-14.

—*Bruce A. Tanner.*

PRACTICAL POINTS

1. It is the privilege of every Christian to be sent forth to labor for the Lord (Matt. 20:1-2).
2. We can be sure that our faithful service will be rewarded by the Lord (vss. 3-5).
3. Diligent, faithful service should characterize every Christian, regardless of his age or circumstances (vss. 6-7).
4. God's rewards are not based on the outward, superficial standards by which people often judge one another; He looks on the heart (vss. 8-13).
5. When we truly grasp the fact that all the blessings we enjoy are gifts of God's grace, there will be less place for envy (vss. 14-15).
6. It is senseless to follow the world's self-centered ways; they do not reflect the values of God (vs. 16).

—Jarl K. Waggoner.

RESEARCH AND DISCUSSION

1. What did all the vineyard workers in Jesus' parable have in common (Matt. 20:2-7)? How did they differ?
2. Does Jesus' parable suggest that our commonly held ideas about "fairness" are flawed (vss. 8-12)? Explain.
3. Are God's rewards for service exactly the same for all His children? Explain.
4. How should a Christian view his labor for the Lord and the Lord's rewards for such labor (vss. 13-15)?
5. In what ways can you illustrate the spiritual principle that "the last shall be first, and the first last" (vs. 16)?

—Jarl K. Waggoner.

ILLUSTRATED HIGH POINTS

Into his vineyard (Matt. 20:1)

"It is not wrong to work," said the pastor. "The Lord wants us to be faithful in the work we do."

Sitting in the congregation was John, a middle-aged, unmarried man who was having a difficult time at his place of employment. John was a cook in a local restaurant. He enjoyed his job and had a good relationship with the other employees.

John's workload had recently doubled when one of the cooks decided to quit and take a job elsewhere. Within a few days, a man who had little experience in cooking was hired as a cook. He started at the same pay level as John. At first, John was going to quit his job. After thinking about it, though, he decided to stay.

John told a friend, "I like my job, and I am getting paid well to do it. Why should I be concerned and upset about what someone else is paid? My responsibility is to do my work to the very best of my ability. The Lord will take care of me."

The last shall be first (vs. 16)

A church missionary committee was discussing raising support for several missionaries. One committee member was a retired missionary who had spent fifty years in missions. Each one spoke of the missionary he would like to see get an increase. Descriptive phrases such as "nice personality," "neat dresser," "very amusing," "good slides," and "good storyteller" were heard.

Finally, the elderly missionary spoke. "I have been a missionary for many years," she said. "I have seen lots of them come and go. I have learned that you cannot determine quality by what you have mentioned here today."

—V. Ben Kendrick.

Golden Text Illuminated

"[The man] said unto them; Go ye also into the vineyard, and whatsoever is right I will give you. And they went their way" (Matthew 20:4).

The Parable of the Laborers in the Vineyard has always provoked much comment. It has much to teach us about how God's ways are higher than our ways. Our golden text focuses on one of the ways this truth should affect our behavior.

After hiring some workers for his vineyard at the start of the day, the employer in the parable finds about three hours later that there are "others standing idle" (vs. 3), and so he hires them as well. The key part of the verse concerns the wages for these new workers. Instead of specifying how much they would receive, as he did with his initial hires, he simply says he will give them "whatsoever is right."

What this points to is one of the foundational teachings of Scripture—that we are to live our lives by faith in God. And this particular parable emphasizes that this faith includes trust in God's goodness.

We are not told why the laborers so readily agreed to the indefinite terms set forth by the employer. The parables of the New Testament are not meant to answer every question like that. We can imagine that they might have been living from day to day and would have been desperate. And perhaps the employer had a reputation for fairness. But whatever we may read into the story, the fact remains that the laborers agreed to the terms.

The vital nature of trusting in God's goodness is a recurring theme of Christ's teaching. In the Parable of the Talents (Matt. 25:14-30), the "unprofitable servant" is thrown "into outer darkness" because he buried His master's money instead of using it to gain more for him. When he was asked for an explanation of his behavior, he said, "I knew thee that thou art an hard man, . . . and I was afraid."

While it is true that this parable does not explicitly say what the master's character was, it is pretty clear he stands for God. With his perception of what the master [substitute with God] was like, he would not serve him. He was punished as one who lacked faith in God.

Returning to this week's parable of the vineyard, we can put ourselves in the laborers' place and imagine being a bit skeptical about this unspecified payment the employer announces. In this fallen world, we can imagine the vineyard owner deciding to give these latecomers next to nothing when the end of the day came.

By trusting in the fairness of the employer (who can again stand for God) these latecomers to the vineyard (which stands for the kingdom of God) would enjoy the same benefits as those who were hired at the start.

At the heart of God's goodness is His grace. If we fail to understand that what we receive from God is not related to the extent or quality of our labor but instead to the simple free grace of the Saviour, we will find ourselves without a true grasp of who we are, who God is, and the only way we can have a relationship with Him.

When we cry out for justice to be done, we need to be careful what we are wishing for. Thank goodness God does not deal with us as we deserve; rather, He is abundantly generous with us. We can trust that He is overflowing in goodness and fairness toward His people.

—*Stephen H. Barnhart.*

Heart of the Lesson

Picture a professional athlete who agreed to play an entire season for one million dollars. Several times throughout the season, the owner signed additional players to contracts, promising them fair payment at the season's end. How would the various players feel if, when the season was over, they all received the same salary? They could choose to rejoice in their mutual well-being, or they could allow themselves to be destroyed by jealousy over the seeming inequity.

1. The arrangements (Matt. 20:1-7). The above situation parallels a parable told by Jesus to answer a question from Peter and to illustrate the statement that the "first shall be last; and the last shall be first" (19:30; cf. 20:16).

Jesus' parable presented God as an employer, so to speak, and a very generous one. A penny does not sound like much to us, but it was a good wage in Jesus' time.

Notice that five different hirings took place throughout the course of the day, yet only one group of workers was assigned a wage. We can be sure, however, that each person hired was grateful for the opportunity—especially those who were hired toward day's end. After all, the vineyard owner could have left them unemployed.

2. The argument (Matt. 20:8-12). The owner elected to be generous to all his workers and this is a major emphasis of the parable. Predictably, the first group to be hired was resentful. They felt that unequal work had resulted in equal pay.

3. The application (Matt. 20:13-16). The vineyard owner had a very simple answer. He had kept his word to the initial group. After watching the last group, they might have been thinking that they would receive a bonus. As the owner pointed out, though, he had fulfilled his word to them. Giving generous wages to the other workers was his decision alone.

"This parable is intended to teach one simple truth, that a man's reward will be, not according to the length of his service, not according to the notoriety of his service, but according to his fidelity to the opportunity which is given to him" (Morgan, *The Gospel According to Matthew,* Revell).

J. Vernon McGee shared an illustration that points to what Jesus was saying. "I have always felt that the Lord will someday reward a dear little lady who may have been a member of my church. I will turn to a member of my staff to say, 'Do you know her?' He will say, 'I have never heard of her. She did not sing in the choir, she was never president of any of our societies, and she never taught a Sunday school class. That woman didn't do anything, and look at the way the Lord is rewarding her!'

"We will probably find out that this dear lady was a widow with a young son. She never spoke to thousands of people like some evangelists and preachers, but she faithfully raised her one little boy, and he became a missionary who served God on a foreign field. The widow had been faithful in the task God had given her to do.

"Somebody might protest, 'Well, she sure didn't work as hard as I did!' That might well be true, but God is not going to reward you for the amount of work you have done. He will reward you according to your faithfulness to the job which He called you to do" (*Thru the Bible with J. Vernon McGee,* Nelson).
—Ken Schafer.

World Missions

The parable of the workers in the vineyard (Matt. 20:1-16) is a beautiful picture of the sovereign grace, goodwill, and large-hearted generosity that God extends to outcasts, to sinners, and to latecomers through Jesus. "Go ye also into the vineyard, and whatsoever is right I will give you" (Matt. 20:4).

One group of Christians who are ceaseless in reaching sinners for Jesus Christ, who are unremitting in making known God's large-hearted generosity of eternal life through faith in Jesus Christ, are those involved in The JESUS Film Project, a ministry of Cru (formerly Campus Crusade for Christ International).

The "JESUS" film is a biblically based film on the life of our Lord and Saviour, Jesus Christ. The film, now in four hundred languages, has been shown throughout the world by hundreds of traveling "JESUS" film teams.

Since the film has a clear and compelling gospel presentation, many of the outcasts and sinners who see it come to know of God's amazing generosity evidenced through the Person and work of Jesus. Many respond to the message about Jesus Christ—His love, His sacrificial death, His resurrection, His lordship—and put their trust in Him.

Many uncultivated vineyards are being cultivated for Jesus. On Christmas Eve 1996, Palestinian authorities on the West Bank allowed gospel literature and the "JESUS" film to be distributed in Manger Square. The results were amazing.

A Palestinian Campus Crusade for Christ worker recalled that twenty thousand people had gathered that night and that 80 percent were Muslim. "We had," he said, "Arabic New Testaments, 'JESUS' film videos, and audio cassettes. They gave us a special location in the square. I want to tell you something. People came to us like a wave. . . . They came by tens and hundreds, stretching out their hands, pushing and shouting. I asked them, 'Do you know what this is?' 'Yes, it is the Bible. We want it!'"

When the evening came to a close, thousands of Bibles and "JESUS" videotapes and cassettes had been distributed. A vineyard had been cultivated for Jesus Christ. Opportunities revealing God's sovereign grace had been made available to thousands of outcasts and sinners.

Elsewhere, the film has not only cultivated but also reaped a significant harvest. After the film was translated into Yao for 1.4 million people who live in Mozambique—a nation in southeast Africa—a premiere showing of the film took place. About 3,500 Yao people came to hear and understand the gospel. For four days, the "JESUS" film teams (consisting of 35 people) presented the film at schools during the day and held open-air showings at night.

While retelling the event in a May-June 1997 newsletter, the director of the Jesus Film Project, Paul Eshleman, said, "In total, 39,000 Yao saw and understood "JESUS" and 6,000 publicly indicated decisions for Christ. And this was in a Muslim area where a profession of faith can cost you your livelihood, your family, or your life."

Since those early days, the Jesus Film Project has reached 10 million views of their films digitally, with more than 100,000 installs of their media app on phones. In 2014, the "JESUS" film was remastered in HD. Pray for its continued success.

—*Herbert W. Bateman, IV.*

The Jewish Aspect

The Lord's parable in Matthew 20:1-16 was set during the time of grape gathering. This was usually in early September in Israel, when the sun-kissed land blossomed with beauty and fruitfulness. It was a time for the people to rejoice in God's goodness.

Many varieties of grapes are produced in the Holy Land, and all are superior quality. When ripe, grapes are eaten fresh, dried as raisins, or pressed for juice. Some fruit is boiled in large caldrons to produce *dibs,* or grape honey.

Since time out of memory, everyone is pressed into service when the grapes are ripe. The choicest grape-producing land in Israel is the Carmel district in the north. It is said that all roads lead to Carmel for the harvest (Unger, *Unger's Bible Dictionary,* Moody).

Early in the 1900s, most of the settlers in Carmel were of Russian origin. In the recent exodus of Jews from Russia in the 1970s and 1980s, the new immigrants expected to join the earlier Russian settlers in the grape-producing area. The Israeli government feared overpopulation would damage the delicate ecosystem in Carmel, so they planned to move these new citizens to the arid south. Newly arrived Russians left their aircraft and sat down on the landing field, refusing to go anywhere but to Carmel. The government relented and settled the immigrants in the north.

In the Lord's parable, the vineyard produced a bumper crop. This speaks of the quality of life that will be the norm in the kingdom reign of Christ. All the Old Testament references to agricultural yield in the millennial kingdom speak of bountiful crops.

In reviewing the history of Israel as God's vineyard, the psalmist pointed out that the Lord (whom the householder in Matthew 20:1 represents) "brought a vine out of Egypt" (Ps. 80:8). When he had displaced the heathen, God planted the vine which then flourished (vss. 9-10).

The extension of God's vineyard Israel is seen in that "she sent out her boughs unto the sea, and her branches unto the river" (Ps. 80:11). In other words, God's plans are for Israel to stretch from the Mediterranean Sea to the Euphrates River. The vineyard has not yet reached that size. This is a kingdom promise awaiting fulfillment.

The psalmist sadly reported that the vineyard had been despoiled. The walls of the vineyard were broken down, wild beasts devoured it, and it was burned with fire (Ps. 80:12-16). This is a picture repeated again and again in the history of Israel, and it is a picture of the land in the Great Tribulation.

The psalmist prayed, "Let thy hand be upon the man of thy right hand, upon the son of man who thou madest strong for thyself" (Ps. 80:17). The "son of man" is the Messiah, who shall bring the vineyard to a state of fruitfulness never seen before.

There will probably always be those who complain about the terms of remuneration God gives, thereby losing the joy of the Lord in His harvest. J. Dwight Pentecost wrote, "By this parable the Lord desired those who had asked what they would receive (Matt. 19:27) to learn the lesson that they were to work in the vineyard and leave their reward to Him" (*The Words and Works of Jesus Christ,* Zondervan).

—Lyle P. Murphy.

Guiding the Superintendent

Peter spoke for the disciples when he asked Jesus what reward He would give them for having to leave their homes and families to follow Him (Matt.19:27). Part of Jesus' reply was a parable illustrating a wrong attitude toward kingdom rewards.

DEVOTIONAL OUTLINE

1. The contract workers (Matt. 20:1-2). Jesus said that His kingdom is like a man who owned a vineyard and went early in the morning to hire men to work in it. Soon he found men who agreed to work all day for one denarius (a common day's wage), and he sent them to work.

2. The trusting workers (Matt. 20:3-5). The marketplace was the typical place to find laborers in that culture. At about nine in the morning, the landowner went there and told the men he found waiting there that if they would work in his vineyard, he would pay them whatever was right. These men were willing to trust his word and went to work.

The landowner went and hired workers in the marketplace again at noon and at three o'clock. These men also went to work on the terms that he would give them whatever was right.

3. The last set of workers (Matt. 20:6-7). Finally, the landowner found men standing idle in the marketplace with only one hour left in the workday. In contrast to his previous dealings, he mentioned nothing about the pay but simply told the men to go work in his vineyard. They obeyed, apparently without hesitation.

4. Payment of the workers (Matt. 20:8-12). At the end of the workday, the landowner told his foreman to pay the workers. One significant stipulation, however, was that the last workers hired were to be the first ones paid. To the surprise of the men who had made a contract with the landowner, those who had worked only one hour were given a full day's wages.

The first workers assumed that since they had done more work, they would be paid more than the others. They began to grumble, therefore, when they were paid one denarius as well. They complained that the landowner had made them equal to the laborers who had worked only one hour.

5. The just landowner (Matt. 20:13-16). The landowner made it clear that he had not wronged the workers. They had agreed to work all day for one denarius, and he had given it to them. He had the right to give the other workers whatever he chose. They had no reason to impugn his goodness and generosity.

Are we willing to serve God without receiving payment in this life? In God's kingdom, rewards are not given on the basis of human ways of thinking.

AGE-GROUP EMPHASES

Children: Our relationship with the Lord is based on our willingness to trust Him. Children should be shown that He is a good and loving God who is just in everything He does.

Youths: The young people should recognize that they can always trust in God's goodness. It is unwise to try to make deals with such a generous Father.

Adults: Many times we slip into a contractual way of thinking in our Christian lives, believing that if we do right, God must protect us. We must learn to serve Him out of love.

—Todd Wiliams.

SCRIPTURE LESSON TEXT

LUKE 18:9 And he spake this parable unto certain which trusted in themselves that they were righteous, and despised others:

10 Two men went up into the temple to pray; the one a Pharisee, and the other a publican.

11 The Pharisee stood and prayed thus with himself, God, I thank thee, that I am not as other men *are,* extortioners, unjust, adulterers, or even as this publican.

12 I fast twice in the week, I give tithes of all that I possess.

13 And the publican, standing afar off, would not lift up so much as *his* eyes unto heaven, but smote upon his breast, saying, God be merciful to me a sinner.

14 I tell you, this man went down to his house justified *rather* than the other: for every one that exalteth himself shall be abased; and he that humbleth himself shall be exalted.

NOTES

God's Great Mercy

Lesson Text: Luke 18:9-14

Related Scriptures: Matthew 18:1-5; 23:1-12;
Luke 16:14-17; Romans 3:10-30

TIME: TIME: A.D. 30   PLACE: on the way to Jerusalem

GOLDEN TEXT—"Every one that exalteth himself shall be abased; and he that humbleth himself shall be exalted" (Luke 18:14).

Introduction

We are regularly reminded of the importance of prayer in the life of every believer. We also regularly hear believers confess that they feel their prayer life is lacking. That is probably true of the majority of us.

Many of us remember that as children, we were present and part of the weekly prayer service in our churches. This was especially true for those of us who grew up in small, maybe rural, churches where there was not an over-abundance of group activities keeping us on the run all the time. We had the privilege of singing with the adults and listening to them pray. Being thus exposed to the attitudes and spiritual activities of those adults helped us grow. This is now missing in many of today's churches.

The tendency now is to have special activities for those in every age group instead of having everyone together in the church services. While there are benefits to this approach, there is loss in not being exposed to adult praying.

LESSON OUTLINE

I. **ILLUSTRATION BY WAY OF PARABLE**—Luke 18:9-10

II. **TWO ATTITUDES OF PRAYER**— Luke 18:11-13

III. **APPLICATION OF THE PARABLE**—Luke 18:14

Exposition: Verse by Verse

ILLUSTRATION BY WAY OF PARABLE

LUKE 18:9 And he spake this parable unto certain which trusted in themselves that they were righteous, and despised others:

10 Two men went up into the temple to pray; the one a Pharisee, and the other a publican.

A parable with a purpose (Luke 18:9). {This chapter begins with two parables told by Jesus. In the first, He emphasized how important persistent prayer is; in the second, He contrasted the prayers of two people with entirely different attitudes. Taken together, they show us that the prayer life of a believer is most important but that prayer per se can be ineffective if a person has a wrong attitude.}[Q1] Jesus had a specific purpose in telling the first parable, and Luke spelled it out.

"And He spake a parable unto them to this end, that men ought always to pray, and not to faint" (Luke 18:1). The word translated "always" is the Greek word *pantote,* "at all times." The phrase "not to faint" is from the word *ekkakeō,* meaning to "lack courage, lose heart, be fainthearted" (Vine, *Vine's Expository Dictionary of New Testament Words,* MacDonald). We should never get tired or weary of praying. Instead, it should be a source of joy and strength for us to communicate with our Father.

It was the common practice of the Jews to pray three times a day, so the idea of continuous praying would have been revolutionary to them. To engage in this level of communication with our Heavenly Father means we are keeping our requests before Him constantly. It does not mean endless repetition or long, painful sessions. Faithful communication is part of living by faith, because we are determining not to be discouraged even when God does not answer us as quickly as we would like. When He delays, we wait, trusting He has good reasons.

The illustration Jesus used featured an emotionally impassive judge receiving a request from a woman who needed protection from an adversary. He finally acceded because of her persistence. Jesus followed this with another parable, this one with a contrast. Once again there was a purpose, although this time it was stated by Luke in a more indirect fashion. There were those listening to Jesus who felt self-righteous to the degree that they were looking down on others they thought less spiritual.

This was especially an attitude of the religious leaders, who considered themselves to be the perfect examples of righteousness. Everyone else was looked upon as no more than ignorant sinners. An attitude of pride is always a hindrance to our spiritual growth or, perhaps, as in the case of these leaders, evidence of no spiritual life whatsoever. The believer being guided by the indwelling Holy Spirit of God will have compassion on others and a genuine concern for their spiritual well-being.

Two men with a purpose (Luke 18:10). {Jesus began this parable by referring to two individuals who came to the temple to pray. The contrast between them was as stark as imaginable, the one being a prominent spiritual leader of the community and the other one of the most-hated individuals in the community.}[Q2] Publicans worked for the Roman government, collecting taxes from fellow Jews in order to turn the money over to Rome. These tax collectors were notorious for collecting exorbitant amounts in order to get wealthy.

Although it is not the point of this parable, we recognize that God loved both of these individuals. No matter what status we might have in life, He will gladly accept and forgive and welcome us into His family (cf. Pss. 5:4; 11:5). What counts most is the attitude of the heart with which we approach God. Very religious people are not necessarily in a right relationship with Him, but they are always welcome. Other people might not be in a right relationship with Him, either, but God is always welcoming to them too.

Jesus was again telling a parable with a specific purpose in mind. {He began by stating that these two individuals had a purpose in attending the temple. Their purpose was to pray.}Q3 That in itself was certainly a good thing, and this had already been pointed out in the preceding parable. It would be good to remind ourselves that parables were simply commonly understood incidents from daily life meant to teach one particular truth. They are not meant to be interpreted in every detail but understood as illustrations.

Warren Wiersbe wrote, "Throughout His public ministry, Jesus exposed the self-righteousness and unbelief of the Pharisees (see Luke 11:39-54). He pictured them as debtors too bankrupt to pay what they owed God (Luke 7:40-50), guests fighting for the best seats (Luke 14:7-14), and sons proud of their obedience but unconcerned about the needs of others (Luke 15:25-32). The sad thing is that the Pharisees were completely deluded and thought they were right and Jesus was wrong. This is illustrated in this parable" (*The Bible Exposition Commentary*, Cook).

TWO ATTITUDES OF PRAYER

11 The Pharisee stood and prayed thus with himself, God, I thank thee, that I am not as other men are, extortioners, unjust, adulterers, or even as this publican.

12 I fast twice in the week, I give tithes of all that I possess.

13 And the publican, standing afar off, would not lift up so much as his eyes unto heaven, but smote upon his breast, saying, God be merciful to me a sinner.

A prayer of pride (Luke 18:11-12). The Pharisees were meticulous about their religious practices, so it is no surprise that when this Pharisee arrived in the temple, he prayed. What is surprising, however, is the prayer he uttered. While he said he thanked God, there is really no element of praise in his prayer. Rather, what we read is an expression of negative contrast and self-exaltation! He used other people as his standard for righteousness rather than the standards of God and His demands for righteousness.

{His first words thanked God that he was not like other men. He immediately put all those who were not of his social and religious class in a category of inferiority and despicability, and he quickly made a specific contrast with the tax collector who was there with him. His attitude was that he was better than most other people, and he justified it by mentioning some of the people considered to be the most ungodly people in society: extortioners, the unjust, and adulterers.}Q4

{He then pointed out specific areas in which he considered himself to be faithful in religious practice. No doubt the two things he mentioned were intended to be examples that included other activities as well. He faithfully fasted twice a week (not just the required once), and he scrupulously tithed on everything. This was probably the truth. The problem in his doing of such things was that they were done with the wrong attitude and served only to increase his personal sense of pride.}Q5

"This Pharisee's actions and his prayer provide a picture of his life and occupation—he was a separatist, but his separation and desire to remain clean before God had hardened into a lifestyle of self-righteousness. . . . The words of this prayer, . . . while probably true, were not prayed in the correct attitude of humility before God. It was as if this Pharisee was trying to trade his good deeds for God's grace" (Osborne, ed., *Life Application Bible Commentary*, Tyndale).

His basic attitude seems to have been that he had no sins that he needed to confess. He was so spiritually mature that he needed nothing more from God than His praise. It is somewhat ironic that he would feel a need to remind God of how good he was! Surely God had already noticed and was beside Himself with pleasure over such an outstanding man!

A prayer of humility (Luke 18:13). "An entirely different kind of prayer came from the tax collector's lips. It was a prayer of humility, dependence, and desperation. . . . The Pharisee was proud and confident; the tax collector grieved over his own condition as a sinner. The Pharisee described his righteousness; the tax collector begged for mercy to escape the judgment his sin deserved. Which one of them truly prayed?" (Anders, ed., *Holman New Testament Commentary,* Broadman & Holman).

{The publican stood at a distance from the Pharisee, giving an indication that he felt most unworthy of being in the presence of God or a religious leader.}[Q6] He wanted to stay as far away as possible. Little did he realize that he was the more godly one and was keeping distant from one not approved by God! An additional evidence of his sincere humility and sense of sinfulness is seen in the fact that he refused to even raise his eyes toward heaven. He felt a profound unworthiness. It was genuine humility, not a sham.

Furthermore, he stood and beat his chest, apparently as a physical indication of his recognition of the enormity of his sin and that it was keeping him at a distance from his God. It was also an expression of his deep and sincere contrition. As opposed to the Pharisee, who considered himself to be such a godly prize for the people, this man felt totally unworthy of being in God's presence. Unlike the Pharisee, his standard of comparison was God instead of other people. This gave him a more realistic evaluation.

It is never good for us to compare our spirituality to that of other people. It will always be true that some believers are much more mature than others, and it will always be true that some will be extremely immature. We should not compare ourselves to either except to use our observations to challenge ourselves to be continuously growing in the Lord. However, that growth can come only as we set God as our standard of righteousness and desire to reach that.

{The publican's prayer was that God might be merciful to him.}[Q7] The word "merciful" means "to be conciliated" or "propitious" (to be favorable toward someone). He was asking God to see his repentant spirit and thus be satisfied with him. He had nothing else to offer for his sinful condition beyond his humble spirit that recognized his need.

APPLICATION OF THE PARABLE

14 I tell you, this man went down to his house justified rather than the other: for every one that exalteth himself shall be abased; and he that humbleth himself shall be exalted.

{It was the publican who went home justified in God's eyes, not the religious leader.}[Q8] Jesus' emphasis was so much on the changed life of this man that He simply referred to the Pharisee as the other person while He pointed out the one who was truly righteous at this point. It was no doubt true that the Pharisee had not been an extortioner, an unjust person, or an adulterer. He did not, however, realize that he was still a sinner, and this was the critical truth that kept him from being justified, leaving him in a lost condition.

"He [the Pharisee] was deluded about the publican who was also in the temple praying. The Pharisee thought that the publican was a great sinner, but the publican went home justified by God while the proud Pharisee went home only self-satisfied" (Wiersbe).

{Being justified before God means being declared righteous and therefore innocent of all charges against us.}Q9 This can never happen to someone who does not acknowledge that there are charges. We must accept the fact that we are sinners in need of a Saviour if we are to be born again. When we recognize our sinfulness and humble ourselves before God in sincere repentance, the redemptive payment of Jesus' blood is immediately applied to our sin, and we are received into the family of God as forgiven sinners.

Such humility is in the heart, where God looks to see what a person is really like. Self-exaltation is external and visible to others as well as to God. Genuine humility is internal and can be seen in its entirety only by God, even though it will sometimes be recognized by others who also know Him well. {God brings down those who are proud but exalts those who are genuinely humble.}Q10 "Surely he scorneth the scorners: but he giveth grace unto the lowly" (Prov. 3:34).

It cannot be emphasized too often that self-righteousness is completely worthless when it comes to being saved and becoming a part of God's family. One of the saddest statements being made these days is that a high percentage of people who faithfully attend church every week are, in reality, not born again. Many of these precious folks give regularly, participate in the church activities, and faithfully invite others to attend their church. The most important element, however, is missing.

It is good to remember that no amount of good works, even faithful church attendance, can provide access into heaven. Just as the Pharisee's outwardly pure life was no guarantee of salvation, neither is it so for any of the rest of us. It is only acknowledging our sinful condition and receiving Jesus as Saviour that will give us eternal life.

—Keith E. Eggert.

QUESTIONS

1. What did Jesus cover in the two parables He told?

2. Who were the two personalities Jesus used for His teaching in the second parable?

3. What was their purpose in going to the temple?

4. How did the Pharisee view himself, and what was his standard of comparison that led him to these conclusions?

5. How did the Pharisee emphasize how he viewed his religious activities?

6. What did the publican do to reveal a sense of unworthiness?

7. What was his prayer request?

8. What did Jesus declare about him and the Pharisee?

9. What does it mean that a person is justified?

10. What principle did Jesus state in Luke 18:14 about how God deals with people?

—Keith E. Eggert.

Preparing to Teach the Lesson

Pride was the first sin (Isa. 14:13) and continues to have a dominant influence in the world today. Our society is so full of pride that even we Christians may not recognize it in our lives—we may think it is normal!

As you prepare this study from Luke 18, let the Lord first work in your heart regarding pride you may be harboring in some areas. Then pray for the Lord to use the Scripture to help your learners see the pride in their lives, realize the consequences of their pride, and take intentional steps to move away from it.

TODAY'S AIM

Facts: to recognize pride as a primary source of sinful problems in the world today.

Principle: to examine our lives to find open and hidden instances of pride.

Application: to adopt a humble spirit in all areas of life.

INTRODUCING THE LESSON

Our world is characterized by a great amount of corruption and degradation. While sin in general is at the heart of these problems, perhaps the sin of pride is the primary source of the corruption. What problems do we see in the world that are the result of pride? (Allow your learners to respond. They may suggest such problems as terrorism, marriage break-ups, and financial or moral scandals. Point out how these problems stem from pride.)

Pride is not just the problem of lawbreakers and immoral people. We Christians are prone to it as well. Our study today from Luke 18 will help us uncover the sin of pride in our lives.

DEVELOPING THE LESSON

1. Pride (Luke 18:9-12). In one of our Lord's teaching times, He knew that some in His audience "trusted in themselves that they were righteous, and despised others," so He spoke a parable to them.

The parable involved two men—a Pharisee and a publican—who both went to the temple to pray. The Pharisees were self-righteous leaders of Israel who considered themselves better than others (Matt. 23:1-39; Luke 7:36-50; 15:1-2; John 9:13-34). The publicans, or tax collectors, were often not well received in Israel because of their unethical practices, but that did not mean God could not reach them by His grace (Matt. 9:9-13; 11:19; Luke 15:1; 19:1-10).

Even before we read the Pharisee's "prayer," we note two indications of pride. First, he stood to pray. Standing to pray is not wrong, but apparently he stood in full view of people since we read that the tax collector stood far away (Luke 18:13). The second indication of the Pharisee's pride is that he "prayed thus with himself" (vs. 11). He was seemingly more concerned about himself than about speaking to God.

The Pharisee's prayer also shows his pride. "God, I thank thee, that I am not as other men are, extortioners, unjust, adulterers, or even as this publican" (vs. 11). In essence, he said that he was better than other people, including the publican who was also there at the temple praying. He even thanked God that he was better! To reinforce his claim, he boasted, "I fast twice in the week, I give tithes of all that I possess" (vs. 12). This man obviously did not have a true understanding of himself or God.

2. Humility (Luke 18:13-14). In contrast to the Pharisee, the publican "standing afar off, would not lift up so much as his eyes unto heaven, but smote upon his breast, saying, God be merciful to me a sinner." This man was so consumed with his sinfulness that he did not even look to heaven to pray. He did not consider himself better than anyone else. In deep contrition he recognized his own sinfulness and hopelessness; and as a result of his faith, he asked God to be merciful to him.

The Lord concluded His parable by saying, "I tell you, this man went down to his house justified rather than the other: for every one that exalteth himself shall be abased; and he that humbleth himself shall be exalted" (vs. 14). The publican was justified because he acknowledged his need of God's mercy. The Pharisee was not justified because he did not admit any need in his life.

The lesson for us is that those who follow the humble attitude of the publican will be exalted in the Lord's eyes. Those who follow the self-righteous attitude of the Pharisee will be abased.

ILLUSTRATING THE LESSON

Instead of thinking *I am better,* one should think *I am unworthy.*

CONCLUDING THE LESSON

Our study today has shown us clear examples of pride and humility. We may never express the "I am better" thoughts the way the Pharisee did, but we may harbor that same thinking in our heart. Let us take a couple of minutes now to examine our hearts to uncover any of that same proud thinking. (Give your learners about two minutes to pray and examine their lives to uncover areas of pride. Encourage them to think about their attitudes toward people in their family, at work, or even at church.)

I know we all want to renounce that proud spirit and move away from it. To help us do that, let us think of short, two-sentence prayers that express our desire to adopt an "I am unworthy" attitude. An example of such a prayer is "Lord, I realize how sinful I am and how great You are. Help me have a better understanding of myself and see that I am not better than others."

(Make sure your students have paper and pens. Give them time to write one or two such prayers. When they have completed their prayers, ask several to read what they wrote, or ask the class to turn in their papers so that you can read the prayers aloud.)

Fighting an "I am better" attitude is a lifetime struggle. Let us examine our lives daily to see where we still harbor that attitude and move away from it. May we always strive to exhibit an attitude of humbleness as a testimony of our Christian faith.

ANTICIPATING THE NEXT LESSON

Next week begins a new quarter and a new unit of study on success and failure. To be successful in serving Christ, we must strive to be faithful in our obedience to Him. Disobedience brings only failure.

—*Don Anderson.*

PRACTICAL POINTS

1. All self-righteousness is a matter of vastly misplaced trust (Luke 18:9).
2. If we look down on others with contempt, we can be sure our righteousness is not from God.
3. Praying to ourselves could be an apt description of what we do if we are not careful (vss. 10-11).
4. Too many public prayers are little more than thinly veiled bragging sessions (vs. 12).
5. We cannot approach a holy God without recognizing our need for mercy (vs. 13).
6. Humility is needed to avoid humiliation (vs. 14).

—Kenneth A. Sponsler.

RESEARCH AND DISCUSSION

1. Why is it so easy to think we are high up on the scale of righteousness and most other people are doing much worse (Luke 18:9)?
2. What was the reason for going to the temple to pray (vs. 10)? What modern equivalent might we follow today?
3. Few of us would likely be so obviously boastful in our prayers as the Pharisee was (vss. 11-12). In what subtle ways might we fall into such a trap?
4. If we know we have been saved by grace, do we still need to ask for God's mercy (vs. 13)? Why or why not?
5. How do we know we are being truly humble and not putting on a show of humility in order to be honored for it (vs. 14)?

—Kenneth A. Sponsler.

ILLUSTRATED HIGH POINTS

And despised others (Luke 18:9)

A Washington state college professor who believes that goodness and education are synonymous watched a news piece with a small group of people. After the piece aired, she commented that her view of the situation differed from the common sentiment.

The piece exposed an injustice done to an innocent man who had spent more than twenty years behind bars. It was later discovered that the prosecuting attorneys had intentionally withheld the evidence that eventually cleared him. When the story finished airing, the professor asked the group to consider what the cost would have been had the prosecutors come clean regarding their misconduct. The world, she contended, would have been robbed of good lawyers with college educations. It was far better for all concerned, she insisted, that only this poor, uneducated man was removed from society as he, she quipped, had little to contribute.

If "self-righteous" is stamped on one side of a coin, "contempt for others" is surely etched on the other.

I am not as other men are (vs. 11)

Eyewitness testimony is commonly thought to be largely reliable. But the human eye can be an untrustworthy instrument. Humans have a significant area called a scotoma, or blind spot, in each eye. Our brains compensate for the blind spots by interpolating from the existing visual information and filling in the missing portions with inventions. We see what is not really there.

We are most likely to suffer spiritual blind spots in how we perceive ourselves. Like the "blind" Pharisees (cf. Matt. 15:14), we may think we see when we do not.

—Therese Greenberg.

Golden Text Illuminated

"Every one that exalteth himself shall be abased; and he that humbleth himself shall be exalted" (Luke 18:14).

I was a good child. I went to church every week, was a good student, participated in many activities, and even volunteered on the side. I was also a braggart. I took pride in my accomplishments—too much so, at times. I tended to parade my deeds like some sort of pedigree. Boasting was common for me.

But one day my grandfather silenced my self-aggrandizement. I was in mid-boast when he interrupted me with a single sentence. He looked up and said, "The preacher who preaches of himself has a congregation of one."

At first, I did not catch the meaning of this. When he explained it, I was outraged that he would apply the saying to me. However, after considering my actions, I realized that he was right. Since then, that old proverb has stayed in my mind.

My problem was that, like the Pharisee in the lesson, I was exalting myself. This Pharisee had "the pedigree." He was someone with the highest standing in the temple. He fasted more than required, tithed every source of income, and was well respected in his community.

In contrast, the publican came from the lowest stratum of society. His occupation made him an outcast. Publicans were known for being liars, so he was shunned by respected members of the community. Since he collected taxes for the government, he was hated by almost everyone.

We find these two at the temple, praying. However, there is a noticeable difference in their prayers. The Pharisee's prayer was an elaborate laundry list of his accomplishments. His prayer was the equivalent of "Thank God I am not as bad as that person over there!" He showed no awareness of sin in his life, let alone remorse or repentance. He did not see his need for God's mercy. His prayer was all for show.

The publican's prayer was sincere and honest. His plea was that God would remember him, despite his sinfulness. He did not highlight any good deeds. He did not look for someone with greater sin and try to pass himself off as better than that person. He merely asked that God show him mercy.

We know whose prayer God honored. Scripture tells us that it was the publican who went away forgiven that day. Why? The Pharisee's prayer was prideful and self-righteous. The publican's prayer was humble.

Humility is one of the great earmarks of a deep faith. We are told that God bestows grace upon the humble (Prov. 3:34) and that He crowns them with salvation (Ps. 149:4). We are also told that humility brings honor to His followers (Prov. 18:12).

Proverbs 18:12 also mentions that pride can bring about a person's downfall. We are also told that God resists the proud (Jas. 4:6).

Paul goes on to tell us that we should esteem others as better than ourselves (Phil. 2:3). Believers should lift others higher, not take a sanctimonious attitude and bring them down. As the old adage states, "There but for the grace of God go I." We should be so occupied with our own sinfulness that we cannot judge the sins of those around us.

Which person are you—self-righteous Pharisee or humble publican? Let us make practicing humility evidence of our authentic faith.

—*Jennifer Lautermilch.*

Heart of the Lesson

It is reported that Martin Luther said the following: "True humility does not know that it is humble. If it did, it would be proud from the contemplation of so fine a virtue." Most people shy away from speaking about humility, fearing what others will say and how they themselves will appear to their hearers. But Jesus had no such reservations.

He who Himself demonstrated the greatest humility in His incarnation (cf. Phil. 2:5-11) often spoke of humility and man's need of it (cf. Matt. 5:5; 21:5). In today's lesson Jesus teaches us that true humility is one clear evidence of real and saving faith.

1. The prayer of a self-righteous Pharisee (Luke 18:9-12). With brevity and clarity, Luke describes those to whom Jesus was speaking as people who thought highly of themselves and looked down on others. As Luke reiterates the parable, one can almost see and hear the Pharisee as he announces to God and everyone within earshot how righteous he is.

The Pharisee started by reminding God of what and who he was not like. As he peered down on the publican, you can imagine his haughty look and the pride that beat within his chest. He had never sold out his nation, nor abetted the Roman occupiers, nor fleeced his fellow countrymen as had this tax collector. He then continued to remind God of all the religious things he had done. He had gone well beyond the requirements of the law.

All of his statements were punctuated with the word "I," for that in reality was what his life was about. He was proud of himself and expected others to share in his exalted self-assessment.

2. The prayer of a self-abasing publican (Luke 18:13). Next, we are introduced to the publican. Publicans were categorized with sinners in Jesus' day. They were looked down on by most respectable and pious Jews. Jesus Himself was disdainfully called a friend of sinners and publicans (7:34).

As the publican came to pray, his heart attitude was clearly seen by his positioning of himself, his posture, and the smiting of his breast. In his few and simple words, the publican clearly revealed that he knew the truth about himself and the truth about God. He was a sinner in need of mercy, and God was the only one who could grant that mercy.

3. Jesus' unexpected pronouncement (Luke 18:14). Perhaps no one listening to Jesus was surprised by the words of the publican; of course he was a sinner. Of course he needed God's mercy. But we can only imagine how they were taken aback by Jesus' pronouncement that it was the publican who went away justified. Before they could recover from their shock, Jesus stated the principle clearly: "For every one that exalteth himself shall be abased; and he that humbleth himself shall be exalted."

A man of humble faith recognizes that no matter how righteous he seeks to be, his efforts cannot justify himself before a holy God (cf. Rom. 3:9-12). Only by repenting of his sins and trusting in the righteous work of Christ can any man go "down to his house justified" (Luke 18:14; cf. Rom. 3:23-28). In what are you trusting?

—Don Kakavecos.

World Missions

A missionary couple at a missions conference one year was memorable, but it was not because they had dynamic personalities or gave inspiring speeches. Both seemed shy, had difficulty mingling, and appeared uncomfortable in general with the questions and attention they were getting.

One husband and wife who had been visiting the church that had the conference decided to support these unlikely missionary candidates. The daughter of the couple thought back to a day in her Christian high school, when a man had come to speak in chapel and had not been a good public speaker. Her mother, a teacher at the school, had pointed out that the man may be a better missionary than someone who could impress a crowd. Those who thrive on stage in their home country may struggle in a small or slow-moving work on the field. Others, who may seem to be terrible in missions because they are not good public speakers in churches, may be just what is needed in more subdued cultures or small settings.

The mother had been right. That shy missionary couple is still serving on the field. They have reached many for Christ.

When a missionary comes to church, we may tend to evaluate them. Consciously or subconsciously, we may notice whether they have a good strong handshake, whether they look us in the eye, or whether they are comfortable behind the podium or talk with ease after the service. Sometimes we rate how they will do as missionaries based on their performance with us.

Luke 18:9-14 reminds us that judging others according to our own perceptions is faulty. God may have equipped your visiting missionary with the exact qualities needed for the work he has been called to do. He may be called to a culture where a firm handshake is considered aggressive, where looking someone in the eye is rude, and where general confidence and ease in conversation is seen as arrogant and ungodly.

In fact, those who do well on deputation may have a difficult time on the field, where people are not encouraging them and lauding their faith and where they have no crowds to show pictures to or children who see them as heroes. People who love speaking to crowds often struggle doing one-on-one ministries, and vice versa.

Next time a missionary comes, whether he impresses the church or not, check for humility of spirit. If his faith is humble, if he longs for God's purpose over his own, God will use him, no matter how he appears.

The same principle applies to anyone we encounter in the ministry. A person may sound very spiritual or look holy but be filled with pride in his own supposed righteousness. Another may appear to be lost beyond hope but have a truly repentant attitude. We should present the gospel message to both. In this week's Scripture text, only one person went home justified, and it was not the one who appeared to be holy.

Appearances can be deceiving, which is why God tells us not to be wise in our own eyes (Prov. 3:7) and not to judge according to looks (Isa. 11:3). If we long to be like Him, we will not look at what is outward but what is in the heart (I Sam. 16:7).

—Kimberly Rae.

The Jewish Aspect

Jesus' parable about the Pharisee and the publican demonstrated the common Jewish attitude toward tax collectors (Luke 18:11). They were distrusted, hated, and avoided. Why did Jews have such contempt for them?

Rome collected taxes from all its provinces. It needed revenue to survive. Tax collectors, therefore, had legal authority, and troops to enforce it. Rome usually collected taxes through the means of private individuals. Those tax collectors were to gather the taxes and send them to Rome. This meant that in Israel the publicans were Jews and were considered to be traitors and apostates. They had sold out to the enemy, Rome.

Two kinds of publicans worked in Jesus' day. The common publican sat at a custom house, on a trade route, or at the gate of a major city. He examined all the goods that passed by and assessed a tax on them. Matthew was this kind of publican (Matt. 9:9). The second type of publican was more like a tax commissioner. He was in charge of an entire district and had other publicans working under him. Zacchaeus, "the chief among the publicans" (Luke 19:2), was this kind of tax collector. Jews despised both types.

Publicans collected taxes in Israel at several major places. Along the Mediterranean coast, they worked at Gaza, Ashkelon, Joppa, and Caesarea. Those were all on major trade routes. Moving inland, taxes were collected on the major trade routes passing through Jericho and Capernaum. They were also collected at Jerusalem.

Taxation was often burdensome, since only the publican knew the exact amount of fixed taxes he had to collect. Whatever he could collect above that amount was his to keep. The ethical standard of the publican, therefore, was the only guideline to protect the taxpayer. If a publican was greedy, then he could overcharge and keep the profits. Since publicans had soldiers to support them, the average Jew had no recourse except to pay what was demanded. Rome supported each publican as long as the tax quotas were met.

The Talmud speaks forthrightly about the character of publicans. They could not serve as judges or even as witnesses, for they were no better than robbers (*Sanhedrin* 25b). Because of the publicans' unsavory character, Jews were permitted to lie to them to protect themselves from financial harm (*Nedarim* 27b).

Jews regarded publicans as so unclean that even the handles of their staffs were defiled. If a publican entered a Jewish house, the house was considered unclean. The presence of one publican in a family, according to the Talmud, was enough to disgrace the entire family (*Shebu'oth* 39a).

The Jews of New Testament times knew all these things well. When publicans asked John the Baptist what they should do, he responded, "Exact no more than that which is appointed you" (Luke 3:13).

However, Jesus knew that a publican, like any sinner, could come to faith. Jesus called the publican Matthew to be a disciple (Matt. 9:9), and Matthew then invited his publican friends to a dinner to meet Jesus (vss. 10-13). Jesus later chose Matthew as an apostle (10:3). The chief publican Zacchaeus was radically changed when he came to Christ (Luke 19:8). The salvation of publicans warned Jewish religious leaders that they also needed to repent (Matt. 21:31-32). God's grace is available to all people.

—*R. Larry Overstreet*

Guiding the Superintendent

"William Barclay tells the story of Paedaretos who lived in Sparta in ancient Greece. A group of 300 men were to be chosen to govern Sparta. Though Paedaretos was a candidate, his name was not on the final list. "Some of his friends sought to console him, but he simply replied, 'I am glad that in Sparta there are 300 men better than I am.' He became a legend because of his willingness to stand aside while others took the places of glory and honor" ("Willing to Stand Aside," bible.org).

In this week's lesson, we discover the spiritual priority that the Lord Jesus placed on humility through His use of a parable of contrast that included the positive picture of humility and the negative picture of religious pride.

DEVOTIONAL OUTLINE

1. A proud Pharisee (Luke 18:9-12). Jesus realized that He was in the presence of people who struggled with pride. These people had two distinctive characteristics: they ascribed to themselves a sense of importance that resulted in not only self-reliance but also in a self-righteous attitude, and they treated others with contempt.

Jesus' parable concentrated on two men, one a respected religious leader and one a despised tax collector, who went to the temple to pray. The religious leader assumed a posture of prayer that was characteristic of the Pharisees (cf. Matt. 6:5). It was a posture of eminence, solemnity, and seriousness; but it was also a posture that brought excessive attention to the religious leader.

The Pharisee's prayer consisted of an arrogant depiction of moral superiority and religious commitment. What was lacking, though, was a sense of humble dependence on God.

2. A humble publican (Luke 18:13-14). In stark contrast to the Pharisee's prayer, the publican's prayer was saturated with a sense of personal unworthiness. The publican's distance from the temple court, his downcast countenance, and animated physical gestures demonstrated his belief that he was in need of God's grace and mercy.

Jesus concluded His use of imagery by stating that the publican departed having been granted God's acceptance and favor. That was not the case for the Pharisee.

AGE-GROUP EMPHASES

Children: Children communicate with honest and forthright language that sometimes surprises people who have become used to indirect and vague words. Encourage your children to talk to the Lord in prayer with the same straightforward honesty. God loves that kind of prayer.

Youths: A major part of growing up involves movement from self-centeredness toward consideration of others. Help your young people embrace the truth that humility is a sign of mature strength and not immature weakness. Encourage them with the words of James, who wrote, under the guidance of the Holy Spirit, "But he giveth more grace. Wherefore he saith, God resisteth the proud, but giveth grace unto the humble" (Jas. 4:6).

Adults: Some of your adults may be struggling with spiritual lethargy. They simply are tired and frustrated with their efforts to please God by performance-oriented Christianity. Remind your tired adults that God is not interested in their religious works; rather, He is interested in their humble repentance and faithfulness.

—*Thomas R. Chmura.*

loyal servants. As Jesus gathered and appointed the apostles, He was beginning a frontal assault on the kingdom of Satan. Those who were oppressed and downtrodden were the first to recognize the wonder and blessing of Christ's work. But the Jewish rulers, who were assumed to be God's earthly representatives, fought viciously against Christ's mission of mercy. They were the tares among the wheat (Matt. 13:25, 28). How clearly Jesus exposed their hypocrisy in His parables. Yet, they could not understand because they were incapable of hearing truth (vss. 11-15).

Jesus taught His followers to pray for God's kingdom to come (Luke 11:2). He went on to say that this involves God's good will being done on earth just as it is done in heaven. While we long for a day when God's kingdom is unchallenged around the globe, we should never discount the reality of God's sovereign control (Acts 2:34-36). He has all power, and He is working out His sovereign plan (Isa. 14:24, 27).

When we look around and see the many evils that plague this world, though, we may wonder, What is God's purpose right now? Why has He not removed the wicked and instituted His full righteous control over humanity? Surely God gives us many wonderful reminders that Satan is a defeated enemy. It is essential that we not succumb to the faulty perception that evil forces are actually prevailing. Note that every lesson we will study this quarter shows that the kingdom of God prevails in the face of all opposition.

All of this encouraging truth makes little difference in our lives, however, unless we act upon it. Our daily lives should show that our choices are made in light of the victorious nature of Christ's kingdom. Too often discouragement creeps into our thinking. Too often we fail to advance in faith. So many times we give up territory to the enemies of God because we are timid or uncertain about the power of God working in us.

Let us carefully focus our minds on God's overcoming power. We can do this through prayer and the study of God's Word. We can enjoy victory in Christ every day. May this quarter of study move us toward a more faithful and compelling life of obedience as true and courageous soldiers in God's victorious kingdom.

Tares That Tarry

Todd Williams

In World War II, the Office of Strategic Services found a way to disguise explosives as flour used for baking. Curiously, this explosive mixture could actually be used to bake edible bread and muffins! This helped greatly in veiling its true purpose if the enemy ever got suspicious. In His parable about the tares, Jesus referred to a plant that disguises itself as wheat. The Greek word for tare (*zizania,* Matt. 13:25) almost certainly denotes the invasive weed commonly known as darnel (*Lolium temulentum*) that sometimes plagues wheat fields. Before it develops its poisonous fruit, the stalk of this weed is virtually indistinguishable from wheat.

Jesus' parable was no doubt readily understood by the agricultural society in which He ministered. We have no way of knowing whether it was typical for farmers to wage agricultural warfare on each other using the enemy's tactic Jesus described here, however. But none of Jesus' listeners missed the fact that this was an especially malicious way to hurt a rival's crops.

The meaning behind the parable of the tares gives us some valuable insights. First, it offers a glimpse into the affairs of the unseen realm by exposing the diabolical tactics of the evil one. And second, it provides insight into the Lord's dealings with those people who represent evil in the world.

The interpretation of the parable in a nutshell (Matt. 13:36-43) is that the Lord is willing to endure evildoers (tares) for a time for the good of true believers (wheat). In the end, however, He will bring down the wicked with the terrible judgment (fire) that they richly deserve. As we ponder the proclamation of God's kingdom in this quarter's topics, note how Jesus' teaching about the tares seems to resonate in nearly every lesson. Impostors and pretenders seem always to be lurking around, not too far from the wonderful kingdom truths we will be learning.

Let us first consider the glimpse we have of Satan's work as it is characterized in the parable of the tares. Satan has sown his crop of evil people in the world, even while God cultivates His own crop of those who are bound for glory. While both crops are immature, they look alike, but as they mature, they are known by their fruits—one is good while the other is poisonous!

But surprisingly, Jesus' parable indicates that uprooting the evil weeds before the time of harvest would devastate the good crop (Matt. 13:29-30), since their roots are closely intertwined. This reminds us that God graciously allows people time to show their true colors.

Our lessons this quarter identify various frauds who tip their hand and who might be detected by discerning believers. We recognize these impostors as the guests who decline to attend the banquet (lesson 6—Luke 14:18-20), as the "goats" who ignored the needy (lesson 8—Matt. 25:41-43), and as the complaining vineyard workers (lesson 12—20:11-12). Look to spot others in our lessons this quarter who pretend to obey God but are truly His enemies.

Finally, what wisdom can we discover about how God handles those who are tools of Satan? Is it really better to allow impostors to remain alongside the true citizens of God's kingdom? If we were in charge, we might desire to judge all the evil ones immediately, since they so often infiltrate the church with their fleshly thinking and deceptive behavior (Gal. 1:7; 2:4; II Cor. 11:13, 20; II Pet. 2:1-2).

But thankfully, God's wisdom is much greater than ours. He sees that by remaining patient with evildoers, He is able to much more clearly reveal the great riches of His grace to His true followers (Rom. 9:22-23). Jesus Himself allowed Judas to remain with the apostles, knowing full well that he was "a devil" (John 6:70). Peter shockingly denied Christ three times, but eventually, through God's forgiveness and abundant grace, he revealed himself as a true servant of Christ.

The greatness of God's mercy is so much more clearly understood and appreciated when set alongside the darkness of evil and pride. This reality is repeatedly emphasized in this quarter's lessons: Jesus contrasted the rejoicing of the blessed against the reviling of their persecutors (lesson 1—Matt. 5:10-12); He underscored God's wonderful mercy for Lazarus by focusing on the selfishness of the rich man (lesson 7—Luke 16:19-31); He drew attention to the gratefulness of the last vineyard workers by stressing the grumbling of the early workers (lesson 12—Matthew 20:1-16); and He juxtaposed the pride of the Pharisee alongside the humility of the publican (lesson 13—Luke 18:9-14). Without these kinds of contrasting characters, we surely would have less humility and undervalue God's immeasurable mercy toward us.

God's kingdom is truly upside-down to the world's way of thinking, and His patient dealing with the "tares" is one of the best ways to help us realize that. Moreover, God's forbearance with evil should teach His children to be patient as well. It is sometimes very tempting for us to rush to judgment in the cases of those who do not think or behave exactly as we think they should. It is vitally important for us to understand that just as it takes time for true believers (wheat) to grow, mature, and eventually to bear fruit, so too will evildoers (tares) one day be fully exposed and justly judged for their crimes. Let us not be in a hurry to prematurely label others in the church as phonies or frauds (cf. Rom. 14:1).

As we think about God's kingdom this quarter, may we reject our fleshly thinking and repeatedly discover God's great wisdom in His plan for this world. Let us rejoice that one day the evil will be judged and that God's people will be gloriously revealed and exalted (cf. Rom. 8:18-25).

TOPICS FOR NEXT QUARTER

PARAGRAPHS ON PLACES AND PEOPLE

PEREA

Although not mentioned by this name in the Bible, this region east of the Jordan River has a rich biblical history. The area, called Gilead, was given to the tribes of Reuben, Gad, and Manasseh as an inheritance (Josh. 22:9). It is believed to be the same region where the prophet Elijah was from (I Kgs. 17:1). In the time of Christ's ministry, it was part of the territory ruled by Herod Antipas, and it is where John the Baptist preached and baptized (John 1:28-29). When Jews were traveling between Jerusalem and Galilee, the preferred route passed through this area to avoid Samaria. Many of Jesus' teachings and miracles took place here, "beyond Jordan" (Matt. 4:15, 25; Mark 3:8; John 3:26; 10:40).

ABRAHAM'S BOSOM

This place of comfort and blessing is spoken of by Jesus in the story of Lazarus and the rich man (Luke 16:22-23). Jewish apocryphal writings describe "Abraham's bosom" as a place of blessing in *Sheol* for those who are awaiting the final judgment. Those who were wicked, like the rich man, would be sent to Gehenna—a place of torment in *Sheol*—to await final judgment. The image Jesus painted may reflect the Jewish custom of reclining to eat with the most favored guest positioned next to the host, leaning on his bosom (cf. John 13:23). "Abraham's bosom" is also considered by many to be an alternative term for heaven, where the righteous ones of God await their resurrection.

THE MULTITUDES

In a general sense, the multitudes referred to in the Gospels were the crowds that followed Jesus (Matt. 4:25; Mark 5:24; Luke 12:1). Translated from the Greek word *ochlos,* "multitude" is found primarily in the Gospel accounts. When used, it was usually describing a gathering of the common people that did not have a specific leader (Matt. 9:36). The multitudes were amazed at Jesus' teaching and miracles (Matt. 9:8, 33; Mark 11:18; Luke 13:17). Jesus is recorded as having compassion for the multitudes (Matt. 15:32; Mark 8:2). This is in contrast to the religious leaders, who had disdain for the multitudes (cf. John 7:31, 32, 40-49). The multitudes were easily swayed to turn on Jesus at His trial, calling for His crucifixion (Matt. 27:20-25; Mark 15:11-13).

THE TWELVE

Jesus called twelve men to be His closest disciples (Mark 3:14-19). The number twelve matches the number of the twelve tribes of Israel and looks forward to the twelve foundations of the New Jerusalem (Rev. 21:14). These men were with Jesus day in and day out during His three-year ministry. They learned His ways and the ways of God's kingdom. Jesus ordained them and sent them out (Greek: *apostel-lō*) to preach, heal, and deliver the people of Israel in His name. Later this mission was expanded beyond Israel to include all people (Matt. 28:18-20). The names of all twelve men are given in three places: Matthew 10:2-4, Mark 3:16-19, and Luke 6:14-16. The Twelve are: Simon (Peter) and his brother Andrew, James and his brother John, Philip, Thomas, Bartholomew (Nathanael), Matthew (Levi), James (son of Alpheus), Thaddaeus (Judas the brother of James), Simon (the zealot), and Judas Iscariot. After Christ's ascension, Matthias was chosen to replace Judas Iscariot (Acts 1:13-26).

—Kelly Hawver.

Daily Bible Readings for Home Study and Worship

(Readings are for the week previous to the lesson topics.)

1. June 4. Upside-Down Kingdom

M —Comforted by Repentance. II Cor. 7:8-13.
T —Humility Draws God's Attention. Isa. 66:1-2.
W—New Heaven and New Earth. Rev. 21:1-4.
T —Suffering Prophets. Heb. 11:36-38.
F —Who Receives God's Blessing? Ps. 24:1-6.
S —The Beatitudes. Luke 6:20-26.
S —Who Are Kingdom Citizens? Matt. 5:1-16.

2. June 11. A Perfect Kingdom

M —Unbelieving Israel. Rom. 9:30—10:4.
T —Building on the Foundation of Christ. I Cor. 3:11-15.
W—Mercy over Judgment. Jas. 2:10-13.
T —Common Grace. Acts 14:8-18.
F —God Hates Evil. Ps. 5:4-8.
S —Understanding God's Laws. Matt. 5:31-37.
S —God's Standard for His Kingdom. Matt. 5:17-18, 21-22, 27-28, 38-39, 43-44.

3. June 18. A Victorious Kingdom

M —A House Divided. Matt. 12:22-32.
T —Jesus Overpowers Satan. Luke 11:14-23.
W—Sin That Leads to Death. I John 5:14-17.
T —The Twelve Are Sent. Matt. 10:1-15.
F —The Seventy-Two Sent. Luke 10:1-12.
S —Lord of the Sabbath. Luke 6:1-5.
S —Authority over Satan. Mark 3:13-19; 6:6b-13.

4. June 25. Growing God's Kingdom

M —Small Beginnings. Mark 4:26-32.
T —Increasing Influence. Luke 13:18-21.
W—Setting Up God's Kingdom. Dan. 2:24-47.
T —The Returning Christ. Matt. 24:29-31.
F —Evil Removed from the World. Matt. 13:36-43.
S —The Final Harvest. Rev. 14:14-20.
S —Good and Evil Grow Together. Matt. 13:24-33.

5. July 2. Praying to God

M —Song of Praise. I Chr. 16:23-34.
T —Extolling the Lord. Ps. 145:1-21.
W—Daily Bread for Israel. Ex. 16:15-22.
T —Seeking the Face of the Lord. Ps. 27:7-14.
F —All Are Unrighteous. Rom. 3:10-20.
S —Honest Prayer. Matt. 6:5-8.
S —Teach Us to Pray. Luke 11:1-13.

6. July 9. Accept God's Invitation!

M —Unprepared for the Kingdom. Matt. 22:1-14.
T —The Stone Rejected. Matt. 21:42-44.
W—Gospel Scorned by the Jews. Acts 13:44-52.
T —A Place of Honor. Prov. 25:6-7.
F —The Proud Will Be Humbled. Isa. 2:10-12.
S —Hospitality to the Poor. Luke 14:12-14.
S —Two Critical Warnings. Luke 14:7-11, 15-24.

7. July 16. A Warning for the Hard-Hearted

M —What Does Your Heart Treasure? Matt. 6:19-21.
T —Give to the Poor. Luke 12:32-34.
W—Heavenly Treasure. Mark 10:17-22.

T —Judgment of the Dead. Rev. 20:11-15.
F —The Lake of Fire. Rev. 21:5-8.
S —Unbelieving Hearts. Heb. 3:7-19.
S —The Rich Man and Lazarus. Luke 16:19-31.

8. July 23. Separating the Sheep and the Goats

M —Authority Given to the Son of Man. Dan. 7:9-14.
T —A Coming Judgment. Matt. 16:24-28.
W—Judging the World in Righteousness. Ps. 9:1-10.
T —Evidence of Faith. Jas. 2:14-20.
F —Pure Religion. Jas. 1:22-27.
S —God Judges Rightly. II Thess. 1:3-10.
S —Judgment of the Nations. Matt. 25:31-46.

9. July 30. Ears to Hear

M —Listen to My Instruction. Ps. 78:1-8.
T —Receiving God's Word. Matt. 13:18-23.
W—Hearing Without Understanding. Isa. 6:8-12.
T —Revealed Mystery of Christ. Rom. 16:25-27.
F —Taught by the Spirit. I Cor. 2:6-16.
S —Imperishable Seed. I Pet. 1:22-25.
S —Hearing God's Word. Matt. 13:9-17.

10. August 6. Forgiving One Another

M —Love and Forgive Enemies. Luke 6:27-38.
T —Much Love with Much Forgiveness. Luke 7:36-50.
W—Mercy to the Unfaithful. Ps. 78:32-40.
T —Called to Forgive. Col. 3:12-17.
F —Always Willing to Forgive. Luke 17:3-4.
S —Forgiveness Through the Blood. Eph. 1:3-10.
S —Repeated Forgiveness. Matt. 18:21-35.

11. August 13. A Story of Forgiveness

M —Firstborn's Portion. Deut. 21:15-17.
T —Grace of the Father. Matt. 7:7-12.
W—Prayer for Mercy. Ps. 86:1-7.
T —Turn from Sin and Live. Ezek. 18:21-23.
F —Welcome the Repentant. Luke 15:25-32.
S —God Will Comfort the Repentant. Isa. 57:15-21.
S —Repentance and Reconciliation. Luke 15:11-24.

12. August 20. God's Gracious Rewards

M —A Rich Man's Sorrow. Matt. 19:16-22.
T —Salvation Only by God's Grace. Matt. 19:23-30.
W—Beware of Envy. Jas. 3:13-18.
T —The Last Will Be First. Luke 13:22-30.
F —God Will Assign Us Our Place. Matt. 20:20-23.
S —Not Demanding Our Privileges. Matt. 17:24-27.
S —God's Grace Illustrated. Matt. 20:1-16.

13. August 27. God's Great Mercy

M —No Place for Boasting. Rom. 3:21-26.
T —Fast in Secret. Matt. 6:16-18.
W—God Knows the Heart. Luke 16:13-15.
T —The Proud Humbled. Matt. 23:1-12.
F —Faith like a Child's. Matt. 18:1-5.
S —Turn from False Worship. Isa. 1:10-17.
S —Humble Faith. Luke 18:9-14.

REVIEW

What have you learned this quarter?

Can you answer these questions?

Christ Proclaims the Kingdom

UNIT I: Understanding God's Kingdom

June 4

Upside-Down Kingdom

1. Who was listening to Jesus at the beginning of the Sermon on the Mount, and how did that change?
2. What three basic types of followers do we see in Jesus' ministry?
3. What is the true meaning of "blessed" in these verses?
4. What does "poor in spirit" (Matt. 5:3) refer to?
5. What is the meek person like?

June 11

A Perfect Kingdom

1. In what ways did Christ fulfill the law?
2. What was a "jot" and a "tittle" (Matt. 5:18)?
3. What is the meaning of the word "Raca" (vs. 22)?
4. What kind of danger is one in when calling someone a fool?
5. What is the background behind the Greek word translated "hell"?

June 18

A Victorious Kingdom

1. What important decision did Jesus have to make at this time?
2. Why was it so important, and how did He prepare for making it?
3. For what two purposes did Jesus choose the twelve men He did?
4. Why was it so important that the Twelve spend time with Jesus before going out on their own?

5. What special authority did Jesus confer upon these men?

June 25

Growing God's Kingdom

1. What preceded the parable of the tares?
2. Are "kingdom of heaven" and "kingdom of God" the same or different? Explain.
3. What are some differences between the parable of the sower and the parable of the tares?
4. What were tares? How did they get into the field in Jesus' parable?
5. What do the tares represent? Where might we see tares today?

UNIT II: Responding to God's Kingdom

July 2

Praying to God

1. Why did the disciple want Jesus to teach them how to pray?
2. What is suggested by addressing God as "our Father" (Luke 11:2)?
3. What does "hallowed" mean? How do we hallow God's name?
4. What request in Jesus' model prayer precedes all others?
5. What should motivate us to pray for Christ's imminent return?

July 9

Accept God's Invitation!

1. What had Jesus observed as He watched the people coming in?
2. How did Jesus say they should act when attending such an event?
3. What principle did Jesus set forth regarding being exalted?
4. What lesson about self-exaltation can we learn from this?
5. What statement did one of the guests make to Jesus after this?

July 16
A Warning for the Hard-Hearted
1. What is the traditional name given the rich man? Where does it come from?
2. How is the rich man's lifestyle described?
3. Who was Lazarus, and how is he described?
4. What happened to both men once they died?

July 23
Separating the Sheep and the Goats
1. When will the event that Jesus speaks of in Matthew 25:31 take place?
2. How did Jesus refer to the two groups of people?
3. Which group will be invited to enter the kingdom?
4. What is the significance of the right-hand side in Scripture?

July 30
Ears to Hear
1. What type of people among those listening to Jesus could not comprehend what He was saying?
2. What question did the disciples ask Jesus, and why?
3. At what point in His ministry did Jesus begin to use parables more extensively?
4. What were the first two reasons Jesus gave for using parables?
5. What does the phrase "to them it is not given" mean (Matt. 13:11)?

August 6
Forgiving One Another
1. What had caused Peter to wonder about how often to forgive?
2. How do we know his concern was about fellow believers?
3. How did Jesus respond to Peter's seemingly generous offer to forgive seven times? What did He mean?
4. How does the concept of debt relate to our need to forgive?
5. What was Jesus portraying in the first servant's huge debt?

UNIT III: Entering God's Kingdom
August 13
A Story of Forgiveness
1. How did the father respond to his son's arrogant request?
2. What persons or groups are portrayed by the parable?
3. What was especially degrading about the son's circumstances and employment?
4. What brought him to his senses, and what did he decide to do?

August 20
God's Gracious Rewards
1. Why did Jesus use parables as He described what the kingdom of heaven is like?
2. What agreement did the owner make with the first shift of workers?
3. At what times of the day did the owner recruit workers?
4. How did the owner instruct the steward to pay the workers?

August 27
God's Great Mercy
1. What did Jesus cover in the two parables He told?
2. Who were the two personalities Jesus used for His teaching in the second parable?
3. What was their purpose in going to the temple?
4. How did the Pharisee emphasize how he viewed his religious activities?